International AIR BAND RADIO HANDBOOK

The guide to world-wide air traffic control

David J. S

Patrick Stephens Limited

First published in 1995

A Catalogue record for this book is available from the British Library

ISBN 1 85260 467 0

Library of Congress catalog card no 95-79120

Patrick Stephens Limited is an imprint of Haynes Publishing, Sparkford, Nr Yeovil, Somerset BA22 7JJ

Printed and bound in Great Britain by Biddles Limited, Guildford and Kings Lynn

As part of our ongoing market research, we are always pleased to receive comments about our books, suggestions for new titles, or requests for catalogues. Please write to: The Editorial Director, Patrick Stephens Limited, Sparkford, Near Yeovil, Somerset BA22 7JJ.

Contents

Introduction

Air band radios offer a unique insight into the world of aviation. You can be right there in the cockpit, whether it be of a civil airliner, a military jet, or a private aeroplane. You do not even have to live near an airport to be able to listen. The UK-orientated *Air Band Radio Handbook*, first published in 1986, is now in its fifth edition, an indication of the popularity of the hobby; but since many British aviation enthusiasts travel widely in pursuit of their interest, it was felt that an international version would be a highly useful addition. Inevitably, there is some overlap of content with the original book because it is intended that, for the benefit of overseas readers, the present volume should also be able to stand on its own. However, the opportunity has been taken to include many subjects of general interest for which there was insufficient space in the previous book. These include Flight Plans and a list of airport codes, as well as emergency and interception procedures. There is even a list of standard French R/T phraseology for private pilots venturing across the Channel! Conversely, readers from abroad will find much of interest in the original volume, including airline operational messages and military aeronautical communications.

Air band listening is not a uniquely British pastime; it is also popular in the USA, and I have had letters from places as diverse as India and the former Yugoslavia, describing what is to be heard on the local air waves. Nor is an expensive scanner essential; a cheap pocket radio with air band will do the job for you, although it does have its disadvantages, as you will read in Chapter 12. The subject is obviously vast but, since basic procedures are virtually identical world-wide, the sections on individual countries are confined to local differences and general information. The USA section has, however, been made as comprehensive as possible, partly because American methods are so highly developed, and also because of the number of British visitors who take their air band radios on holiday over there. Complete lists of VHF frequencies are, of course, impracticable, but all major airports are covered, especially if they handle international traffic.

As before, I have aimed the book at several levels of interest: the air band enthusiast, obviously, whether he or she is a beginner baffled by radio jargon, or an experienced listener who wants to learn more; the student pilot or PPL holder, and also the general reader who is curious about the workings of air traffic control on an international basis. For younger readers considering a career in ATC, I hope the book will provide a useful overview of the profession. Finally, I regret having to use so many abbreviations and acronyms but it is impossible to write a book of this nature without them. All, however, are listed below and explained in the text!

Acknowledgements

For their help in the preparation of this book, I would like to thank Terry House of Siemens Plessey Systems, British Airways Aerad, UK Civil Aviation Authority, Ian Doyle, Paul Howard, Leo Marriott, Ken Rodgers and Bob Womersley. Ken Cothliff and Andy Rackham of Air Supply, near Leeds-Bradford Airport, were supportive as ever, seeking out some of the more obscure documentation on my behalf. Thanks also go to Ken Barker for permission to use the list of Principal Worldwide Air Routes from *High in the Sky*, published by The Aviation Hobby Shop. In addition *Transmit*, the Journal of the Guild of Air Traffic Control Officers, and *The Controller*, the Journal of IFATCA, the International Federation of Air Traffic Controllers' Associations, were an extremely valuable source of reference, as was the *ICAO Journal*.

I freely admit that some of the entries for individual countries are sketchy in the extreme, reflecting the lack of available information in English, rather than any regional bias. I would welcome any further input on overseas ATC systems for use in future editions.

Abbreviations and Q-Codes

ACARS*	Aircraft Communications Addressing and Reporting System	ASDE	Airport Surface Detection Equipment	EATCHIP*	European ATC Harmonization and Integration Programme
ACAS	Airborne Collision Avoidance System	ASECNA*	French acronym for the Security of Aerial Navigation in Africa	EATMS	European Air Traffic Management System
ACC	Area Control Centre	ATC	Air Traffic Control		
ACF	Area Control Facility	ATD	Actual Time of Departure	ECAC	European Civil Aviation Conference
ADD	Allowable Deferred Defect	ATFM	Air Traffic Flow Management	EFAS	En-Route Flight Advisory Service
ADF	Automatic Direction Finder	ATIS*	Automatic Terminal Information Service	ETA	Estimated Time of Arrival
ADIZ*	Air Defence Identification Zone	ATM	Air Traffic Management	ETD	Estimated Time of Departure
ADR	Advisory Route	ATS	Air Traffic Services	ETOPS*	Extended Range Twin Engine Operations
ADS	Automatic Dependent Surveillance	ATZ	Aerodrome Traffic Zone		
ADT	Approved Departure Time	BAA	British Airports Authority	FAA	Federal Aviation Authority
AEIS	Aeronautical En-Route Information Service	BFO	Beat Frequency Oscillator	FANS*	Future Air Navigation Systems
AFB	Air Force Base	CAA	Civil Aviation Authority	FDPS	Flight Data Processing System
AFI	Africa (ICAO region)	CANAC*	Computer Assisted National ATC Centre	FIC	Flight Information Centre
AFIS*	Aerodrome Flight Information Service	CCA	Continental Control Area	FIR	Flight Information Region
AFTN	Aeronautical Fixed Telecommunications Network	CFMU	Central Flow Management Unit	FIS	Flight Information Service
AGL	Above Ground Level	CTA	Control Area	FL	Flight Level
AIP	Aeronautical Information Publication	CTZ	Control Zone	FM	Frequency Modulation
		CVFR	Controlled Visual Flight Rules	FMS	Flight Management System
AIS	Aeronautical Information Service	D/F	Direction Finding	FPS	Flight Progress Strips
		DFR	Departure Flow Regulation		
AIREP*	Air Report (Met)	DGPS	Differential Global Positioning System	FSS	Flight Service Station
AMSL	Above Mean Sea Level	DME	Distance Measuring Equipment	GA	General Aviation
ARINC*	Aeronautical Radio Incorporated	DoD	Department of Defense (USA)	GLONASS*	Global Orbiting Navigation Satellite System
ARSA	Airport Radar Service Area	DVOR	Doppler VHF Omni-Directional Range	GMC	Ground Movement Control
ARTCC	Air Route Traffic Control Centre	EAT	Expected Approach Time	GMP	Ground Movement Planning

GNSS	Global Navigation Satellite System	OLDI*	On-Line Data Interchange	SID*	Standard Instrument Departure
GPS	Global Positioning System	ORCAM*	Originating Region Code Allocation Method	SOTA*	Shannon Oceanic Transition Area
HF	High Frequency	OTS	Organized Track System	SRA	Surveillance Radar Approach
HMR	Helicopter Main Route	PAL	Pilot Activated Lighting	SSB	Single Side Band
HPZ	Helicopter Protected Zone	PANS*	Procedures for Air Navigation Services	SSR	Secondary Surveillance Radar
IAS	Indicated Air Speed	PAR	Precision Approach Radar	STAR*	Standard Terminal Arrival Route
IATA*	International Air Transport Association	P-DME	Precision Distance Measuring Equipment	STCA	Short-Term Conflict Alert
ICAO*	International Civil Aviation Organisation	PIREP*	Pilot Report (Met) (pronounced Pie-Rep)	STOL*	Short Take-Off and Landing
IFR	Instrument Flight Rules	PTS	Polar Track Structure	TA	Traffic Advisory
ILS	Instrument Landing System	QAR	Quick Access Recorder	TACAN*	Tactical Air Navigation
IMC	Instrument Meteorological Conditions	QDM	Magnetic track to the airfield with nil wind	TAS	True Air Speed
INO	Indian Ocean (ICAO region)	QFE	Barometric pressure setting at aerodrome level	TCA	Terminal Control Area
INS	Inertial Navigation System	QGH	Controlled descent through cloud	TCAS*	Traffic Alert and Collision Avoidance System (Tee-kass)
LARS*	Lower Airspace Radar Advisory Service	QNH	Barometric pressure at sea level	TIBA*	Traffic Information Broadcasts by Aircraft
kHz	Kilohertz	QSY	Change frequency to. . .	TMA	Terminal Manoeuvring Area
MDH	Minimum Descent Height	RA	Resolution Advisory	TOS	Traffic Orientation Scheme
METRO*	US military met office (pronounced Mee-tro)	RCC	Rescue Co-ordination Centre	TRACON*	Terminal Radar Control
MHz	Megahertz	RDP	Radar Data Processing	TRSA	Terminal Radar Service Area
MLS	Microwave Landing System	RMI	Radio Magnetic Indicator	TWEB	Transcribed Weather Broadcast
MNPS	Minimum Navigation Performance Specification	RNAV*	Random Navigation	UHF	Ultra High Frequency
MTI	Moving Target Indicator	R/T	Radio Telephony	UIR	Upper Information Region
NACS	Northern Area Control System	RTOW	Regulated Take-Off Weight	USAF	United States Air Force
NDB	Non-Directional Beacon	RTTY*	Radio Teletype (pronounced Ritty)	UTC	Universal Time Co-ordinated
NFM	Narrow Frequency Modulation	RVR	Runway Visual Range	VDF	VHF Direction Finder
NM	Nautical Miles	SAR	Search and Rescue	VFR	Visual Flight Rules
NOTAM*	Notice to Airmen	SARPS*	International Standards and Recommended Practices	VHF	Very High Frequency
OACC	Oceanic Area Control Centre			VLF	Very Low Frequency
OAT	Operational Air Traffic *or* outside air temperature	SATNAV*	Satellite Navigation	VMC	Visual Meteorological Conditions
		SCATANA*	Security Control of Air Traffic and Air Navigation Aids	VOR	VHF Omni-Directional Range
OCA	Oceanic Control Area			WAFS	World Area Forecast System
OCH	Obstacle Clearance Height			WFM	Wide Frequency Modulation

*The abbreviations marked with an asterisk are normally spoken as a complete word.

Chapter 1

ICAO and Air Traffic Control

The International Civil Aviation Organisation (ICAO)

The United Nations, for all its laudable aims, is often less than effective in carrying them out. However, one of its specialized agencies, the International Civil Aviation Organisation, with its headquarters in Montreal, is acknowledged to be the most successful international body of all. Universally referred to as I-Cayo, it was created in 1944 to respond to the immediate needs of civil aviation in the post-war era. Since then it has been responsible for all the technical standards, as well as for building the legal framework, which has made the orderly development of civil aviation possible.

This standardization has been achieved primarily through the adoption of specifications known as International Standards and Recommended Practices (SARPS). They are published in 18 sections designated as Annexes, which cover the whole spectrum of aviation activity. A Standard is a specification whose uniform application is recognized as necessary for the safety or regularity of international air navigation and to which contracting states will conform. A Recommended Practice is one agreed to be desirable and to which states will endeavour to conform. The Annexes cover such subjects as licensing of personnel, rules of the air, meteorology, aeronautical charts, units of measurement, nationality and registration marks, airworthiness, telecommunications, air traffic services, aerodromes, aeronautical information services, and aviation security. After a Standard is adopted it is put into effect by each ICAO member state which, for all practical purposes, is the entire world. If, for various reasons, a state is unable to comply, a so-called Difference must be filed with ICAO for publication in the appropriate air navigation documents.

In addition to the SARPs which are developed by its Air Navigation Committee, ICAO also formulates Procedures for Air Navigation Services (PANS). These consist of operating practices and material considered too detailed for SARPS. Not all aviation problems can be dealt with on a world-wide scale and many subjects are considered on a regional basis. ICAO, therefore, recognizes nine geographical areas: European-Mediterranean (EUM), Middle East (MID), Africa/Indian Ocean (AFI), South East Asia (SEA), Pacific (PAC), South American (SAM), Caribbean (CAR), North American (NAM), and North Atlantic (NAT). Each must be treated individually for planning the provision of air navigation facilities and services required on the ground by aircraft flying in the area. The regions are served by seven ICAO offices: Bangkok (SEA and PAC), Mexico City (CAR and NAM), Cairo (MID), Dakar (AFI West), Nairobi (AFI East), Lima (SAM), and Paris (EUM).

In each region careful planning is needed to produce the network of air navigation facilities and services upon which the aircraft depend, as well as the aerodromes, the meteorological and communications stations, and the search and rescue organizations. This planning is done at ICAO regional air navigation meetings held at regular intervals, where the need for each facility or service is carefully considered and decided upon. The plan which emerges from a regional meeting is so designed that when the states concerned put it into action, it will lead to an integrated, efficient system for the entire region.

As financial and technical resources vary widely between nations, and because air transport's demands involve such complex and costly equipment and well-qualified personnel, there may be uneven implementation of air navigation plans. ICAO helps with its Technical Assistance activities and has succeeded also, in a few cases, in arranging for joint financing. For example, certain facilities in the North Atlantic region, such as navigation aids in Greenland and Iceland, have been paid for by the states whose airlines make use of them. The heavy costs of running modern ATC systems can largely be offset by the navigation charges levied on their users. For example, a country such as Romania, with little tourist industry of its own, handles a great deal of overflying traffic from Western Europe to and from Greece and Turkey. Its newly-installed radar equipment was obtained with international financing and the loans will be paid off by user fees. In due course the system will become self-supporting.

ICAO pays special attention to promoting civil aviation in developing countries where topography renders road and rail networks inadequate or non-existent. With the help of the appropriate ICAO Annexes and associated publications, as well as an ICAO technical assistance mission if necessary, many a small country with no aviation background has been able to set up an efficient if basic system of air traffic control, navigational aids, and aerodromes.

Air Traffic Control

By ICAO definition, the objectives of the air traffic services are to: (1) prevent collisions between aircraft; (2) prevent collisions between aircraft on the manoeuvring area and obstructions on that area; (3) expedite and maintain an orderly flow of air traffic; (4) provide advice and information useful for the safe and efficient conduct of flights; (5) notify appropriate organizations regarding aircraft in need of search and rescue aid, and assist such organizations as required. Each ICAO contracting state determines the extent to which ATC will be provided at its aerodromes and within its airspace. In some cases, by mutual agreement, responsibility for ATC in certain areas may be delegated to a neighbouring state without loss of national sovereignty. Airspace over the high seas or areas of undetermined sovereignty is administered on the basis of regional air navigation agreements. Air traffic control comprises three basic services: Area Control, Approach Control, and Aerodrome Control, as well as Flight Information Service to accomplish objective 4 above and Alerting Service to carry out objective 5. All are described in later chapters.

ATC uses radio to communicate with aircraft – VHF for relatively short ranges, and HF for longer distances over oceans and wilderness areas. It is possible to listen to much of this radio traffic if one has a receiver with the appropriate air band frequencies. The following chapters describe how to do this, what can be heard, and what it all means.

Chapter 2

Air Traffic Control Terminology

The messages between air traffic control and pilots are constructed in a verbal shorthand designed to impart the maximum amount of unambiguous information in the shortest possible time. English is often claimed to be the international language for aviation radio communications but, in countries where English is not the first language, this is only true for major airports and route systems used by international air services. At smaller aerodromes the national language is almost certainly in universal use. Controllers handling international flights often speak to fellow-countrymen in their own tongue, a particularly common practice in Greek, Italian and Spanish airspace. English-speaking pilots complain about it because it prevents them from building up a mental picture of the traffic situation. (They also suspect that local pilots sometimes jump the queue for landing by negotiating with controllers in a foreign language!) ICAO in fact spec-

Typical mix of general aviation aircraft at Halim Airport, Jakarta, Indonesia. (Paul Howard)

ifies an alternative language to English in each of its regions – Spanish in the SAM (South America) Region, for example.

ICAO fudges the issue somewhat in its recommendations for ATIS weather broadcasts: 'Pending the development of a more suitable form of speech for universal use in aeronautical R/T communications, ATIS (Automatic Terminal Information Service) broadcasts provided at aerodromes designed for use by international air services should be available in the English language.' Esperanto has been suggested as an alternative radio language but the idea has few supporters! It is fair to say, however, that R/T English is extremely concise and has become so well established that it is difficult to imagine a better alternative.

Aviation pre-dates the computer industry in its use of jargon, much of which is incomprehensible to the outsider. The air waves are full of strange words and abbreviations – squawk, radial, QNH, sigmet, localizer, Tee-Cass, and so on; this book will explain them all to you.

The terms QNH, QFE, and Flight Level are the first to puzzle the newcomer to air band listening, simply because they are heard so frequently. The first two are codes rather than abbreviations and refer to the current atmospheric pressure at sea level and aerodrome level respectively. When the value in millibars, hectopascals, or inches of mercury is set on the aircraft's altimeter the instrument will indicate the distance above the appropriate datum. The new term hectopascal has virtually replaced millibar (both measures are identical), while inches are used mainly in the USA and Canada.

Above a point known as the Transition Altitude, varying in different countries – the highest being 18,000 ft in the USA – a standard setting of 1013.2 millibars or 29.92 inches is used, producing what is termed a Flight Level (abbreviated to FL). This ensures that all aircraft, particularly within controlled airspace, are flying on the same altimeter setting and can thus easily be separated vertically by the required amount. It also solves the problem of continually adjusting the altimeter and climbing or descending to allow for local pressure variations over the route, any error being common to all aircraft in the system. FL 70 is roughly equivalent to 7,000 ft, FL 230 to 23,000 ft and so on.

Times are given in the form of two figures; for example 14, pronounced one-four, indicates 14 minutes past the hour, four-two 42 minutes past the hour, and so on. The standard worldwide ATC time is Universal Time Constant, known as UTC or, less often, Zulu. The second term used to refer to Greenwich Mean Time (GMT) which, for all practical purposes, was the same as UTC. The use of UTC ensures that there is no confusion with Flight Plans on aircraft crossing time zones.

The word *squawk* is often heard, especially in route clearances, along with a four figure code. This is set on the aircraft's transponder, a device which responds to automatic interrogations from a ground station by sending a return signal in coded form. The information appears on the radar screen as a label giving callsign, height, and destination, adjacent to the appropriate aircraft position symbol. The word blip is obsolete, the image on the display (screen is obsolete too!) on modern radars being produced electronically via a computer. The centre sweep familiar in films is now rarely seen as even relatively old radar equipment can be processed to produce an excellent picture.

The term clearance or cleared is a legal one meaning that the aircraft may proceed under certain explicit conditions and that it will not be impeded by other traffic. It has, in the past, been rather over-used by controllers in circumstances where its application was unnecessary so the authorities have narrowed it down considerably. It is now confined mainly to route clearances and runway occupancy for take-off and landing, thus avoiding any possible confusion with the meaning.

Directions are given in degrees magnetic so that if an aircraft is heading 360° it is flying due north, 090° due east and so on. Note the difference between heading and actual path over the ground (track). If there is a strong cross-wind an aircraft may be pointing (heading) in a particular direction but travelling over the ground in a considerably different direction. There is an analogy here with rowing a small boat across a fast-flowing river; although you may be aiming for a point on the opposite bank, the current will also be deflecting you sideways. Simple right and left are used for direction changes, as in the instruction 'Turn right heading 340', port and starboard being long out-of-date in aviation.

Speed is expressed in knots, one knot being equal to one nautical mile per hour. The exception to this is on transatlantic and similar long-haul flights where a Mach Number is employed, speed being expressed as a ratio of the speed of sound. Jet transports cruise at around Mach 0.8 and Concorde at Mach 2, or twice the speed of sound. Above 25,000 ft the use of Mach Numbers overcomes considerable airspeed indicator errors caused by low air density and varying temperatures.

Distances are measured in nautical miles (approx 2,025 yd). References to DME, as in 'Report 25 DME Rodos', relate to the Distance Measuring Equipment carried aboard aircraft. It receives radio transmissions from ground beacons and enables the distance to or from the particular position to be presented automatically to the pilot as a continuous read-out in miles and tenths, as well as a 'time to go' to the beacon.

Runways are designated by two numbers derived from the heading in degrees magnetic. The runway at Heraklion, Crete, for example, is 09/27. This is rounded down from the actual direction of 092/272° magnetic, with the resulting final zeros omitted. Similarly a heading of 056/236 would be presented as 06/24. Other examples are 07 Left/25 Right and 07 Right/25 Left at Frankfurt, and 09/27 at Amsterdam. Note that small annual changes in the bearing of the Magnetic Pole can affect the designation of runways. For example, London Heathrow's directions were 10/28 until 1987 when the exact alignment became nearer to 090/270° than 100/280° magnetic and they were redesignated 09/27. An anomaly is Northern Canada, where runway designators are given in degrees true because the proximity of the Pole means gross differences in magnetic variation. Parallel runways are suffixed Left, Right, or – where there are three – Central. However, at many locations in the USA parallel runways are given separate designators to try to prevent confusion: for example 8/26 and 9/27 at Houston Intercontinental. (Note the deletion of the initial zero as is the practice in the USA.) Los Angeles has four parallel runways which are known as 6L/24R and 6R/24L and 7L/25R and 7R/25L. Conversely, at Milwaukee two runways which diverge by more than ten degrees are given the 'parallel' designators 7L/25R and 7R/25L. Runways for STOL aircraft are sometimes suffixed S, as in 18S/36S at Dallas-Fort Worth. At present, the only parallel runways in Europe with separate designators are 09/27 and 10/28 at Charles de Gaulle.

Somewhat confusing to the layman are the terms VFR, IFR, VMC, and IMC, so I shall explain them at some length because they are of paramount importance in ATC. Flight conditions are divided thus: (a) Visual Flight Rules (VFR) which apply under Visual Meterological Conditions (VMC); and (b) Instrument Flight Rules (IFR) which apply under Instrument Meteorological Conditions (IMC).

The minima for VFR flight are quite complicated but can be summarized as follows. At or below 3,000 ft AMSL at an indicated air speed (IAS) of 140 knots or less, an aircraft must remain in sight of ground or water and clear of cloud in a flight visibility of at least 1,500 metres. If the IAS is more than 140 kt up to a limit of 250 kt, the flight visibility must be at least 6 km. Above 3,000 ft up to FL 100 the minima are 5 km visibility and at least 1,500 metres horizontally, or 1,000 ft vertically clear of cloud. At FL 100 and above, the speed limit no longer applies and the visibility minimum is increased to 8 km.

Since it is his or her responsibility to keep clear of other traffic, the pilot must maintain a good look-out. Furthermore, under certain conditions climbs or descents maintaining VMC may be authorized for aircraft flying under IFR so as to expedite traffic; it is then the pilot's responsibility to

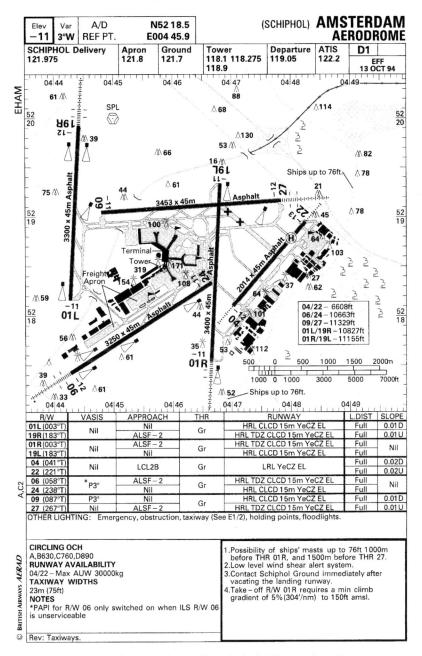

Elev −11	Var 3°W	A/D REF PT.	N52 18.5 E004 45.9		(SCHIPHOL) **AMSTERDAM AERODROME**		
SCHIPHOL Delivery 121.975		Apron 121.8	Ground 121.7	Tower 118.1 118.275 118.9	Departure 119.05	ATIS 122.2	**D1** EFF 13 OCT 94

R/W	VASIS	APPROACH	THR	RUNWAY	L.DIST	SLOPE
01L (003°T)	Nil	Nil	Gr	HRL CLCD 15m YeCZ EL	Full	0.01 D
19R (183°T)		ALSF−2		HRL TDZ CLCD 15m YeCZ EL	Full	0.01 U
01R (003°T)	Nil	ALSF−2	Gr	HRL TDZ CLCD 15m YeCZ EL	Full	Nil
19L (183°T)		Nil		HRL CLCD 15m YeCZ EL	Full	
04 (041°T)	Nil	LCL2B	Gr	LRL YeCZ EL	Full	0.02D
22 (221°T)					Full	0.02U
06 (058°T)	*P3°	ALSF−2	Gr	HRL TDZ CLCD 15m YeCZ EL	Full	Nil
24 (238°T)		Nil		HRL CLCD 15m YeCZ EL	Full	
09 (087°T)	P3°	Nil	Gr	HRL CLCD 15m YeCZ EL	Full	0.01 D
27 (267°T)	Nil	ALSF−2		HRL TDZ CLCD 15m YeCZ EL	Full	0.01 U

OTHER LIGHTING: Emergency, obstruction, taxiway (See E1/2), holding points, floodlights.

CIRCLING OCH
A,B630,C760,D890
RUNWAY AVAILABILITY
04/22 – Max AUW 30000kg
TAXIWAY WIDTHS
23m (75ft)
NOTES
*PAPI for R/W 06 only switched on when ILS R/W 06 is unserviceable

1. Possibility of ships' masts up to 76ft 1000m before THR 01R, and 1500m before THR 27.
2. Low level wind shear alert system.
3. Contact Schiphol Ground immediately after vacating the landing runway.
4. Take – off R/W 01R requires a min climb gradient of 5% (304'/nm) to 150ft amsl.

© BRITISH AIRWAYS *AERAD*

Rev: Taxiways.

A.C2

Amsterdam Aerodrome Chart (British Airways Aerad.)

avoid other traffic. In R/T transmissions the terms VFR or Victor Fox are used freely. In the same way, VMC may be referred to as Victor Mike. The phrase 'VMC on top' means that the aircraft is flying in VMC conditions above a cloud layer.

IFR comes into force when the visibility requirements described above cannot be met, and at all times during the hours of darkness. It is then mandatory for an aircraft to be flown on instruments by a suitably qualified pilot. It must also carry a minimum scale of navigational and other equipment. Within controlled airspace, responsibility for separation from other aircraft is in the hands of the ground controllers.

Outside controlled airspace, pilots flying above the transition altitude must reset their altimeters to the standard setting of 1013.2 millibars or 29.92 in and fly in accordance with what is known as the quadrantal rule. This is intended to ensure that aircraft on converging headings at levels below 24,500 ft remain clear of each other by at least 500 ft, as the following table explains:

Magnetic track	*Cruising level*
Less than 90°	Odd thousands of feet
90° but less than 180°	Odd thousands of feet plus 500 ft
180° but less than 270°	Even thousands of feet
270° but less than 360°	Even thousands of feet plus 500 ft

Above 24,500 ft the semi-circular rule applies:

Magnetic track	*Cruising level*
Less than 180°	25,000 ft
	27,000 ft
	29,000 ft or higher levels at
	intervals of 4,000 ft
180° but less than 360°	26,000 ft
	28,000 ft
	31,000 ft or higher levels at
	intervals of 4,000 ft

A final variation on the IFR/VFR theme is Special VFR, an authorization by ATC for a pilot to fly within a control zone, even though he is unable to comply with IFR, and in certain airspace where provision is made for such flights. Depending on the visibility, amount of cloud and its height, and the limitations of the pilot's licence, a Special VFR clearance may be requested and issued.

Standard separation is provided between all Special VFR flights, and between such flights and other aircraft operating IFR. In practice much use is made of geographical features to keep Special VFR traffic apart, routeing along opposite banks of an estuary, for instance. When flying on this type of clearance a pilot must comply with ATC instructions and remain at all times in flight conditions which enable him to determine his flight path and to keep clear of obstructions. It is implicit in all Special VFR clearances that the aircraft stays clear of cloud and in sight of the surface. ATC almost always imposes a height limitation which will require the pilot to fly either at or below a specific level.

Phonetic alphabet

To overcome the problems of confusing similar sounding letters like 'B' and 'P', or 'M' and 'N', an international spelling alphabet is in use. Certain universally accepted codes and abbreviations, such as QNH, QFE, ILS, SRA, and QDM are not put into phonetics but said as written. Others are turned into a word – ATIS (Ay-Tiss), TCAS (Tee-Cass), and SID (Sid). There is also a standard way of pronouncing numbers and the word decimal, as used in radio frequencies, is supposed to be said as 'dayseemal', although this rarely happens in practice. (The Americans use 'point' instead.)

Phonetic alphabet

A – Alpha	J – Juliet	S – Sierra
B – Bravo	K – Kilo	T – Tango
C – Charlie	L – Lima	U – Uniform
D – Delta	M – Mike	V – Victor
E – Echo	N – November	W – Whiskey
F – Foxtrot	O – Oscar	X – X-Ray
G – Golf	P – Papa	Y – Yankee
H – Hotel	Q – Quebec	Z – Zulu
I – India	R – Romeo	

Transmission of numbers

0 – Zero	4 – Fower	8 – Ait
1 – Wun	5 – Fife	9 – Niner
2 – Too	6 – Six	Thousand – Tousand
3 – Tree	7 – Seven	

Examples of number transmissions are: 10 – Wun Zero; 583 – Fife Ait Tree; 2,500 – Too Tousand Fife Hundred; 3,000 – Tree Tousand. Frequencies are passed in the form: 118.1 – Wun Wun Ait Day-see-mal Wun; 120.375 – Wun Too Zero Day-see-mal Tree Seven (the final digit being omitted).

Q-Code

A further note concerns the Q-Code, long obsolete in aviation apart from certain enduring terms like QGH, QNH, and QFE. It was an expansion of the Q-Code already in use by the merchant marine and it became possible to exchange information on practically all subjects that might be needed in aviation communications. These three-letter groups could be sent by

Wireless Telegraphy (W/T) in morse with great speed, and overcame any inherent language difficulties. For example, an operator would send the code 'QDM' to a ground station, which meant 'What is my magnetic course to steer with zero wind to reach you?' The ground operator would transmit 'QDM' and the appropriate figure.

ICAO standard words and phrases used in R/T communications

Word/Phrase	Meaning
Acknowledge	Let me know that you have received and understood this message.
Affirm	Yes.
Approved	Permission for proposed action granted.
Break	Indicates the separation between messages.
Break Break	Separation between messages transmitted to different aircraft in a very busy environment.
Cancel	Annul the previously transmitted clearance.
Check	Examine a system or procedure (no answer is normally expected).
Cleared	Authorized to proceed under the conditions specified.
Confirm	Have I correctly received the following..? or Did you correctly receive this message?
Contact	Establish radio contact with…
Correct	That is correct.
Correction	An error has been made in this transmission (or message indicated). The correct version is…
Disregard	Consider that transmission as not sent.
Go ahead	Pass your message.
How do you read	What is the readability of my transmission?
I say again	I repeat for clarity or emphasis.
Monitor	Listen out on (frequency).
Negative	No, or permission not granted, or that is not correct.
Over	My transmission is ended and I expect a response from you.
Out	My transmission is ended and no response is expected.
Read back	Repeat all, or the specified part, of this message back to me exactly as received.
Recleared	A change has been made to your last clearance and this new clearance supersedes your present clearance or part thereof.
Report	Pass required information.
Request	I should like to know…or I wish to obtain…
Roger	I have received all your last transmission. (Note: under no circumstances to be used in reply to a question requiring a direct answer in the affirmative (affirm) or negative (negative).
Say again	Repeat all, or the following part of your last transmission.
Speak slower	Reduce your rate of speech.
Standby	Wait and I will call you.
Verify	Check and confirm with originator.
Wilco	I understand your message and will comply with it. (Abbreviation for 'will comply'.)
Words twice	As a request: Communication is difficult. Please send every

word, or group of words, twice. As information: Every word, or group of words, in this message will be sent twice.

The words over and out are now rarely used in practice but the original form of *affirmative*, superseded in 1984 by *affirm*, is still to be heard, especially in the USA. Note that some ICAO phrases such as 'go ahead' and 'recleared' are not approved for use in the UK, although you will certainly hear the latter!

The clarity of radio transmissions is expressed by the following scale:

Readability 1 – Unreadable;
Readability 2 – Readable now and then;
Readability 3 – Readable but with difficulty;
Readability 4 – Readable;
Readability 5 – Perfectly readable.

Another phrase in common usage is 'Carrier wave only', indicating that an unmodulated transmission is being received by the ground station, i.e. it is just noise without the accompanying speech.

Communications

Aeronautical ground stations are identified by the name of the location, followed by a suffix which indicates the type of service being given.

Suffix	*Service*
Control	Area Control Service
Radar	Radar (in general)
Director	Approach Radar Controller dealing only with arriving traffic
Arrival	Equivalent to *Director*; used in USA etc
Departure	Approach Controller dealing only with departing traffic.
Approach	Approach Control
Tower	Aerodrome Control
Ground	Ground Movement Control
Delivery	Clearance Delivery
Clearance	Alternative form of Clearance Delivery
Precision	Precision Approach Radar
Talkdown	Precision Approach Radar (Military)
Information	Flight Information Service
Radio	Air/Ground Communications Service
Homer	Direction-Finding Station
Apron	Apron Control
Ramp	Ramp Control
Dispatch	Company Dispatch

In the former Soviet Union the suffix *Krug* (Russian for circuit) is used for approach radar units, *Ground* is known as *Taxying*, and some *Tower* facilities as *Start* (Tbilisi Start, for example) after the code name for a data processing system. Other anomalies include *Gonio*, equivalent to *Homer* (from the French 'goniometer') for D/F equipment, *Sol* (the French for ground), and *Flight Data* instead of *Delivery*.

When satisfactory two-way communication has been established, and provided that it will not be confusing, the name of the location or the call-sign suffix may be omitted. The basic rule is that the full call-signs of both stations must be used on the first transmission. For example:

Aircraft: De Gaulle Tower Air France 123.
ATC: Air France 123 De Gaulle Tower pass your message.

Aircraft call-signs may take various forms, but they must remain the same throughout the flight. However, if aircraft on the same frequency have similar call-signs ATC may instruct them to alter the format temporarily to avoid confusion.

The recommended methods of presenting callsign information are summarized below.

	Example	
Type of callsign	**Full**	**Abbreviated**
(a) The five-character callsign corresponding to the registration marking of the aircraft, the first one or two letters being the national prefix	OOABC	OBC
(b) The five-character callsign referred to in (a) above, preceded by the R/T designator of the aircraft operator	Sabena OOABC	Sabena BC
(c) The five-character callsign referred to in (a) above, preceded by the type of aircraft (An American practice which is very slowly spreading to Europe)	Citation N526J	Citation 26J
(d) The R/T designator of the aircraft operator, followed by the flight identification	Speedbird 835	No abbreviation permitted
(e) Alpha-numeric callsign corresponding with the aircraft registration marking	N786AQ	86AQ

In practice other variations are to be heard, some pilots using their company three-letter designator and flight number rather than the normal company callsign and flight number, eg PNR 232 for *Skyjet* 232 (the Spanish operator Panair). Either is correct and it is quite common for controllers, faced with an unfamiliar company designator on a flight progress strip – or simply forgetting what it stands for – to revert to the three-letter prefix. Poor long-range HF reception is another reason for the use of three-letter designators. The aim is to prevent incidents and potential accidents caused by callsign ambiguities, but they still occur in sufficient numbers to cause concern.

Private aircraft normally use the aircraft registration letters or numbers as a callsign, as do some taxi and executive aircraft, and sometimes airliners on training or empty positioning flights. Otherwise, commercial operators use their company designator and flight number as in (d) above. Intensive use of flight numbers often leads to callsign confusion when two aircraft with the same flight number are on frequency together, for example Air France 422 and Air Malta 422. The problem is under constant scrutiny and a possible solution is the use of alpha-numerics. Further confusion has been caused by callsigns resembling flight levels or headings, so operators have agreed, as far as possible, not to allocate flight numbers which end in zero or five. In practice, this means figures below 500. There are several standard suffixes to flight numbers which include *P* for a positioning flight, *T* for a training flight and *F* for a freight operation. The suffix *Heavy* on the initial call reminds ATC that an aircraft is wide-bodied with a powerful vortex wake and that following aircraft may require increased separation.

Glossary of aviation terms heard on radio
See also Abbreviations and US list on pages 160-162.

Abeam	Passing a specified point at 90 degrees to the left or right.
Abort	Abandon take-off or return prematurely.
Active	The runway-in-use.
Actual	The current weather conditions.
Alternate	Alternate airfield if unable to land at destination
Approach plate	Another term for approach chart.
Approach sequence	Position in traffic on to final approach.
Approved Departure time	See page 61.
ATIS (Ay-Tiss)	Automatic Terminal Information Service.
Backtrack	Taxi back along the runway.
Base turn	The turn on to final from an instrument approach when it is not a reciprocal of the outbound track.
Blind transmission	A transmission from one station to another when two-way communication cannot be established but where it is believed that the called station is able to receive the transmission.
The Boundary	Boundary between Flight Information Regions or alternatively the edge of a Control Zone.
Box	Radio, Box One being the main set and *Box Two* the standby.
Breakthrough	Transmissions on one frequency breaking through on to another.
Build-ups	Cumulo-nimbus clouds.
CAVOK	See page 89.
CB	Also referred to as Charlie Bravo. Cumulo-nimbus clouds.
Charlie	That is correct (common HF usage).

Clearance limit	A specified point to which an ATC clearance remains effective.
The company	As in 'Follow the company', i.e. an aircraft belonging to the same operator as the subject.
Conflict alert	See page 54.
Conflicting traffic	Other aircraft in the vicinity which may prove a hazard.
Crosswind component	Strength of wind from the side on final approach.
The Data	Temperature, QNH, runway-in-use, etc.
Direct	Flying from one beacon or geographical point straight to another one.
Drift	The effect of wind on an aircraft (see page 13).
Established	Aligned or 'locked on' with the ILS.
Expected approach time	See page 73.
Flag	Warning flag on cockpit instrument that ILS or other ground-based aid has failed or is not being received correctly.
Glidepath	The final descent path to the runway on an ILS approach.
Go around	Overshoot runway and rejoin circuit or carry out missed approach procedure.
GPU	Ground Power Unit.
Guard frequency	International Distress Frequency which is monitored continuously by aircraft flying long-distance routes.
Heavy	See page 21.
Heading	Direction in which the aircraft is pointing. (See also Track.)
Intentions	Course of action after a missed approach etc.
Jet A-1	Turbine fuel.
Localizer	See page 32.
Mach	Speed expressed as a ratio of the speed of sound, Mach 1.
Navex	Navigational Exercise.
Notam	Notice to Airmen
Off blocks	The time the aircraft commenced taxying.
On blocks	Time on parking stand.
Orbit	Circle, usually over a specified point.
Pattern	American equivalent of circuit.
Pax	Passengers.
Practice asymmetric	Engine failure simulation on multi-engined aircraft.
Procedure turn	Similar to base turn except that the aircraft retraces its steps on an exact reciprocal of the outbound leg.
QAR	Quick Access Recorder.
QFE	Barometric pressure at aerodrome level.
QNH	Barometric pressure at sea level.
QSY	Change frequency to . . .
Radar overhead	Radar blind spot above aerial.
Radar vectoring	Specified headings given by radar (see page 74).
Radial	Magnetic bearing line from or to a VOR.
Released	Control of a particular aircraft formally handed over from air ways controller to approach.
Regional	The QNH for a defined area.

Resume own navigation	Revert to self-navigation after a period of radar vectoring.
Runway heading	Climb straight ahead after take-off.
RVR	Runway Visual Range (see page 89-90).
Sector	Each leg of a series of (usually) scheduled flights. Also sub-divisions of an area control service.
Selcal	Selective Calling (see pages 81-82).
SID	Standard Instrument Departure.
SIGMET	Significant met conditions (see page 90).
Slot time	See page 61.
SNOCLO	Airfield closed during snow-clearing operations.
SNOWTAM	See pages 90-91.
Speed limit point	Position before which an inbound aircraft entering a TMA must have slowed to the speed limit (normally 250 kt). For departing traffic, speed restriction is lifted here.
Squawk	SSR code (see pages 62-63).
Stand	Numbered parking position on apron.
Standard missed approach	Procedure to be followed if an aircraft is unable to land from an instrument approach.
Stepdown fix	A defined point on the final approach track indicating that a critical obstacle has been safely overflown and descent to the next specified level may be commenced.
Stratus	Low-lying cloud layer.
TAF	Terminal Aerodrome Forecast.
Teardrop	A 180 degree turn to land back on the runway from which one has just departed. Often used by circuit training aircraft when runway-in-use is changed.
Tech stop	En route diversion for technical reasons.
Three greens	Indication of wheels down and locked.
Track	The path of an aircraft over the ground.
Traffic	Other aircraft known to be in the vicinity.
U/s	Unserviceable.
Volmet	See page 91.
Vortex wake	See pages 50-51.
Wake turbulence	Alternative form of vortex wake.
Waypoint	A pre-selected geographical position used with a Flight Management System.
Wind shear	See page 90.

Apart from callsign presentation, there are certain other basic R/T rules with which pilots must comply. Aircraft flying in controlled airspace must obtain permission from the controlling authority before changing frequency to another station. Another important point is that an ATC route clearance is *not* an instruction to take off or enter an active runway. The words *take-off* are used only when an aircraft is cleared for take-off. At all other times the word *departure* is used – the disaster at Teneriffe in 1977 was caused mainly by a flight crew interpreting a route clearance as also implying a take-off clearance. They must have known better but there were pressing distractions and so the fatal error was made.

There is a stringent requirement to read back route (or airways) clearances because of the possible seriousness of a misunderstanding in the transmission and receipt of these messages. If the controller does not receive a read-back, the pilot will be asked to give one. Similarly, the pilot is expected to request that instructions be repeated or clarified if any are not fully understood. The following ATC instructions *must* be read back in full by the pilot: Level instructions; heading instructions; speed instructions; airways or route clearances; runway-in-use; clearance to enter, land on, take off on, backtrack, hold short of, or cross an active runway; Secondary Surveillance Radar operating instructions; altimeter settings; VDF information; frequency changes; and type of radar service.

Examples are:

ATC: LNABC cleared to cross Bravo 1 at BLUFA Flight Level 180.
Aircraft: Cleared to cross Bravo 1 at BLUFA Flight Level 180, LBC.
ATC: Iberia 179 contact Madrid Approach 119.9.
Aircraft: 119.9 Iberia 179.

Levels may be reported as altitude, height, or Flight Level, according to the phase of flight and the altimeter setting, but a standard form of reporting is adhered to. An aircraft climbs, descends, maintains, passes, leaves or reaches a level, the following ATC instructions clarifying this:

Shamrock 920 climb FL 190.
Speedbird 58 report passing FL 160.
Swissair 842 report reaching FL 190.
Alitalia 481 maintain altitude 3,500 ft.
Aircraft: Lufthansa 401 request further descent.
ATC: Lufthansa 401 descend FL 60.
Aircraft: Lufthansa 401 leaving FL 190 for FL 60.

Sometimes a changing traffic situation may necessitate an intermediate halt to a descent or climb. 'Shamrock 920 stop descent FL 150.' Occasionally, for traffic reasons, a higher than normal rate of climb or descent may be requested to avoid eroding separation. 'Shamrock 920 climb to FL 190, expedite passing FL 150.'

Chapter 3

Divisions of Airspace

Flight Information Region/Upper Information Region (FIR/UIR)

The world is divided into FIRs which, above a certain Flight Level varying between states, become UIRs. The current total is around 350. Their boundaries normally follow geographical state borders, but over international waters and parts of the world having good relations with their neighbours they are able to assume straight lines in accordance with ICAO recommendations. Each FIR/UIR takes its name from an important city, particularly if it is the location of an Area Control Centre (ACC). Sometimes the country itself lends its name to the FIR. Over the oceans the word Oceanic is added, e.g. New York Oceanic FIR. Alaska is a special case with three FIRs: Anchorage Arctic, Anchorage Continental, and Anchorage Oceanic.

Airspace classifications

Within the FIR/UIRs, different types of airspace are classified internationally by ICAO so that it is perfectly clear to pilots from anywhere in the world which flight rules apply and what air traffic services they can expect inside a particular area. The designations are as follows:

Class A: IFR flights only are permitted, all flights are subject to ATC service and are separated from each other.
Class B: IFR and VFR flights are permitted, all flights are subject to ATC service and are separated from each other.
Class C: IFR and VFR flights are permitted, all flights are subject to ATC service and IFR flights are separated from other IFR flights and from VFR flights. VFR flights are separated from IFR flights and receive traffic information in respect of other VFR flights.
Class D: IFR and VFR flights are permitted and all flights are subject to ATC service, IFR flights are separated from other IFR flights and receive

traffic information in respect of VFR flights, VFR flights receive traffic information in respect of all other flights.

Class E: IFR and VFR flights are permitted, IFR flights are subject to ATC service and are separated from other IFR flights. All flights receive traffic information as far as is practicable.

Class F: IFR and VFR flights are permitted, all participating IFR flights receive an air traffic advisory service and all flights receive flight information service if requested.

Class G: IFR and VFR flights are permitted and receive flight information service if requested.

Aerodrome Traffic Zones

Air Traffic Control is not necessarily provided at each and every airfield. Where traffic is light and VFR applies at all times, pilots will have no difficulty in fitting themselves into the traffic pattern. ICAO's guideline is that when the anticipated traffic density reaches a point where the pilots 'cannot be expected to take the responsibility of deciding the correct action necessary to ensure a safe and expeditious flow of air traffic, an aerodrome control service should be established'. It should be manned by qualified personnel provided with facilities ranging from flag signalling equipment and signal lamps, if these simple aids are deemed adequate, to a complete system of ATC based on the use of VHF radio. Responsibility will extend only a short distance from the aerodrome – the Aerodrome Traffic Zone (ATZ). A compromise is the Aerodrome Flight Information

ATC is rare on Pacific island airstrips like this one in Melanesia. (Paul Howard)

Service (AFIS), which provides advice and information (but *not* control) to pilots. They then decide their own course of action to achieve a safe operation.

Control Zones

When, in further development, it is decided that an aerodrome should handle IFR traffic, it becomes necessary to protect such traffic by extending control to IFR flights and by placing additional restrictions on VFR flights. To accomplish this, controlled airspace should be established to protect the arrival, departure, and holding paths of the IFR flights. The basic unit is the Control Zone (CTZ), which extends from the surface up to a specified level. Typically it is circular in shape with a radius of five nautical miles from the aerodrome.

Control Areas

When it is essential to provide ATC service over a wide area to allow for radar vectoring and instrument approaches, additional controlled airspace, known as a Control Area (CTA) or Terminal Control Area (TCA), should be established to supplement the Control Zone. Sufficient vertical clearance is left beneath the CTA to avoid unduly restricting the operation of VFR flights outside the CTZ. In some cases uncontrolled corridors within controlled airspace may be provided to enable uncontrolled VFR traffic to have access to small aerodromes within the area or to cross it without a lengthy diversion round its boundaries.

Airways and Advisory Routes

When the density of traffic flowing between two or more aerodromes increases significantly, control should be extended to en route traffic. The controlled airspace around each of the aerodromes concerned should then be linked by Control Areas of various types, either in the form of airways or covering the route structure throughout the whole of the airspace between the different points. The type of traffic flow is a major factor in the determination of the shape of a Control Area. Where the traffic is at random and does not conform to specific routes, a CTA over the whole airspace is desirable. Where it is channelized an airway is more suitable. The available navigation aids are another important factor; VOR/DMEs will encourage direct flights, NDBs will dictate narrow airway type navigation. Ideally, routeings and procedures for aircraft overflying TCAs or CTZs should be designed so as permit these aircraft to operate though such areas without impeding the movement of arriving and departing aircraft. Airways are generally 10 miles wide (five miles each side of the centreline) but in some regions they are narrower, 10 km over the CIS portion of the former USSR, for example. Minimum flight altitudes allow for a clearance of at least 1,000 ft (300 m) above the highest obstacle within the area concerned.

In some of the less developed parts of the world where air traffic is relatively light, an Advisory Route may be established instead of an airway. It is still a narrow corridor but positive control is not imposed, merely the passing of information to enable pilots to maintain their own separation. Collectively, airways and Advisory Routes, as well as Arrival and Departure Routes, are known as Air Traffic Services (ATS) Routes and each is identified by a unique designator allocated by ICAO. Some are major trunk routes extending for thousands of miles, others are short regional links. Until 1987 they were named after colours followed by a number between one and 999 – Amber, Blue, Green, and Red, plus White for Advisory Routes – but the system became inadequate to cater for specialized applications such as Area Navigation and Supersonic Routes. The initial letters of the five colours already in use were adopted phonetically as the basis of the new system, Amber One becoming Alpha One, Blue One Bravo One and so on. The allocations are as follows:

(*a*) A, B, G, R for routes which form part of the regional networks of ATS routes;
(*b*) L, M, N, P for area navigation routes which form part of the regional networks of ATS routes;
(*c*) H, J, V, W for routes which do not form part of the regional networks of ATS routes and are not area navigation routes;
(*d*) Q, T, Y, Z for area navigation routes which do not form part of the regional networks of ATS routes.

Where applicable, one supplementary letter is added as a prefix to the basic designator in accordance with the following:

(*a*) K (spoken as 'Kopter') to indicate a low level route established for use primarily by helicopters;
(*b*) U (spoken as 'Upper') to indicate that the route or portion thereof is in the upper airspace;
(*c*) S (spoken as 'Supersonic') to indicate a route established exclusively for use by supersonic aircraft during acceleration, deceleration, and while in supersonic flight.

Where advisory service only is provided a supplementary letter D is added to the end of the designator. A supplementary letter F indicates that flight information service only is provided on the route. It should be noted that some trunk routes have common segments bearing dual or even triple designators. An example is G472/G463 over western Thailand. The 'Victor' or VOR airway designator is peculiar to the USA and a few other countries including Japan, Turkey, and Saudi Arabia. (See page 154).

Upper Air Routes

Most follow the line of normal airways below, using the prefix U as in Upper Romeo One, but in some cases only the upper portion of the route exists. Lower limit is usually FL 250 but it can be less than this.

Random Navigation (RNAV) Routes

Based on extensive use of Area Navigation (RNAV) (see pages 34-35), a new RNAV designator has been allocated to each European Trunk Route for its entire length. In practice the new network will integrate with the existing upper airways system rather than replace it. When segments of the new Trunk Routes are superimposed on conventional airways, states maintain a 'double designator' – the new RNAV and the conventional designator. This allows the utilization of these segments by both RNAV and non-RNAV equipped aircraft. Although the new European network is confined to the airspace above FL 330, phased extension to lower levels is planned. RNAV is already in common use in the USA and a few other parts of the world.

Helicopter Routes

The increasing number of offshore oil and gas installations around the world, with their busy helicopter support operations, has meant the introduction of protected airspace. The North Sea within the UK, Norwegian, Danish, and Dutch FIRs is a good example. Helicopter Main Routes (HMRs) are established when helicopters are flying on a regular basis from and to the mainland or between offshore platforms. A Helicopter Protected Zone (HPZ) may be established around two or more installations and a flight information and alerting service is supplied when a Helicopter FIS is present. Although the airspace (apart from the East Shetland Basin in which procedural separation is provided) is non-controlled, its dimensions are published and military and civil pilots must obtain clearance to penetrate an HPZ and keep a good look-out when in proximity to HMRs.

Special Use Airspace

This includes Danger Areas such as military weapons ranges, Prohibited Areas around critical installations, Restricted Areas for various defence purposes, Military Training Areas, and Air Defence Identification Zones. Details of the last can be found in Chapter 10.

Chapter 4

Navigational Aids

To enable a pilot to navigate along airways and to help controllers keep accurate track of his progress in relation to other traffic when no radar is available, extensive use is made of radio beacons. They also provide a means of holding in a particular area, locating an aerodrome, or as a fix for a let-down procedure in bad weather. Certain other aids are used for long range navigation and landing approaches and all are described below.

Non-Directional Beacon (NDB)

This most basic of aids is still used in less developed areas to mark air routes, its useful range being up to 100 miles. It remains the most common worldwide approach and landing aid, sometimes referred to as a Locator Beacon, with a range of about 15 miles in this application. The NDB consists of a radio transmitter in the medium frequency band which sends out a continuous steady note in all directions. A callsign of two or three letters in Morse code is superimposed at regular intervals as a check that the desired beacon has been selected.

The Automatic Direction Finder (ADF), or radio compass, fitted in an aircraft will, when tuned to the appropriate frequency, indicate the relative position of the transmission source by means of a needle on the Radio Magnetic Indicator (RMI). Unfortunately, NDBs suffer greatly from interference. Their signals can be deflected by high ground and coastal refraction and, if there is a thunderstorm in the area, the needle may point to its most active cell in preference to the beacon!

VHF Omni-Directional Range (VOR)

For the last 40 years VOR has been the ICAO standard international short range navaid, both to delineate airways and as an approach aid. It consists of a ground beacon which sends out a signal from which an airborne receiver can determine the aircraft's bearing (or radial, as it is termed) from the beacon. The receiver can add 180° to the 'From' indication and instruct the pilot which way to fly 'To' the station. A 'To/From' flag on the

Doppler VOR at Tahiti. (Thomson-CSF)

instrument face tells the pilot in which mode it is operating. Accuracy is increased by the addition of Doppler (DVOR), by which fluctuations in frequency wave motion emitted by an object moving at speed can be calculated. Most new and replacement installations are now DVORs.

VOR's great advantages are ease of use and freedom from static interference. With two VORs an accurate fix can be obtained from radial intersections. VORs can also be employed for ATIS broadcasts. Disadvantages are that the VHF signals are line-of-sight and thus can be cut off by mountains and man-made obstructions. For the same reason, a large area of coverage requires numerous expensive beacons and in some parts of the world NDBs may have to be interposed to maintain navigation assistance along an airway.

Distance Measuring Equipment (DME)

DME gives the pilot range information from a DME facility which, in the case of en route aids, is normally co-located with a VOR site. DME is increasingly coupled with Instrument Landing Systems, which makes fixed ground outer marker and middle marker beacons unnecessary. A special transmitter in the aircraft transmits pulses in all directions which are received at the DME ground station. As each pulse is received, an answering pulse is transmitted automatically and this is picked up in the aircraft. It is, in fact, the reverse of Secondary Radar (qv).

As the speed of radio waves is constant, a computer in the aircraft, which measures the time interval between the transmission of the pulse and the receipt of the response, is able to convert this interval into a distance and display it to the pilot in nautical miles and tenths (km in some cases). With more advanced equipment the 'time-to-go' to the beacon can also be displayed. Because DME measures slant range rather than ground distance, an aircraft at 30,000 ft overhead the facility will get an indication of approximately 5 nm. For practical purposes, however, this discrepancy is not a major problem. Combined with VOR, DME provides an extremely accurate position fix.

Instrument Landing System (ILS)

ILS is a pilot-interpreted aid which gives a continuous indication of whether the aircraft is left or right of the final approach track and also its position in relation to an ideal glide path to the runway. The latter is a standard 3°, giving an approximate rate of descent of 300 ft per minute. Certain airfields may have greater angles owing to high ground on the approach or other local considerations.

This information is augmented by marker beacons on the ground showing range, the outer marker at about four miles from touchdown and a middle marker at around 3,500 ft. As the aircraft passes over them they give an audible signal. The outer marker transmits low-toned dashes and the middle marker alternate dots and dashes on a medium tone. These markers cannot only be heard, they also illuminate lamps on the instrument panel. The outer marker activates a blue lamp and the middle an amber, each flashing in time with the codes. These signals are transmitted on a standard 75 MHz. Increased use of airport-sited DME is slowly phasing out the markers because the pilot now has a continuous read-out of his range from touchdown. It should be noted in passing that identical beacons, known as fan markers, were once common on airways. I believe that a few are still in use in some parts of the world.

A transmitter with a large aerial system known as the Localizer is sited at the far end of the runway, transmitting its signals on either side of the centreline of the runway and approach. These signals, called blue on the right of the approach path and yellow on the left, overlap in a beam about 5° wide exactly along the approach centreline. A second unit, the glide path transmitter, is sited at the nearer end and slightly to one side of the runway. Aboard the aircraft there is an instrument with two needles: one, which pivots from the top of its case, moves like a windscreen wiper and is actuated by the signals from the Localizer, while the other, which pivots on the left side of the case, moves up and down and is operated by the transmissions from the glide path aerial. When the two needles are crossed at right angles, the aircraft is lined up perfectly for a landing. Any deviation can rapidly be corrected by an experienced pilot. Localizer/DME systems dispense with the glide path beam, but the DME ranges enable the pilot to monitor his rate of descent. Some Localizers are designed to radiate a back-beam or back-course in the opposite direction. This can be used to provide directional guidance when going around from the instrument runway or for providing a back-course ILS to the reciprocal runway. In some parts of the world – the USA, for example – back-course approaches are quite common but they are regarded as unreliable and not air-calibrated for accuracy. The needle indications on a back-course are reversed.

Initial approach on to the ILS is normally achieved by Approach Radar, the aim being to place the aircraft on a closing heading of about 30° to the final approach at a range of between seven and nine miles. The aircraft should be at an appropriate altitude so that the glide path can be intercepted from below rather than attempting to 'chase' it from above. The final turn-on can be done by radar direction, but these days it is usually done automatically by coupling the ILS with the FMS or autopilot. Where no radar is available a procedural ILS is flown, similar to an NDB approach with the exception that the procedure turn will intercept the ILS and enable the pilot to establish himself on it.

ILSs are divided into three categories as follows:

Cat 1 – Operation down to 60 m decision height with Runway Visual Range in excess of 800 m.
Cat 2 – Operation down to 60 m decision height with RVR in excess of 400 m.
Cat 3 – Operation with no height limitation to and along the surface of the

ILS localizer antenna array at Helsinki-Vantaa. (Finnish CAA)

runway with external visual reference during the final phase of landing with RVR of 200 m.

Sub-divisions are Cat 3b, with RVR of 45 m, and a planned Cat 3c, with RVR of zero. They both require guidance along the runway and the latter also to the parking bay. Special ground lighting is required for Cat 2 and 3 ILSs, together with safeguarded areas around the sensitive aerial systems to avoid fluctuations caused by vehicles or taxying aircraft. Localizer/DME approaches are non-precision and therefore uncategorized.

Microwave Landing System (MLS)

MLS, which works in the much higher microwave frequency band around 5,000 MHz, was once nominated by ICAO as the future replacement for ILS but the target date for implementation gradually crept further away and the plan has now been shelved. The main reason for this is that satellite navigation is likely to make it redundant and, therefore, apart from Canada (which is now having second thoughts!) no one is willing to invest in universal MLS installations until the capabilities of SatNav are proved. The USA has already announced that it will adopt SatNav rather than MLS as its future universal approach aid.

The disadvantage of ILS is that it provides a single, fixed approach to the runway which all aircraft, regardless of flight characteristics, must follow. MLS uses two scanning beams, one lateral and one vertical, to provide a variety of approach paths for different aircraft types, ranging from airliners through STOL aircraft to helicopters. The lateral (azimuth) scanning beam allows curved approaches to be made with more efficient integration and separation of approach paths in complex airspace with major airports in close proximity. The well-known dog-leg approach to Runway 13 at Hong Kong would also be smoothed out by MLS. Distance information is provided by Precision DME (P-DME).

Autoland

The modern auto-pilot is able to accept ILS signals to fly the aircraft along both the Localizer and the Glide Path. Technical advances in both ground and aircraft equipment mean that suitably equipped aircraft with radio altimeters and auto-throttle can now perform automatic landings in zero visibility in perfect safety.

Area Navigation Systems or RNAV (Random NAVigation)

These permit aircraft to operate on any desired flight path within coverage of ground or satellite-based navaids or within the limits of self-contained aids or a combination of them. In other words, an aircraft can fly across country instead of from one beacon to another. For the moment RNAV is confined chiefly to oceanic airspace where the provision of surface navaids is obviously impracticable. However, approved RNAV routes are being established in upper airspace in various parts of the world. There are a number of systems, and modern Flight Management Systems are able to combine data from them to ensure very accurate navigation. The assumed performance of RNAV equipment envisages two levels of navigational accuracy for en route purposes. These are: (a) Basic RNAV, having a performance equal to or better than a track-keeping accuracy of plus or minus 9.5 km (5 nautical miles), which is similar to that achieved by aircraft without RNAV operating on routes defined by VOR or VOR/DME; and (b) Precision RNAV, having a performance equal to or better than a track-keeping accuracy of plus or minus 0.93 km (half a nautical mile) standard deviation.

Inertial Navigation System (INS)

A totally self-contained aid which uses gyros and accelerometers to measure continuously the acceleration of an aircraft and from this computes velocity and position information. Correct alignment is absolutely essential before starting or moving the aircraft. The latitude and longitude of the parking stand (published in navigation documents) is fed into the computer and the INS equipment automatically stabilizes itself to true north. This has to be checked at every new starting point. Thereafter, all the positions for the planned route are put into the computer in their correct order. These en route positions are known as way-points and INS will direct the aircraft via the FMS.

The INS computes Great Circle tracks (the shortest distance over a curved surface, i.e. the globe) between two way-points. As the aircraft approaches each way-point the system will draw the attention of the pilot to the fact. If a turn is to be made on to a new track, the aircraft will automatically commence its turn before arriving overhead the way-point so as to avoid overshooting it. The system also has the ability to return to the original flight path after temporary track deviation for weather avoidance.

Doppler

Another aid independent of ground transmitters, it uses a radar pulse transmitted by an aircraft at a certain frequency, which is reflected back to the aircraft at a different frequency according to its speed. This difference – the Doppler Shift – is proportional to the velocity of the aircraft. Doppler is of limited use over calm seas which do not reflect very well and so is used as a back-up aid rather than a primary system such as INS.

LORAN-C

A long-range navigation system which uses a master and three slave stations, each group being known as a chain. The master emits a series of uniformly spaced pulses per second, the slaves a corresponding precisely tuned series at a different phase. A computer on the aircraft, which must be able to receive the master and at least two of the slaves, measures the difference between the times taken for the master and slave transmissions to reach the receiver. Until recently it was necessary to plot the figures on a specially gridded LORAN chart but the aircraft computer will now display track and distance to go to a desired position, as well as other information such as ground speed. LORAN-C is in extensive use in the USA and is the principal navaid employed by oil industry helicopters over the Gulf of Mexico.

Decca

This operates on a similar principle to LORAN, using a chain of long wave transmitters, but is confined mainly to the British Isles and surrounding waters. The information received enables a pen on a moving map display to trace the path of the aircraft over the ground.

Omega

Eight VLF (Very Low Frequency) radio transmitters are situated at strategic points on the globe (Argentina, Australia, Hawaii, Japan, Liberia, North Dakota, Réunion Island, and Trinidad) so that aircraft and shipping with a simple receiver and Omega charts can find their position wherever they are. Omega is really a very long range form of LORAN.

VLF Navigation

This system employs 10 transmitters around the world (Australia, England (Rugby), Hawaii, Japan, Maine, Maryland, Norway, Panama, Puerto Rico and Washington State), which are used by the US Navy for communications with nuclear submarines. The transmitters are much more powerful than the similar Omega and therefore of extremely long range. The two systems are now often used in combination as VLF/Omega.

Flight Director or Flight Management System

A computer which simultaneously accepts information from all navigation and air data instruments and translates it into a single read-out or pictorial display, which tells the pilot what action to take in order to achieve the desired result. In most installations flight directors are then coupled to an autopilot which accepts their instructions and flies the aircraft accordingly – an integrated flight control system.

Transponder

The transponder is not a navigational aid in the true sense, but its use certainly enhances the service which ATC is able to provide. A small airborne transmitter waits until a radar pulse strikes its antenna and then instantly broadcasts, at a different frequency, a radar reply of its own – a strong synthetic echo. Since ordinary 'skin return' (the reflection of the ground radar pulse from the aircraft structure) is sometimes quite weak, especially at great distances or with small aircraft, the transponder helps the radar operator to track targets that might return an echo too weak to display.

The transponder is simple in concept but in practice is a complex, sophisticated device. It is triggered into either of two modes of reply by the nature of the ground radar pulse. Without delving too deeply into the technicalities, Mode A is employed for identification and Mode C for altitude information. Mode B is in military use only and Mode S is a datalink which will be further described below. At advanced Area Control Centres, radar replies are channelled into a computer which decodes the pulses, converts them into a letter and number display, and places a label alongside the appropriate target on the radar screen. The information includes the callsign and altitude of the aircraft. Secondary Surveillance Radar (SSR) has many advantages. One of the most important is that aircraft identification is easy to achieve and eliminates the necessity of requesting a turn of at least 30° from the original heading to confirm which blip is which on the screen. R/T loading is reduced considerably because altitude information is presented continuously to the controller and the pilot no longer needs to make constant checks.

Secondary radar differs from primary radar in that the 'echo' returned to the ground station is augmented by an authentic signal triggered from the aircraft's transponder equipment. Interference from weather and other causes is virtually eliminated. This is not the case with primary radar, which is not quite the magic eye some would believe; it suffers from all sorts of interference. Depending on the wavelength of a particular radar, weather clutter can swamp the screen with returns from rain and snow. There are ways of removing, or at least reducing, this clutter, but the aircraft echo can be lost too, especially if it is a small one. It is not uncommon, therefore, to hear a controller say that he is unable to give a radar approach due to rain clutter and offer an alternative, such as an ILS approach.

In North-West Europe the presence of too many secondary radars leads to another kind of problem: over-interrogation of aircraft, which 'garbles' the data. The answer is monopulse SSR, which is gradually replacing previous equipment. It requires only a limited number of interrogations to identify and locate aircraft and is able to differentiate between two aircraft in close proximity. Its accuracy and Mode S capability mean the controller can isolate one aircraft target among many and concentrate a flow of information upon it. (The 'S' in Mode S stands for 'Selective'.)

Traffic Alert and Collision Avoidance System (TCAS)

When Traffic Alert and Collision Avoidance System (TCAS) is fitted to aircraft, the equipment reacts to the transponders of other aircraft in the vicinity to determine whether or not there is the potential for a collision. TCAS is currently under worldwide evaluation, and in the USA is already mandatory for public transport aircraft having 30 or more seats. Warnings are given in two steps: typically 40 seconds before the assumed collision, a Traffic Advisory (TA) warning indicates where the pilot must look for the traffic; then between 20 and 30 seconds before the assumed collision a Resolution Advisory (RA) gives the pilot advice to climb, descend or remain level. The two warnings, TA followed by RA, can only be received if the conflicting aircraft is transponding on Mode C or Mode S. Where both aircraft in an encounter are fitted with TCAS Mode S, the transponders will communicate with each other to agree which aircraft is to pass below, and which above, the other. Warnings appear on a small cockpit display indicating the relative positions of the conflicting aircraft in plan view and ele-

Siemens Watchman-S radar head. The gate antenna is the SSR element. (Siemens)

vation, together with an aural warning spoken by a synthetic voice.

Datalink

Mode S datalink is an air/ground data communications facility using advanced SSR technology. SSR itself is a basic one-way datalink, automatically transferring to the ground, on request from the ground station, aircraft identity and height information from the aircraft avionics. This information is known as Mode A/C data and Mode S is a development of this function, allowing two-way transfer of much larger amounts of information to and from suitably equipped aircraft. Its advantages include the transfer of information without further cluttering busy VHF voice channels, better intelligibility because datalink messages are not subject to language confusion or radio interference, and higher integrity as automatic error detection and correction is possible. Mode S also provides better computer compatibility as airborne and ground systems can communicate without human involvement, allowing enhancements to ground radar and flight data processing systems.

Global Positioning System (GPS)

It is generally acknowledged that GPS is on the brink of revolutionizing aircraft navigation and will in time replace most existing navaids. Based on a series of satellites, it is capable of fixing an aircraft's position anywhere on the globe to within a few metres. It is already under trial on certain transoceanic flights and has the potential to become the major aid for instrument approaches during the next few years. GPS was conceived originally for US military use, the first dedicated satellite being launched in 1978. The completed system consists of 21 satellites with three on-orbit spares. The master control station is located in Colorado and is supported by monitoring stations on Ascension Island, Diego Garcia, Kwajelein, and Hawaii, spaced at nearly equi-distant points around the earth. The satellites require constant attention from the ground, including data uploads and orbital positioning adjustments. Without this maintenance it is said that the system would 'gracefully degrade' to complete uselessness in about two weeks! Comms are uplinked in S band at 2227.5 MHz and confirming messages are downlinked on 1783 Mhz.

GPS equipment in the aircraft measures the time that it takes the satellite signal to reach the receiver. To do this accurately, it needs the exact time the signal leaves the satellite. An error of a mere 1,000th of a second would put the position fix out by about 180 miles! Hence each satellite carries four atomic clocks which use the oscillation of cesium and rubidium atoms to keep unbelievably accurate time (one second tolerance to 30,000 years!).

Despite its sophistication, GPS works on the classic navigational principle of triangulation. However, instead of the position being the point at which three lines from different radio beacons intersect, a GPS position is derived from the intersection of three 'circles' transmitted from three satellites. The circles are in reality spheres around each satellite.

The receiver also checks a fourth satellite and if the fourth line of position does not pass through the other three, the receiver assumes that its own internal clock is out of synchronization. It then resets its clock automatically until all four position lines cross at the same point. This ingenious self-setting method means that a GPS receiver can operate with a simple quartz internal clock which is accurate over relatively short periods of time as long as it is reset often.

There are two distinct levels of positional accuracy: a Common Acquisition code, which has an accuracy of 100 metres and is available for all users; and a Precision code, encrypted for military use only, down to 16 metres. These errors can be reduced still further by the use of Differential GPS where an accurately surveyed site is used to provide correction factors for other GPS users.

Unfortunately, because of the military applications of GPS for target finding, the US Department of Defense currently applies what it calls 'selective availability'. This is the reason why the system is only accurate to within 100 metres, caused by intentional meddling with the satellite clocks' accuracy. Obviously, in various flashpoint areas of the world, the system might be cut off or interfered with at will to the detriment of civil users. For GPS to be adopted as the universal aircraft navaid, its integrity must be guaranteed but the DoD has yet to be persuaded to give this assurance. Since the United States voluntarily offered the satellite system for civil use as long ago as 1983, one assumes that this hurdle will be overcome in due course. GPS, by the way, is available to the general public in hand-held form for little more than the cost of a scanner!

Also operational is GLONASS, the GLobal Orbiting NAvigation Satellite System developed by the former USSR. A joint system combining the GLONASS and GPS satellites is planned so that worldwide coverage will be increased significantly and a greater measure of redundancy introduced to guard against satellite failure. GNSS 1 (Global Navigational Satellite System 1) is the term for joint GPS/GLONASS. The existing civil INMARSAT system, intended mainly for marine use, will provide a back-up pending a switch to a civil-controlled SatNav system designated GNSS 2. Differential GPS (DGPS) could provide an alternative to ILS and MLS by using a ground-based datalink signal as a cross-check of the accuracy of the satellite-derived position. Similarly, an American scheme proposes a

network of ground stations which will continuously monitor the accuracy
of the satellite signals.

Automatic Dependent Surveillance (ADS)

This is a technique which uses the positions derived from the aircraft's flight
management system, transmitted via a geostationary satellite to the ground.
FMS readings can also be sent so that controllers can compare the aircraft's
actual heading, speed, and climb rate with the flight plan filed before departure. The data consists of the aircraft's latitude, longitude, and altitude.
Already operational over parts of the Pacific, it eliminates huge gaps in
oceanic radar coverage by producing what is, in effect, a synthetic radar picture. An electronic display provides an easily interpreted image of both the
present situation and the predicted future to aid traffic management.

Aircraft Addressing and Reporting System (ACARS)

ACARS was developed in the USA by ARINC to reduce voice communications. For example, an exchange of routine ops information taking up to
one minute of congested VHF air time can be compressed by ACARS into
less than a second. A ground computer converts it into a print-out. As well
as a flight deck unit for keyboard data entry, an aircraft equipped with
ACARS is fitted with sensing devices which send data automatically to the
ground station when the aircraft has performed certain manoeuvres, such
as push-back from the departure gate, take-off, landing, and gate arrival.
SITA, the European communications company, has a version known as
AIRCOM which is compatible with ACARS. Use is increasing on this side
of the Atlantic and it is possible for the amateur to decode the messages
with the aid of a personal computer and equipment such as the *Airmaster*
produced by Lowe Electronics (see addresses on page 99). In the USA,
ARINC utilizes frequencies 129.125 and 131.55 for the datalink. In Europe
131.725 is allocated. The system is also expected to be adapted for HF use.
It has, however, great potential for routine ATC messages, as proved by
Canada and the UK, which have been passing oceanic clearances to selected airlines for several years via VHF datalinks and ACARS. Pilots must
still, however, request the clearance and acknowledge receipt by voice but
in the next phase of the trial a single button push on the ACARS unit will
confirm reception.

Chapter 5

Primary Tools of Air Traffic Control

VHF frequencies

Its clarity and lack of interference make VHF ideal for short-range aviation communications. The VHF air band was first established as 118–132 MHz in 1947 and extended downwards in 1959 to 117.975. Later the upper limit was increased to 136 and, very recently, to 137 MHz, by the International Telecommunications Union (ITU), which is the primary body controlling the allocation of all radio frequencies. There are, theoretically, 760 channels between 118.0 and 136.975 inclusive, with a spacing of 25 kHz between them. (117.975 and 137.0 are left unallocated as an interference buffer against adjoining bands.) ICAO recognizes that in some regions 100 kHz or 50 kHz spacing may provide an adequate number of frequencies suitably related to international and national air services and equipment having this spacing will remain acceptable.

A crisis is looming in European civil VHF frequency allocations because of increasing traffic and the new ATC sectors required to control it, as well as VHF datalink development. A proposal to reduce channel spacing to 8.33 kHz for high-level traffic in Europe has been adopted by ICAO. Implementation will solve the problem but it is likely to be some years before it becomes operational. It will mean that more digits will have to be transmitted (e.g. 133.33, 133.41, etc) but an alternative of using channel numbers on R/T instead of the full frequencies has been suggested.

Air band frequencies are allotted in blocks for different operational services but there are many anomalies, so the following is merely a rule-of-thumb. 118–121.4 are generally tower and approach channels; 121.5 is the VHF emergency frequency, with 123.1 as an auxiliary; 121.6–121.975 inclusive are reserved for ground movement, pre-flight checking, clearance delivery, and associated operations; 130–132 inclusive are company ops frequencies; 136.9–136.975 are reserved for air/ground datalink. In general, Area Control channels are to be found at the higher end of the band.

Immediately below the air band is the VHF navigation sub-band which begins at 108 MHz and is used for VORs and ILS localizer installations. Some VORs also carry speech communications in the form of continuous weather broadcasts for the associated airport. NDBs use the medium frequency band between about 200 and 400 kHz. Above the civil air band, from about 137 to 150 MHz, are a number of frequencies used by military ops and ATC units. The military UHF band extends from 225 to about 420 MHz, using 25 kHz spacing. More details can be found in Chapter 16 of *Air Band Radio Handbook*. Airfield fire and maintenance vehicles which need to go on the runways and taxiways are controlled on a UHF domestic frequency. They are not published but can be found in the range 455–461 MHz (NFM). Most operate on a split frequency (duplex) where the base station transmits on, for example, 455.6375 and the mobile on 460.9375. At many smaller airfields vehicle control will be done on the VHF tower frequency.

Since VHF transmissions follow approximate lines-of-sight, those from high altitudes carry many hundreds of miles. This means that a larger number of separate frequencies have to be allocated or the protection range between a single frequency shared by two Area Control Centres greatly increased. The recommended limits for contacting the larger airports are 25 nautical miles at 4,000 ft for tower and 25 miles from 10,000 ft for approach. Mutual interference can also arise under conditions of enhanced radio propagation even whilst operating within protected limits. Such conditions normally exist very briefly and the planning of frequency allocation takes account of all but the worst of these situations. All pilot/controller conversations are recorded automatically for use in incident and accident investigations. Radar and computer exchange data is also recorded, although, since this is an ICAO recommendation only, the practice is not universal.

For long-distance communications over oceans and undeveloped areas, HF radio is used in many blocks of frequencies between 2 and 30 MHz single side-band (SSB). It suffers from several disadvantages which are covered in more detail in Chapter 9.

Reporting Points and Beacons
Defined by ICAO as 'designators for significant points not marked by the site of a radio navigation aid', reporting points are sometimes described by the American term 'waypoint'. The hypothetical point is established at the intersection of published bearings and distances from two or more VOR/DMEs. Referred to officially by ICAO as 'name codes' – the five letters must be pronounceable and selected so as to avoid any difficulties in pronunciation by foreign pilots or ATC personnel. They should also

be easily recognizable in voice communications and free of any ambiguity with those used for other significant points in the same general area. Ideally the code should be unique, but if this requirement cannot be met a name code designator should not be repeated within 11,000 km (6,000 nm) of the location of the significant point where it was first used. The Regional Offices of ICAO are responsible for co-ordinating the allocations.

In areas such as the North Atlantic where no system of fixed routes is established, or where the routes followed by aircraft vary depending on operational considerations, significant points should be referred to by geographical co-ordinates in latitude and longitude. However, permanently established points serving as exit and/or entry into such areas should have names. Examples are CHAMP and FISSH on the NE coast of the USA, and ERNAN and BANLO on the east side of the Atlantic. There are many thousands of codes in use within the United States and it has been impossible to allocate recognizable names to each. A lot of them, therefore, are meaningless words. Of course, to an English speaker many of the codes in use in Europe and elsewhere mean nothing but many of them are derived from local geography and language.

The naming of ground-based radio navaids such as VORs and NDBs is much simpler. Whenever practicable they are named with reference to an identifiable and preferably prominent geographical location. Again the name should be easily pronounceable. Where the name of a geographical location in the national language causes difficulties with pronunciation, an abbreviation or contracted version of the name, which retains as much of its geographical significance as possible, should be selected, e.g. Furstenfeldbruck – *Fursty*; Jedrzejow – *Jedow*; Grudziadz – *Gruda*; Trzebielino – *Treblo*. The name should, if possible, consist of at least six letters and form two syllables and preferably not more than three. Each VOR beacon has a three letter code, (two in parts of the world where VORs are few) – the *ident* – associated with the full name, such as DPE (Dieppe) and RDS (Rodos). As well as being transmitted at regular intervals on the beacon frequency, it can be employed also by pilots as a phonetic means of referring to a reporting point, e.g. Delta Papa Echo. The codes should not be duplicated within 1,000 km (600 nm) of the location of the radio aid concerned.

In order to permit ATC to obtain information regarding the progress of aircraft in flight, selected significant points may need to be designated as reporting points either 'compulsory' or 'on request'. The aim is to keep the cockpit and controller workload and air/ground communications load to a minimum, so a compulsory reporting point does not always mean just that. Controllers may instruct an aircraft 'Next report at ABC', thus obviating any reports normally required en route to this point. ATC-approved direct routeing between positions many hundreds of miles apart will also eliminate any intervening reports which would otherwise be necessary.

Flight Plans

Flight Plans are a standard method of providing ATC units with details of intended flights. They are mandatory for most IFR flights, any flight across international borders, and flights into designated areas such as ADIZs, or anywhere the authorities deem to be difficult for search and rescue operations. For VFR flights in relatively densely populated countries such as the UK, Flight Plans are not required but pilots are encouraged to file them, particularly if they are flying over water or mountainous areas. In many Third World states Flight Plans are compulsory for every flight, sometimes because of paranoia over internal security but usually because they provide some clue to where an aircraft might be if it disappears in a wilderness area. The entry in the Uganda Aeronautical Information Publication says it all: 'In view of the great difficulties of search and rescue operations within Uganda, Flight Plans are mandatory for all flights'.

A Plan must be filed at least 30 minutes before departure but sophisticated ATC systems such as the United Kingdom's, require considerably more advance warning than this if the flight is to operate within a complex route network. Scheduled flights to a regular timetable are covered by the so-called Repetitive Flight Plan, better known as a 'stored plan'. This refers to the fact that when a computer is being used to support the air traffic services the information can be placed in what is termed the 'bulk store' and the computer programmed to produce the relevant data at a predetermined time. Where there is no ATC unit at destination, Flight Plans have to be 'closed' by the pilot as soon as practicable after landing to avoid unnecessary SAR operations.

Most Plans are sent via the AFTN (Aeronautical Fixed Telecommunications Network) or simply telephoned, but where no land-lines are available they may be sent by Radio Teletype, known as 'Ritty' from its initials RTTY. Many of these messages can be monitored in the UK on an HF receiver. By means of a personal computer or, alternatively, a RTTY module, the read-out is displayed on screen and printed out if desired. Unfortunately, the aeronautical stations around the world pour out masses of information, much of it weather forecasts and reports, so you may have to wait a long time to intercept a Flight Plan.

Typical Flight Plan

Transmitted in abbreviated form on the AFTN, the Flight Plan message reads: FPL AIH2953 IN EA32/M SDHIR/C EGGP0700 NO436F370 UB3 HON UA1 VEULE UL612 PAS UA41 GRO UA26 CMP DCT LIRA0223 LIRN EET/LFFF0031 LSAS0116 LFFF0117 LIMM0124 LIRR0151 REG/GSUEE SEL/DSAL.

Decoded, this means Airtours Airbus A320, wake turbulence category Medium, callsign AIH2953, IFR flight Liverpool to Rome Ciampino, standard navigation equipment, ETD 0700, true air speed 436 kt at FL 370, routeing via Honiley VOR, VEULE on the French coast near Dieppe, Passeiry VOR near Geneva, Pisa VOR, Grosseto VOR, Ciampino NDB, estimated elapsed time to Rome 2 hours 23 mins, alternate airfield Naples. The estimated elapsed times to each FIR boundary en route are also included, as well as the aircraft registration G-SUEE and SELCAL DSAL. The supplementary information (fuel endurance, total number on board, survival equipment, etc) is not sent but held on file at the departure airport.

Flight Progress Strips (FPS)

Amidst all the high tech hardware of modern ATC, the humble paper flight progress strip, which is slotted into a plastic holder, still has an important part to play. It carries all the basic details of each aircraft's flight plan: its callsign, type, required flight level, true air speed, route and destination, along with spaces in which the controller can annotate and update the information. They are still handwritten at many locations but machine-printed in busier ATC environments. The trend is towards electronic presentation of FPSs alongside the radar display or as a 'window' in the display itself, but it is doubtful if the FPS will ever be replaced in tower control positions.

Separations

The rules for keeping aircraft apart are known as Separation Standards and are agreed internationally. So-called procedural separation is employed when no radar is available and a large proportion of the world's ATC is still carried out in this way. It is safe but, with increasing traffic density, not very expeditious. There are two types: vertical in thousands of feet or the metric equivalent, and horizontal in nautical miles. There are three sub-divisions of horizontal separation, namely lateral, longitudinal, and radar. Separation *must* be provided (a) between controlled IFR flights, (b) between controlled IFR flights and Controlled VFR flights including Special VFR flights, (c) between Special VFR flights, and (d) between Controlled VFR flights in controlled airspace.

FLIGHT PLAN	ATS COPY

PRIORITY ≪= FF   ADDRESSEE(S)

≪≡

FILING TIME — ORIGINATOR ≪=

SPECIFIC IDENTIFICATION OF ADDRESSEE(S) AND/OR ORIGINATOR

3 MESSAGE TYPE	7 AIRCRAFT IDENTIFICATION	8 FLIGHT RULES	TYPE OF FLIGHT
≪= (FPL	K Q A 1 3 3	– I	S ≪=

9 NUMBER	TYPE OF AIRCRAFT	WAKE TURBULENCE CAT.	10 EQUIPMENT
–	E A 3 1	/ H	– S/C

13 DEPARTURE AERODROME	TIME
– E G L L	1 5 3 0 ≪=

15 CRUISING SPEED	LEVEL	ROUTE
– N 0 4 5 0	F 3 7 0	→ UA1 RBT UG32 TOP UB25 BEROK UA41 TAQ DCT

≪≡

16 DESTINATION AERODROME	TOTAL EET HR MIN	ALTN AERODROME	2ND ALTN AERODROME
– L I R F	0 2 0 5	→ L I R A	– ≪=

18 OTHER INFORMATION
– REG/5YBEL
EET/LFFF0030 LFMM0105 LIRR0145

)≪≡

SUPPLEMENTARY INFORMATION (NOT TO BE TRANSMITTED IN FPL MESSAGES)

19 ENDURANCE HR MIN	PERSONS ON BOARD	EMERGENCY RADIO UHF VHF ELBA
–E/ 0 6 3 0	→ P/ T B N	→ R/ X V E

SURVIVAL EQUIPMENT	POLAR	DESERT	MARITIME	JUNGLE	JACKETS	LIGHT	FLUORES	UHF	VHF
→ S / X	D	M X	– J	/ L	F	X	V

DINGHIES

NUMBER	CAPACITY	COVER	COLOUR
→ D / 1 5	→ 3 0 0	→ C	→ YELLOW ≪=

AIRCRAFT COLOUR AND MARKINGS
A/ WHITE RED

REMARKS
→ X / ≪=

PILOT IN COMMAND
C/ GRANT)≪=

FILED BY   SPACE RESERVED FOR ADDITIONAL REQUIREMENTS

CA48/RAF F2919(REVISED NOVEMBER 1985)   Carlo D.O. Org No 8810

Typical Flight Plan; a Kenya Airways Airbus A310 from London/Heathrow to Rome. (CAA)

It can be seen that separation does not apply to all types of flying activity. For example, outside controlled airspace VFR flights can operate on a 'see and be seen' basis. The concept of Controlled VFR flights, by the way, has not been adopted worldwide. It is not, for example, recognized in the UK, but VFR flights within controlled airspace are given traffic information on each other, as are VFR and IFR flights. ICAO states that the main vertical separation is 1,000 ft (or 300 metres in those parts of the world which still use metric measurements for vertical levels) below FL 290 and

Example of flight progress strip; a Monarch Airlines Boeing 737 from Manchester to Rhodes.

2,000 ft (600 m) at or above this level. For supersonic aircraft operating above FL 450 4,000 ft is the norm.

The application of lateral separation depends upon the usable accuracy of the navigational aid being used. Track separation is established by requiring aircraft to fly on specific tracks which are separated by a minimum amount. For longitudinal separation, time and distance are the alternatives, spacing depending on the availability of ground-based navaids. Where they are infrequent, the separation between aircraft following the same track is 15 minutes and over oceanic areas it can be as great as 30 minutes. (Oceanic separations are detailed in Chapter 9.) If navaids permit more frequent determination of position and speed, the time spacing can be reduced to 10 minutes. Where aircraft have departed from the same aerodrome and the preceding aircraft is maintaining a true airspeed (TAS) 20 kt faster than the succeeding aircraft, the separation is five minutes. This can also be applied to en route aircraft which have reported over the same exact reporting point. Where the preceding aircraft is 40 kt or more faster, a three minute separation may be applied.

The rules for aircraft flying on crossing tracks, climbing or descending, or combinations of these, are complex. Again they depend on the quality of information available to the controller. If a navaid can be used to determine that one of the aircraft has passed an exact position, the time spacing can be reduced accordingly. For aircraft crossing tracks at the same level the minimum is 15 minutes, or 10 minutes if the above condition applies. Where an aircraft is climbing or descending through the level of another, separation is either 10 minutes or five minutes.

Longitudinal separation based on distance is applied when VOR/DME is available. Subject to certain safeguards, aircraft on the same track and at the same cruising level will be a minimum of 20 nm apart. If the leading aircraft is 20 kt or more faster this can be reduced to 10 nm. Where aircraft are on crossing tracks and/or climbing or descending DME can be used to reduce separation considerably below the time margins described above.

For aircraft departing from an airport the minimum separation is one minute, provided the aircraft fly on tracks diverging by 45° or more immediately after take-off. Where aircraft are going the same way, and provided the first has filed a true air speed (TAS) 40 kt or faster than the second, the separation is two minutes. With a TAS of 20 kt or more faster than the second aircraft it becomes five minutes and in all other cases it is ten minutes. Radar may reduce some of these times and they are also affected by the demands of wake turbulence separation and local procedures. Normally requests for clearances are dealt with in the order in which they are received and issued according to the traffic situation. Obviously air-

Some examples of procedural separation.
1. *Same route, same speed.*
2. *Descending through another aircraft's level.*
3. *Climbing through another aircraft's level.*
4. *Converging tracks, same level.*
5. *Crossing tracks, same level.*
6. *Diverging tracks immediately after take-off.*
7. *Climbing through a level after departure.*

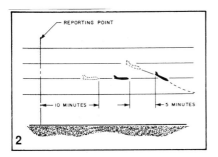

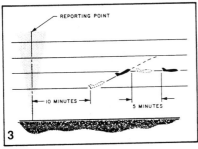

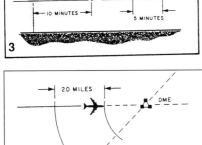

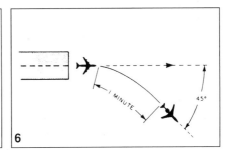

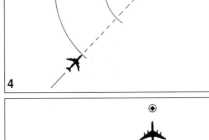

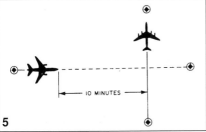

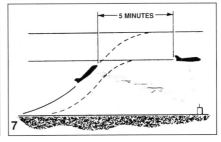

craft in emergency situations are given priority over all others, followed by certain categories of royal and government flights etc, as required by local regulations.

Wake Turbulence (Vortex)

Behind each wingtip of an aircraft in flight and, in the case of a helicopter, the tip of each rotor blade, a trailing cylinder of rapidly rotating air is created, known as a vortex. The heavier the aircraft, the more intense the effect, which is quite capable of rolling a following aircraft on to its back if it gets too close. These hazardous vortices begin to be generated when the nosewheel lifts off the runway on take-off and continue until it touches down on landing. To minimize the danger controllers apply a system of spacing which is outlined below.

ICAO divides aircraft into three wake turbulence categories according to their maximum total weight at take-off:

Heavy – 136,000 kg or more;
Medium – less than 136,000 kg but more than 7,000 kg;
Light – 7,000 kg or less.

The Heavy category includes such aircraft as the Boeing 747 and AN-124, while the Medium category embraces aircraft in the Boeing 737/MD-83 class, together with propeller aircraft such as the Hercules and Electra. Light includes the majority of executive jets downwards. The UK, as well as having a further category (Small), applies somewhat larger separations than the ICAO ones in certain circumstances. (See *Air Band Radio Handbook* Chapter 13.)

Arriving Flights

Where flights are operating visually (IFR flights operating under the reduced minima in the vicinity of aerodromes, VFR flights, or a mixture of the two), pilots are to be informed of the recommended spacing.

For other flights the spacing listed below is to be applied between successive aircraft on final approach.

Leading aircraft	Following aircraft	Minimum distance
Heavy	Heavy	4 miles (7.4 km)
	Medium	5 miles (9.3 km)
	Light	6 miles (11.1 km)
Medium	Heavy	3 miles (5.6 km)
	Medium	3 miles (5.6 km)
	Light	5 miles (9.3 km)
Light	Heavy	3 miles (5.6 km)
	Medium	3 miles (5.6 km)
	Light	3 miles (5.6 km)

Aerodrome Operations

The minimum spacing listed below is to be applied between successive aircraft, both IFR and VFR flights.

(a) Aircraft departing from the same runway or from parallel runways less than 760 m apart (including grass strips):

Leading aircraft	Following aircraft		Minimum spacing at time aircraft are airborne
Heavy	Medium Light	Departing from the same take-off position	2 minutes
Medium	Light	Departing from the same take-off position	2 minutes
Heavy (Full length take-off)	Medium Light	Departing from an inter-mediate take-off point	3 minutes
Medium	Light	Departure from an inter-mediate take-off point	3 minutes

(b) Operations on a runway with a displaced landing threshold if the projected flight paths are expected to cross:

Leading aircraft	Following aircraft		Minimum spacing at time aircraft are airborne or have touched down
Heavy arrival	Medium Light }	departure	2 minutes
Heavy departure	Medium Light }	arrival	2 minutes

(c) Opposite direction runway operations: a minimum of two minutes spacing is to be provided from the time a Heavy aircraft making a low or missed approach crosses over the take-off position of a Medium, Small or Light aircraft departing from the opposite direction runway.

Radar

Fortunately, in much of the world's more congested airspace radar is provided to give the controller a picture of the exact positions of his traffic rather than where the pilots believe they are in relation to sometimes inaccurate radio beacons. The very large safety margins previously deemed necessary can now be reduced dramatically. Vertical separation remains as before but basic lateral separation is usually five miles, reducing to three miles in some terminal areas. Under certain conditions these minima may be higher and will be published in radar unit local instructions. It all depends on the limitations of the radar in use, aircraft distance from the radar head, and several other factors.

However, as has already been mentioned, primary radar suffers from a number of disadvantages, the main one being the display on the screen of many unwanted signals as well as aircraft echoes. Weather clutter can be so intense that it literally swamps the reflected signals from aircraft. Although it can be virtually eliminated by several technical devices, the desensitizing effect on the radar often removes the aircraft echo as well. Ground clutter from buildings, hills and other obstructions can be suppressed by Moving Target Indicator (MTI), but again the detection capabilities of the radar are reduced. A further factor is the size of the aircraft concerned. Obviously, the larger it is, the better the target, but any aircraft will produce fluctuating echoes as its position alters relative to the radar beam.

The answer to most of the shortcomings of primary radar is Secondary Surveillance Radar (SSR), which requires aircraft to carry a piece of equipment known as a transponder. SSR is independent of the aircraft echoing area because the airborne installation has its own transmitter and much less energy is needed than in primary radar for the same operational range. As the airborne response is on a different frequency from the ground interrogator, reflected ground clutter and other unwanted echoes will not be received. The ground-based frequency is 1030 MHz, the aircraft reply is on 1090 MHz.

A further advantage of SSR is that aircraft can be identified without the need for turns, which also reduces the number of R/T transmissions. Unless an aircraft's identity can be confirmed by a handover from another radar unit under certain specified conditions, the process of identification involves establishing the aircraft's current heading and then giving it a turn of at least 30 degrees. Having observed the heading change and obtained confirmation from the pilot that he is steady on the new heading, the controller can now vector the aircraft on to final approach or for transit through his airspace.

SSR's other great advantage is that altitude information can be sent automatically from an aircraft to the ground. This necessitates an altimeter fitted with a coded disc in addition to the normal indicator scale. When interrogated by the ground station, the position of the disc is sensed and the response decoded into numerical form as a direct indication of altitude in hundreds of feet on the controller's display. It is difficult to explain how the interrogation and reply process works without getting too technical. Suffice it to say that the energy pulses for identity and altitude are sent at fixed intervals (8 and 21 microseconds, respectively) and the aircraft transponder is able to recognize this and make the appropriate replies. The identification facility is called Mode A and that for altitude is Mode C.

Mode B is in military use only and Mode D is reserved for future developments. Mode S is a further refinement and provides a datalink enabling much more information to be passed to ground stations automatically.

The reply from the transponder consists of a train of pulses which can produce 4,096 different four-digit codes, the so-called *Squawk* allocated by ATC. Before it can be used for separation purposes, Mode C has to be verified by comparing the pilot's altitude or flight level report with the read-out on the controller's display. If, on verification, there is a variation of plus or minus 300 ft or more between the level read-out and the reported level, the pilot will normally be instructed to switch off Mode C. If independent switching of Mode C is not possible, the pilot will be told to select code 0000 to indicate a transponder malfunction.

Since 1969, ICAO's regional offices have periodically produced lists of SSR codes used for ATC purposes. The aim is to select and co-ordinate the allocation of individual codes by states. They are divided into two distinct categories: transit codes for international use and domestic codes for national use. Transit codes are allocated to specific ACCs for assignment to international transit flights in a system known as ORCAM (Originating Region Code Allocation Method). Aircraft will retain the assigned code beyond national boundaries but not normally beyond Participating Areas. PA West, for example, includes much of Western Europe.

Certain codes are reserved for special purposes on a worldwide scale. They include 7600 for radio failure and 7700 for emergency. There is also a special code for unlawful interference, more familiarly known as hijacking. In all three cases a pulsing effect on the controller's display and an aural alarm will alert him to the situation. Code 2000 is employed by aircraft entering an SSR environment from an adjacent region where the operation of a transponder has not been required. Unfortunately there is a limited number of codes available, but the universal adoption of Mode S will one day enable every aircraft in the world to carry its own unique transponder code.

Radar Data Processing (RDP)

On advanced radar systems automatic radar data processing removes unwanted signals such as ground and weather echoes and limits the information on the radar display to aircraft responses. This computer technology is used to decode the combined radar information from several antenna to produce the best possible picture. It also enables the transponder information to be displayed as a label ('tag' in US parlance) alongside the radar position symbol, a computer-generated 'blip'. RDP can be correlated with Flight Data Processing described below to display callsign, actual flight level, and destination. The aircraft's ground speed and other information can also be displayed as required. All modern radar displays use colour to identify different types of airspace, land and water areas, active and pending traffic, as well as a variety of other operational features specified by the customer.

Flight Data Processing (FDP)

Regardless of the way a country's airspace is organized – controlled or uncontrolled, air routes or direct routes based on RNAV or ground-based aids – FDP can make it safer and more efficient by automating many previously manual ATC tasks. Among its numerous functions are the calculation of estimated flight times between radio beacons, prediction of traffic conflicts, and the alerting of the controller if a cleared route of flight will infringe on the protected airspace of any other flights within the system. It can also provide a data base of 'stored' flight plans for scheduled flights and automatic printing of flight progress strips at appropriate control sectors. Where digitized radar data is available, the processing can be combined, resulting in a fully integrated flight/radar data processing system. FDP is easily interlinked with other computers. For example, Finland's new system transmits flight plan messages to the European Integrated Flight Plan Processing System in Brussels as well as Eurocontrol's Central Flow Management Unit.

Short Term Conflict Alert (STCA)

STCA warns controllers by visual and/or audible means that aircraft are in danger of collision. In busy terminal areas, spurious warnings have always been a problem with ground-based conflict alert systems and the equipment has largely been confined to en route airspace. However, STCA software has now been designed to recognize the high manoeuvring rates of air traffic in TMAs and so minimize false alarms.

Speed Control

Commercial aircraft tended to fly at approximately the same speeds until the advent of civil jets about 30 years ago resulted in considerable differences in performance. Then came the appalling mid-air collision between a DC-8 and a Super Constellation over New York in December 1960. One of the contributory causes was found to be that the DC-8 was flying at far too high a speed for a congested terminal area. As a result the FAA imposed speed limits for aircraft operating in high density areas and below 8,000 ft on certain busy airways. The basic speed limit in TMAs is 250 kt indicated airspeed (IAS) and, subject to this, controllers may ask pilots to increase or reduce speed to maintain the spacing between aircraft on approach. As a general guide, the lower limit for jet aircraft is 170 kt and for multi-propeller aircraft 150 kt, and pilots are required to advise if they are unable to comply with any restriction. For departing aircraft, ATC will endeavour to remove the speed limit as soon as possible, using the phrase 'No ATC speed restriction'. Australia is unusual in declaring that speed control will not be attempted when known turbulence exists.

Continuous Descent Approaches are an American development which has spread to many busy airports in Europe and elsewhere. They are designed to permit a low drag, low power descent profile to be flown in a clean configuration (i.e. no wheels or flaps) until a much later stage of the approach, thus reducing noise and fuel consumption. The usual descent profile approximates to a three degree glidepath from descent points normally a short distance after leaving the holding stack. The choice of predetermined speeds is tailored to suit the overall speed range of aircraft types, but is generally in the order of 210 kt IAS during the intermediate approach. This reduces to 170 kt on base leg and 160 on approach down to a four mile final, after which no speed restriction may be applied.

Speed expressed as a Mach Number, i.e. a proportion of the speed of sound, is generally used on oceanic routes or on certain long overland flights. It is important that pilots maintain the declared or allocated Mach Number because it is used for procedural separation.

Flow Control

By the early 1970s, the traffic density in certain parts of Europe had reached a point where the ATC system was no longer able to cope with the demand. Some states were equipped with radar, others were not, and the result was a considerable variation in traffic handling capacity. Local restrictions to traffic flow tended to move the problem further back down the line and it became obvious that the only solution was international co-operation under the auspices of ICAO. In June 1980, a special European Regional Air Navigation Meeting was held in Paris. Its conclusion was that the ATC system could not be expanded indefinitely but it could be improved, and the provision of an Air Traffic Flow Management (ATFM) service could eliminate most of the difficulties.

This service is designed to ensure an optimum flow of traffic to, or through, areas within which traffic demand exceeds available ATC capacity. In effect, it is a balancing act between traffic demand and the ability of ATC to accommodate it. ATFM's terms of reference are defined as Strategic and Tactical. The former takes place up to 24 hours prior to time of flight and its activities include identifying possible ATC overloads by comparing forecast traffic demands with ATC capacity values and then planning appropriate regional action. The Tactical phase merges with the end of the Strategic phase and continues until the actual handling of the flight, and entails the monitoring of real air traffic demand to ensure that overall ATC capacity is not likely to be exceeded. Where necessary, Flow Control is applied to tailor the demand to safe limits. A further safety net, the so-called RVR Barrier, is used for domestic traffic into certain large airports. Aircraft are not permitted to depart until the RVR at destination has risen above a level at which they will be able to make a landing. The idea is to prevent them occupying limited holding stack levels while waiting for weather improvement. Long haul arrivals with limited fuel reserves and aircraft with Cat 3 approach capability thus gain priority.

The Traffic Orientation Scheme (TOS) forms the basis for the routeing of aircraft on the major traffic flows during the summer peak season, including orientation, i.e. one way or two way. The aim is to balance the demand on Europe's air route system by confining traffic for a specific destination to a particular route, with an alternative in the event of unforeseen en route congestion. Tied in with TOS is the Contingency Routeing Scheme, designed to avoid airspace over the former Yugoslavia.

The initial ATFM Unit areas comprised the following Flight Information/Upper Information Regions: Stavanger, Oslo, Stockholm, Tampere, Malmo, Warsaw, Bratislava, Budapest, Bucharest, Sofia, Istanbul, Ankara, Nicosia, Athens, Rome, Marseille, Barcelona, Seville, Canary, Madrid, Brest, London, Shannon, and Scottish. Within these areas there were 11 separate ATFMUs, plus a twelfth – Moscow – which, technically, was outside the area. They oversaw ACCs within their respective states and immediate neighbours. Copenhagen, for example, was responsible for Stavanger, Oslo, Malmo, Stockholm, Gothenburg, and Helsinki ACCs. The system was very complex, however, and Eurocontrol was given the task of establishing a Central Flow Management Unit (CFMU) which would co-ordinate slot availability and allocation throughout Europe. The number of FMUs was reduced to five – London, Paris, Frankfurt, Rome, and Madrid – using a conference telephone link. By the end of 1995, the new CFMU at Haren, near Brussels, will have taken over all their duties. Towards the end of the decade it is expected that its responsibilities will have extended to Eastern Europe as well. Flow control is not, of course, unique to Europe; the USA has its own system, as has Japan, and both are described later in this book.

Chapter 6

Aerodrome Control

The basic unit of ATC is Aerodrome Control, referred to colloquially as 'The Tower'. In the words of an ICAO document, the tower issues 'information and clearances to aircraft under its control to achieve a safe, orderly and expeditious flow of air traffic on and in the vicinity of the aerodrome with the object of preventing collisions between (a) aircraft flying in the traffic circuits around an aerodrome; (b) aircraft operating on the manoeuvring area; (c) aircraft landing and taking off; (d) aircraft and vehicles operating on the manoeuvring area; (e) aircraft on the manoeuvring and obstructions on that area'. The manoeuvring area, by the way, is defined as 'that part of an aerodrome to be used for the take-off, landing and taxying of aircraft, excluding aprons.' In other words, the runways and taxiways whether paved or natural surfaced.

Amongst its other important responsibilities is alerting the safety services in the event of accident or emergency, and the reporting to pilots of any unserviceable navigational or lighting equipment. Airfield lighting

Zurich's futuristic control tower. (Siemens)

is also operated from the tower. The runway-in-use is selected with due regard for wind strength and direction, and normally a pilot will expect to land or take off as nearly into wind as possible. However, other factors are taken into account by the tower controller, such as runway lengths and the approach and landing aids available, as well as other traffic. If the runway-in-use is not considered suitable, the pilot-in-command is at liberty to request permission to use another one. This will be granted with the proviso that he may thereby incur a delay.

To facilitate the running of the busiest airports it is often necessary to split the duties of Aerodrome Control into Air Control and Ground Movement Control (GMC). The latter's responsibility covers aircraft moving on the apron and aircraft and vehicles on the manoeuvring area except on runways and their access points. At some very busy US airports GMC is further sub-divided with, for example, separate frequencies for inbound and outbound aircraft at Chicago O'Hare and for the two main runways at Atlanta, and separate north and south frequencies at Los Angeles International. Tower (Air Control) may also be split into two for different runways or sectors of an airport. For operations in bad visibility, many airports are equipped with ground movement radar to assist the controllers in monitoring the positions of traffic on the runways and taxiways. Further developments include identity labels added to aircraft images on the radar display and Mode S datalink to confirm position information.

Associated with Ground Control is the Clearance Delivery frequency which, as its name implies, is used to pass route clearances to aircraft prior to taxi. Callsign in Europe is usually *Delivery*, in North America *Clearance*. Major US airports now use Pre-Departure Clearances for participating airlines to relieve congested frequencies. ATC issues the clearance direct to the airline's dispatch office by teletype or computer link and it then goes to the crew as a printed message or via ACARS. Another useful method of reducing R/T communications is the Departure ATIS which, like its Approach counterpart, broadcasts continuous information on QNH, runway-in-use, wind speed and direction, temperature, and any other pertinent information such as taxiway closures and unserviceabilities.

Traditionally, the Aerodrome Controller has had very few aids apart from a wind speed and direction indicator, a pair of binoculars and a signalling lamp for aircraft with radio failure, but ATMs (Air Traffic Monitors) are now coming into wide use. This is a daylight viewing radar using information from the main approach radar but normally confined to a radius of about 10 miles from the airport. It is invaluable for such functions as judging whether or not there is room to clear a departing aircraft for take-off ahead of traffic on final approach, or, in poor visibility, to confirm when a departing aircraft has turned prior to launching a second aircraft whose route takes it straight ahead or turns it the opposite way.

Runway occupancy is governed by the following rules:

(*a*) An aircraft shall not be permitted to begin take-off until the preceding departing aircraft is seen to be airborne or has reported 'airborne' by R/T and all preceding landing aircraft are clear of the runway in use.

(*b*) A landing aircraft will not be permitted to cross the beginning of the runway on its final approach until a preceding departing aircraft is airborne.

ICAO allows landing clearance to be issued when there is 'a reasonable assurance that the separation described above will exist when the aircraft crosses the runway threshold. It must not, however, be issued until a preceding landing aircraft has crossed the runway threshold.' Although frowned upon by most states, particularly the UK, such landing clearances in advance are approved by the FAA and Transport Canada and are a constant feature of US and Canadian airports which have high density traffic. They reduce the possibility of an aircraft having to go around when a controller is occupied with other traffic and is thus unable to issue a landing clearance as soon as the runway is vacated by a preceding aircraft.

Airports outside controlled airspace possess an aerodrome traffic zone

Cardion Airport Surface Detection Equipment (ASDE) in use at Zurich. (Siemens)

through which flight is prohibited without ATC clearance. The circuit ('pattern' in American parlance) is a standard left-hand but at some locations it may be right-hand to avoid built-up areas or high ground. In mountainous countries such as Switzerland the standard circuit in a valley may have to be very close to the airfield with curving cross-wind and base-legs. Circuit height is normally 1,000 ft above surface level but at some airfields it may be different.

The circuit is divided into four legs: crosswind, downwind, base, and final approach. The first aircraft to report downwind will be told to 'report final'. ('Number one' may be added to this.) The second will be told: 'Number two, follow the Cherokee on base'; and so on. If the circuit is very busy the tower may instruct a pilot to 'report before turning base, four aircraft ahead.' When he does this he will be given an update on his position in traffic, there perhaps being only two ahead by this time.

The standard circuit-joining procedure is to arrive overhead the field at 2,000 ft and descend to 1,000 ft on the dead side, i.e. the one opposite the live downwind leg. Whilst watching for departing traffic, the pilot then joins the crosswind leg over the upwind end of the active runway. This should ensure that a joining aircraft does not conflict with one just airborne, as there have been numerous cases in the past of collisions because of careless rejoins a mile or so off the end of the runway. Of course a high performance aircraft can easily be at 1,000 ft by the time it reaches the end of a fairly long runway, so it is up to the tower to make sure that a joining aircraft does not cross its path. At many controlled airports the standard join is not used, aircraft being authorized to join directly onto final, base, or downwind.

Scheduled and other large aircraft are usually fed straight into the final approach, which can sometimes be tricky. One way to achieve this safely, if there is circuit traffic, is to instruct the trainer to extend the downwind leg until he has the arriving aircraft in sight and then follow it. The other solution is an orbit – a 360° turn – always away from the final approach, to be continued until the traffic is sighted. The first method has the disadvantage that a strong tailwind may carry the aircraft out of sight of the aerodrome. An orbit may be impracticable because of following traffic in the circuit. In busy traffic situations when large aircraft are expected, trainers may be told to land and taxi back to the holding point to await further take-off clearance. Another complication is vortex wake, a phenomenon once referred to as slipstream or propwash. As explained earlier, this is a rapidly revolving cylinder of air from each wingtip which can be violent enough to overcome the control forces of a following aircraft and invert it. There are three categories (four in the UK), depending upon maximum total weight at take-off, these being Heavy, Medium, and Light. More details are to be found on pages 50-51.

Helicopter operations are less of a problem than might be imagined, the main one being crossing the active runway. However, they can clear it quickly and can thus be slotted between arriving and departing aircraft, remaining below 500 ft until clear of the traffic zone. The same applies to their arrival, although at places with an adjacent wide river, pilots are understandably reluctant to approach or depart at low level. In this case, the normal procedure is to change the direction of the circuit traffic away from the helicopter. Some large airports have special access lanes for helicopters, designed to deconflict them from fixed wing traffic. Overflying helicopters are treated like any other crossing traffic, either cleared overhead above 2,000 ft if the circuit is busy, or asked to report a few miles away and given traffic information so that they can fly through the pattern without conflict.

The Aerodrome Controller is, of course, pre-warned of arriving traffic by Approach and at some places he handles both functions on the same frequency. Similarly, for departing IFR traffic he will have the flight progress strips on his pending board, made up when the flight plan was filed with ATC. In certain countries with extensive wilderness areas flight plans will be compulsory for VFR flights as well.

Aircraft on IFR flight plans should first request permission to start engines so that ATC can warn of any likely delays and thus minimize fuel burn. If Flow Control measures are in force for its route, the aircraft should already have been given an Approved Departure Time (often known as a 'slot') via the operator or handling agent. A short time is allowed beyond this to cover taxying delays, etc. Alternatively, a time band for crossing an en-route position may be given, for example 'Cross RUGAS between 1420 and 1430.' Sometimes ATC will allocate a start-up time so that aircraft can taxi to the runway in a pre-planned order.

If there is no delay, 'Start up approved' is passed, together with the outside air temperature in degrees Celsius. (Fahrenheit in the USA, Canada and a few other places.) The QNH, QFE, runway-in-use, and wind information may also be given in the same transmission, although this is optional. The alternative is to pass them when taxi clearance is given. In practice, pilots often call in advance for this 'airfield data', acknowledge it and say 'call you again for start'. The presence of a Departure ATIS, of course, makes this unnecessary.

If there are no problems, taxi instructions will be given to the appropriate runway. In the meantime, ATC will have obtained an airways clearance from the parent ACC by land line and this is passed to the aircraft. (Where a Clearance Delivery frequency is used this will already have been done.) Local procedures vary considerably from one airport to another and it may be necessary to contact the ACC again as the subject nears the runway for permission to let it take off. In general terms, the busier the airport the less the co-ordination required. Standard Instrument Departure routes (SIDs, described below) will have been designed to eliminate or at least minimize conflict with those taken by arriving aircraft. Ideally, the sequence of departing aircraft will be organized so that the first will turn on to its desired route one way, the second the other, and a third will climb straight ahead. Various combinations of these will reduce delay to a minimum and the demands of vortex wake separation are also taken into account (See page 50) Immediately after take-off an aircraft will be transferred to Approach, Departure, or Area Control. By local agreement, Area may delegate considerable amounts of airspace to Approach Control for the separation of inbound and outbound traffic. Corfu, for example, handles traffic up to Flight Level 120, as does Naples.

The SSR code, or *squawk* as it is known, is allocated according to a predetermined system. The UK participates in the internationally agreed Originating Region Code Assignment Method (ORCAM), developed by Eurocontrol and endorsed by ICAO. Since there are insufficient code blocks to develop a world-wide system, it has been necessary to group certain countries into Participating Areas, the ICAO EUR region being divided into five of them. ORCAM is designed to reduce R/T and cockpit workload by allocating an SSR code which will

Critical Positions in the Aerodrome Traffic Circuit.

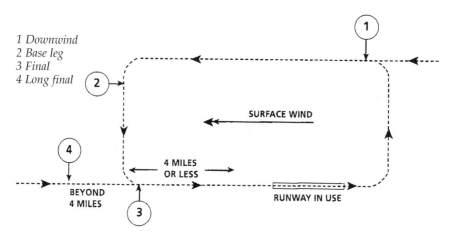

1 *Downwind*
2 *Base leg*
3 *Final*
4 *Long final*

be retained by the aircraft from take-off to touchdown. This helps controllers in forward planning, particularly in areas of radar data processing. Each ACC is allocated two blocks of codes, one for internal flights (Domestic) and the other (ORCAM) for international flights. The ACC with jurisdiction over the airspace first entered by an aircraft will assign a discrete code from one of its blocks. The code will depend on the destination and will be retained throughout the flight within the Participating Area, being transferred from centre to centre along the route. SSR Mode S will solve the problem of the very limited number of codes available (4,096). Mode S transponders employ a unique 'address' for each individual aircraft, 16 million being available worldwide. Unfortunately, the ground interrogator system has its own limitations at present which severely offset the airborne advantages. Approach Control units with SSR capability have their own small block of codes which they can allocate to traffic crossing their area – provided, of course, that the aircraft is transponder-equipped.

Aerodrome Control Phraseology
Aircraft: *Tower Lufthansa 135 request start-up.*
ATC: Lufthansa 135 start-up approved, temperature plus 8.

These start-up requests should always be made by aircraft which intend to fly airways, as there may be unexpected delays. Far better to postpone starting for a few minutes than waste fuel at the holding point. The phrase 'Start-up at your discretion', together with an expected departure time, may be used so that the onus is on the crew to start engines at a convenient time. Note that the words 'at your discretion' are used by controllers to pass the accountability for a course of action firmly into the hands of the pilot. Controllers have very definite responsibilities and they are understandably reluctant to take on any extra ones.

Aircraft: Amsterdam Ground KLM 153 request pushback.
ATC: KLM 153 pushback approved.
Many airports have nose-in parking at the terminal to save apron space and to facilitate passenger handling. Aircraft have to be pushed backwards by a tractor into a position from which they can taxi for departure.

Aircraft: *Tower Skybird 123 request taxi.*
ATC: Skybird 123 taxi Charlie hold Runway 27 via the parallel taxiway, wind 240 at 12 knots, QNH 1008.
Taxi instructions must always specify a clearance limit, which is the point

at which an aircraft must halt and ask for further permission to proceed. The limit is normally the holding point of the runway-in-use but it may also be an intermediate position, perhaps another runway which is in intermittent use. To maintain a smooth operation, controllers try to anticipate calls from taxying aircraft so that they do not actually have to stop at intermediate points. Many airports have complex taxiway systems and each significant section is given a letter, number, or alphanumeric. Some have descriptive names such as North West Taxiway, Parallel, Outer, Inner, and Loop. Chicago O'Hare has several oddities, including the Scenic, Lakeshore Drive, the Bridge, and the Wedge. Holding points are often allocated a letter from Alpha onwards.

The ideal is to establish a circular flow of taxying aircraft so that the ones just landed do not get in the way of those moving towards the hold-

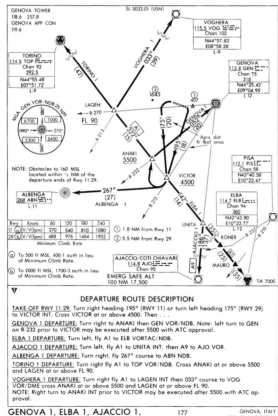

DEPARTURE ROUTE DESCRIPTION

TAKE-OFF RWY 11-29: Turn right heading 195° (RWY 11) or turn left heading 175° (RWY 29) to VICTOR INT. Cross VICTOR at or above 4500. Then . . .

GENOVA 1 DEPARTURE: Turn right to ANAKI then GEN VOR/NDB. Note: left turn to GEN on R-232 prior to VICTOR may be executed after 5500 with ATC approval.

ELBA 1 DEPARTURE: Turn left, fly A1 to ELB VORTAC/NDB.

AJACCIO 1 DEPARTURE: Turn left, fly A1 to UNITA INT, then A9 to AJO VOR.

ALBENGA 1 DEPARTURE: Turn right, fly 267° course to ABN NDB.

TORINO 1 DEPARTURE: Turn right fly A1 to TOP VOR/NDB. Cross ANAKI at or above 5500 and LAGEN at or above FL 90.

VOGHERA 1 DEPARTURE: Turn right fly A1 to LAGEN INT then 033° course to VOG VOR/DME cross ANAKI at or above 5500 and LAGEN at or above FL 90.
NOTE: Right turn to ANAKI INT prior to VICTOR may be executed after 5500 with ATC approval.

GENOVA 1, ELBA 1, AJACCIO 1,   177   GENOVA, ITALY   *Standard Instrument*
ALBENGA 1, TORINO 1, VOGHERA 1 DEPARTURE   GENOVA/SESTRI   *Departure Chart for Genoa.*

ing point. Alas, many airports have inadequate taxiway systems with two-way flows and bottlenecks, perhaps in the worst cases having runway access at only one end. A refusal to give crossing clearance of an active runway is passed in the form: 'Iberia 123 hold short Runway 27.' Permission to continue is: 'Iberia 123 cross Runway 27, report vacated.'

When ready for take-off, permission is sought from the tower. If the runway is occupied by traffic which has just landed, the aircraft will be told to 'line-up', the American equivalent being 'taxi into position'. If there is traffic on final, the aircraft at the holding point may be told: 'Behind the 737 on short final, line up behind'. (Note that this rather clumsy ICAO phraseology is modified in the UK.) Care must be taken that there is no possibility of confusion with another aircraft which may have just landed. Where a preceding aircraft is beginning its take-off roll, the second aircraft may be told: 'After the departing Cessna, line up'. The use of the words 'cleared immediate take-off' means that the aircraft must go without delay to leave the runway free for landing traffic. It is only to be used where there is actual urgency so that its specific meaning is not debased.

I have already covered the circuit joining procedure, so a few examples of phraseology will suffice, using the abbreviated German registration DNK.

Aircraft: DNK five miles east for landing.
ATC: DNK join right hand downwind Runway 05, QFE 1004; or DNK cleared straight-in approach Runway 27 QFE 1004.
Aircraft: DNK downwind.
ATC: DNK Number 2, follow the Cessna 150 on base.
Aircraft: DNK Number 2, traffic in sight.
OR
ATC: DNK extend downwind, number 2 to a Cessna 150 4 miles final on radar approach.
Aircraft: DNK wilco.

The criteria for issuing landing and take-off clearances have already been explained but there are a few other factors. Training aircraft may wish to do a 'touch and go' landing; in other words, the aircraft lands, continues rolling, and takes off again without a pause. The wording 'cleared touch and go' is the only one approved officially, but pilots may ask for a 'roller', the military equivalent. Instructions to carry out a missed approach may be given to avert an unsafe situation, such as when one aircraft is too close behind another on final. 'DNK go around, I say again, go around. Acknowledge'.

Depending on local procedures, a departing aircraft will be retained on the tower frequency until it is clear of the circuit or changed to Approach immediately. Airways flights will be transferred to the ACC just after take-off or as soon as they have been separated from any conflicting traffic by Approach or Departure Control. When the landing roll is complete, the arriving aircraft will be told to clear the runway in the following manner:

ATC: DNK vacate left.
OR
ATC: DNK taxi to the end, report runway vacated.
OR
ATC: DNK take next right. When vacated contact Ground 121.7.

The appropriate taxying instructions are then passed. Pilots may also be given their airborne and landing times by the tower, although there is no official requirement for this. A further detail is defined as 'Essential Aerodrome Information' and refers to any obstruction or unserviceability which is likely to affect operations. It is always prefixed 'caution' and some examples follow:

Caution work in progress ahead north side of the taxiway.
Caution PAPI Runway 27 unserviceable.
Caution large flock of birds north of Runway 27 threshold.

Standard Instrument Departures (SIDs)

SIDs have been developed for the main runways of major airports, the routes terminating at an airway, advisory route or at a radio navigational fix. All aircraft departing from an airport under IFR are required to follow the appropriate SID, unless and until authorized to do otherwise by the relevant ATC unit. Each SID has a designator which incorporates the name of the radio beacon on which it is based. An example is the DOM1F from Runway 14 Left or Right at Cologne/Bonn, based on the Dortmund VOR: 'Initial clearance limit 5,000. Then climb as directed by ATC. Climb straight ahead to 3.5 DME KBO (Koln/Bonn VOR) cross at 1,500 or above, then turn left and proceed via WYP VOR [Wipper] to DOM VOR on 018°. Depart DOM VOR on radial 018 to 6 DME. Then turn left to intercept Airway B5.' Subsequent changes to SIDs result in a new number up to nine, then back to one again. The suffix letter indicates the specific runway or identifies one of several routes established with reference to a particular point. Some airports have separate SIDs for jet and propeller aircraft to take advantage of the former's rapid rate of climb and keep the slower types out of their way.

Chapter 7

Area Control

Aircraft flying on a country's air route system are controlled from one or more Area Control Centres (ACCs). The number of such facilities depends upon the complexity and size of the airspace but the trend is towards reducing the number of ACCs and thus the amount of co-ordination necessary. Chile, for example, aims to consolidate its current five ACCs into a single facility at Santiago. ACCs are not necessarily sited on or adjacent to an airport, although many are. They are fed with data, both verbal and electronic, from remote transmitter/receiver sites and radar aerial heads which are located to provide the fullest coverage of the route system.

For ease of operation the work of an ACC is divided into sectors, each having one or more radio frequencies. Sector boundaries are normally delineated by radio beacons or en route reporting points. In some states upper airspace has its own sector(s). In all cases the controllers work closely together to co-ordinate passage from one sector to the next. The three types of sector control organizations are: (a) procedural control sectors where radar is not available; (b) procedural control sectors assisted by radar; and (c) radar control sectors supported by procedural control. The radar-based system is now the norm in modern ACCs but there are still some high density traffic areas (Greece, for instance) where full coverage has yet to be provided.

The ACC's basic function is thus to separate aircraft using horizontal and/or vertical separation, either by procedural methods or with the aid of radar. Flight Levels are assigned, as far as practicable, according to those requested in the Flight Plan. An aircraft already at a cruising level will normally have priority over other aircraft desiring that cruising level. When two or more aircraft are at the same cruising level, the preceding aircraft usually has priority. The ACC issues route clearances based on information contained in previously filed Flight Plans. These clearances are passed by landline to the departure point. Some are complicated initial routes to establish on an airway, others a simple Standard

Instrument Departure (SID) designator and an SSR *squawk*.

Procedural separation (i.e. where radar is not available) is achieved by calculating in advance the time an aircraft will pass each reporting point along its route, based on its flight planned true airspeed and forecast winds at cruising level. The actual time over each reporting point is monitored by the controller and compared with the pre-computed figure to ensure that the required time separation from a preceding aircraft at the same level is being maintained. Up to FL 290, even levels are allocated to westbound flights and odds to eastbounds. In practice westbound applies to any airway aligned 180º–359º and eastbound to 000º–179º. Above FL 290, greater vertical separation is applied as described on pages 47-48. A typical position report to the standard format is as follows: 'Speedbird 123 GUVAS at 15 Flight Level 310 estimate KOVIS 35 Recife next.'

En-route aircraft are handed over to the next ACC along the route, the estimated time for the boundary being passed well in advance by telephone or other means such as HF radio. This 'transfer of control', as it is

Botswana's Gaborone Area Control Centre is part of the complete airport and ATC system supplied by British company Siemens Plessey Systems. (Siemens)

known, is subject to local agreements between the ATC units concerned, which are often in neighbouring countries. The accepting controller may require the aircraft at a higher or lower level because of confliction with existing traffic or, in exceptional circumstances, to hold at the boundary until the airspace is clear. The latest automated systems, such as On-Line Data Interchange, provide the accepting controller with data on pending traffic without the need for voice liaison.

In some parts of the world, landline communications are non-existent so aircraft details are passed from one ACC to another on the same HF radio frequency in use for communicating with the aircraft themselves. At busy times the result is a cacophony of accented English when three or more centres are calling one another and aircraft are trying to pass position reports, usually in a non-SelCal environment (see pages 81-82). Needless to say, pilots are not happy with the situation and efforts are being made to fund the provision of satellite communications in certain areas.

For aircraft landing within its airspace, an ACC passes a 'release message' to the approach control unit at destination. This information includes callsign and type, point of departure, release point, ETA, and level at the terminal beacon or holding stack. The release point is deliberately made flexible to react to differences in the flow of traffic. It may be a position, time, or level. For example, if the release is 'passing Flight Level 50', approach may not alter the heading of the aircraft until he has received a 'passing Flight Level 50' report. The reason for this is that Area Control may have been separating the inbound aircraft from other traffic above FL 50.

Advisory and Flight Information Services
In less developed parts of the world, comprehensive area control will not exist and airways will be downgraded to Advisory Route status. The aim is to make information on collision hazards more effective than it would be in the mere provision of flight information service. However, advisory service does not afford the same degree of safety and cannot assume the same responsibilities as air traffic control service in the avoidance of collisions. The reason for this is that available information regarding the disposition of traffic in the area concerned may be of doubtful accuracy and completeness. (Aircraft are entitled to fly IFR along advisory routes or cross them without contacting the ground station, but this is obviously not good airmanship.) To make this clear, advisory service does not issue clearances but only 'advisory information' and it uses the words 'advise' or 'suggest' when a course of action is proposed to an aircraft.

IFR flights electing to use the advisory service when operating within advisory airspace are expected to comply with the same procedures as those applying to controlled flights. However, it is for the pilot to decide whether or not he will comply with any advice or suggestions and notify the unit providing the advisory service of his decision without delay. A further complication is that some advisory routes may revert to full airway status when crossing a national or FIR/UIR boundary. Advisory airspace is administered by a Flight Information Centre (FIC), the Lusaka FIC in Zambia, for example. Sometimes it may be co-located with an ACC, such as the Christchurch ACC/FIC in New Zealand.

All ATC units provide a flight information service (FIS) in addition to issuing instructions to aircraft under their control. FIS is defined by ICAO as 'a service provided for the purpose of giving advice and information useful for the safe and efficient conduct of flights.' It can take many forms including, most importantly, *Sigmets* (see page 90), information on changes in the serviceability of navigation aids, and details of airfield runways affected by snow, ice, or significant depth of water. Also available are reported or forecast weather conditions at departure, destination, and alternate airfields, and traffic information for aircraft operating in Airspace Classes C, D, E, F and G. Another example is the provision of available information to VFR flights concerning traffic and weather conditions along the intended route that are likely to make operating under VFR impracticable. Aerodrome Terminal Information Service (ATIS) is another form of FIS.

An extension of FIS in the USA is Flight Watch or EFAS (En Route Flight Advisory Service). Its nationwide frequency is 122.0 and as well as the normal information service it is able to supply emergency assistance in the form of D/F, steers, and fixes. Japan has a similar organization known as Aeronautical En Route Information Service (AEIS) using transmitter sites scattered throughout its territory. The US Flight Watch facility is given by certain selected Flight Service Stations. The main function of an FSS is to provide pilot briefing services, relay ATC clearances, process IFR flight plans, and monitor navaids. Further details can be found in the USA section of this book.

Chapter 8

Approach Control

Approach Control is the link between Area and Aerodrome Control, although in some parts of the world it may serve a very wide area in the absence of a proper Area Control service (Port Vila Approach in Vanuatu, South Pacific, for example.) It ensures that IFR aircraft arrive in an orderly sequence and that VFR traffic is given a routeing to a position from which it can join the visual circuit without conflictions with IFR traffic. Approach will have first contact with arriving aircraft operating outside controlled airspace, and at very rudimentary airfields the Approach and Aerodrome service will be combined on a single frequency.

An arriving aircraft is transferred from Area to Approach at a specified release point, a position, time, or level agreed on the telephone by the two controllers shortly before the aircraft comes onto the Approach frequency. Area will already have requested the lowest vacant level at the aerodrome's terminal beacon and cleared the aircraft to descend accordingly. Ideally, the arriving flight should be released in plenty of time to enable it to carry out a straight-in approach and simultaneously lose height. However, should a busy traffic situation exist, it might be necessary to put it into a holding pattern based upon a radio beacon. The patterns are a standard oval 'racetrack', the direction of turn and headings being published in navigation charts or approach plates. ICAO's guideline is to establish an approach sequence in a manner which will facilitate the arrival of the maximum number of aircraft with the least average delay. Priority will, of course, be given to aircraft in emergency, hospital flights, and certain other specified operations.

At airfields without radar, traffic is separated by procedural methods, the first aircraft making an instrument approach from, say, 3,000 ft, aircraft continuing to hold above at 1,000 ft vertical intervals. As soon as the first aircraft reports visual with the ground or approach lights, and there is a reasonable likelihood of a successful landing, the second aircraft is cleared for the approach and so on. If the aircraft carries out a missed approach

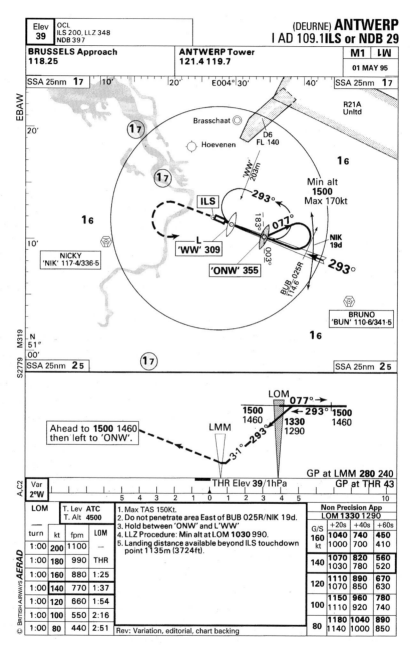

ILS and NDB Approach Chart for Runway 29 at Antwerp. (British Airways Aerad.)

prior to becoming visual, it must climb to the safe terrain clearance altitude, in this instance 3,000 ft. Hence it is not hard to see why this altitude is left vacant at the beacon until the first aircraft breaks cloud.

The Decision Height is the level at which the pilot on a precision approach must carry out a missed approach if he fails to achieve the required visual reference to continue the approach to a landing. A precision approach is defined as being provided by an ILS, MLS, or PAR facility. All other procedures, i.e. NDB, VOR/DME, Localizer/DME approaches, and SRAs, are non-precision and the term Minimum Descent Height is used instead.

The term Expected Approach Time is often heard at non-radar equipped airports. This indicates to a pilot that if he has a radio failure he must not commence an instrument approach until this specific time to allow preceding aircraft to descend and land. 'No delay expected' means that a pilot can begin his approach as soon as he reaches the beacon. If his estimate for the beacon is 12, the next aircraft's EAT will be 19, the third's 26, and so on. When necessary, EATs are passed to Area along with the lowest vacant level in the holding stack – the so-called 'lowest and earliest'.

A standard seven minutes is assumed to complete the let-down procedure and three minutes will be added to this if an aircraft arrives from certain points of the compass and has to realign itself in the correct direction for the descent (A sector join). The controller will calculate the figures and update them as necessary. Note that EATs are not issued in busy TMAs when the delay is likely to be less than 20 minutes. If it is likely to be more, inbound aircraft are given a general statement about anticipated delay and EATs are issued as necessary.

Pilots' interpretations of instrument let-downs vary enormously, the seven minute standard ranging from five to 10 or more, depending upon wind strength, aircraft performance, and other factors. One other phrase used in connection with EATs is the rarely heard 'delay not determined.' This is used to meet certain eventualities, such as a blocked runway, when it is not known how long an aircraft may have to hold.

ICAO approve a Timed Approach Procedure which seems to be little used except in Japan. A suitable point on the approach path marked by a radio beacon serves as a check point in timing successive approaches. Aircraft are given a time at which to pass the specified point inbound. The time is determined with the aim of achieving the desired interval between consecutive landings on the runway while maintaining minimum separation at all times, including the period of runway occupancy.

Where Approach Radar is in use, as well as giving a release the ACC also transfers radar identity in what is called a handover (a 'handoff' to the Americans). The Approach Controller is thus certain that the aircraft he is directing on his radar display is the correct one. The object is to pass headings (vectors) to the pilot to enable him to lock on to the ILS beam by the shortest practicable route commensurate with losing height. If there is no ILS, a Surveillance Radar Approach (SRA) will be given or, when the weather is suitable, radar positioning to a visual final.

In effect a radar directed circuit is flown, the terms downwind, base leg, and final (see page 62) all being used where necessary, although the area of sky covered is far bigger than in the normal visual traffic pattern. A closing heading of about 30° is recommended so that when the aircraft intercepts the ILS only a gentle turn is necessary to lock on. The aim is to intercept the standard 3° glide path at approximately seven to eight miles out on the extended centreline of the runway. As a 3° glide path is roughly equal to 300 ft of descent per mile, the aircraft should be between 2,000 ft and 2,500 ft at this point.

Subsequent landing aircraft are vectored not less than five miles behind, or further depending upon the vortex wake category of the preceding traffic (See Chapter 5). Bigger gaps may also be built in to give space for departing traffic at single-runway airports. At certain locations reduction of the separation to three miles is authorized to ensure maximum utilization of the arrival runway. The wake turbulence rules still apply, of course. Great skill is needed to arrange traffic in line astern with the correct spacing, particularly at airports served by multiple holding stacks. Speed control is also used extensively to even out the flow, a minimum of 170 kt being permissible for jets and 160 kt for large propeller-driven aircraft. (According to the book, any speed restriction must be lifted at four miles on final approach, but pilots often press on to help the traffic flow.) Within the TMAs during the intermediate stages of the approach, a speed limit of 250 kt is imposed on all traffic to make the radar controller's task a little easier.

The Approach Controller passes an eight mile check on intercom to his colleague in the tower who will already have details of the arriving aircraft. If there are no pending departures at the runway holding point, a landing clearance may be given at this juncture but it is more usual to give it at the four mile range. Alternatively, once the pilot reports established on the ILS, Approach may tell him to contact the Tower who will give landing clearance when available.

Pilots expect to receive a landing clearance at around four miles on final approach, but this is not always possible owing to departing traffic or a previous landing aircraft being slow to clear the runway. Two miles is the absolute minimum for large transport aircraft because a go-around is a fairly major operation. The phrase 'expect late landing clearance' is sometimes heard because light aircraft in a busy circuit may, of necessity, only receive one on very short final. They may even be told to go around if they get too close to traffic in front.

For a runway not equipped with ILS the radar controller is normally able to offer a Surveillance Radar Approach. If the weather is poor this can be down to half a mile from touchdown, assuming that the radar is approved for this purpose. With certain types of radar, approaches to two miles only may be allowed. This ensures a reasonable chance of seeing the approach lights and making a successful landing in all but the worst weather.

Where only one Approach Controller is on duty and the ILS fails, he may be unable to offer a half-mile SRA because of the necessity for continuous transmissions during the last four miles of the approach. This means, of course, that any other traffic cannot communicate with him until the talkdown is complete. If a second controller is available, the first can do a half-mile SRA on a discrete frequency while his colleague continues to sequence traffic on to long final for handover as soon as the preceding aircraft has completed its approach.

SRAs to two miles, however, do not require continuous transmissions and the controller can talk to other traffic as necessary, although he must time his calls so that range checks and the associated advisory heights are passed at the correct intervals. The advisory heights are based upon a glide path of 3°, therefore at six-and-a-half miles the aircraft should be at a height of 2,000 ft. Descent on a 3° glide path is equivalent to about 300 ft per mile. Some airfields have non-standard glide path angles because of local obstructions and other considerations, the advisory heights being adjusted accordingly.

Precision Approach Radar (PAR) is nowadays confined mainly to military ATC but is still in common use at civil airports in the former USSR to monitor ILS and other instrument approaches. PAR requires two radar displays, a conventional one showing the approach centreline in plan view, i.e. from above, and a second showing the glidepath from the side. Height as well as heading corrections can be provided by the controller. Standard phrases include: 'This will be a precision monitored ILS approach Runway 27'; 'Rate of descent is good'; 'On glidepath'; 'Slightly (or well) above (or below) glidepath'; 'Still (number) metres (or feet) too high (or too low)'; 'Coming back slowly to the glidepath'.

General Approach Control phraseology
Since almost all major airports now use radar to direct their traffic, I shall

deal with this aspect first. An aircraft must be identified before it can receive a radar control or advisory service: in other words, the controller must be sure that one particular blip on his screen is the aircraft he is directing. This is simple with a radar handover from another ATC unit or by means of SSR, but at airfields outside controlled airspace, where aircraft may approach from random directions with no prior notification, a standard procedure is observed.

ATC: FGM report heading and Flight Level (or altitude).
Aircraft: FGM heading 140 at Flight Level 55.
ATC: FGM for identification turn left heading 110.

The identification turn must be at least 30° different from the original heading. When the pilot reports steady on the new heading, and the controller is sure that he has related a specific blip on his screen with the aircraft, he transmits: 'FGM identified 12 miles south of (airfield)'.

The service to be given is then added.

ATC: Vectoring for an ILS approach runway (designation).

The weather and pressure settings are then passed as a separate transmission.
   If in the initial call the aircraft makes the turn requested and is still not observed on radar, perhaps because it is out of range, in weather clutter, or below cover, the controller will say 'FGM not identified. Resume (or continue) own navigation'. D/F will then be used to home the aircraft towards the airfield for eventual radar pick-up.

When identified, the aircraft will be vectored, that is given headings to steer to fit it into the approach sequence or, if traffic is light, direct to final approach. Position checks are given at intervals ('Five miles north of the airport downwind') so that the pilot can maintain a mental picture of his geographical position and carry out the appropriate cockpit checks in good time. Outside controlled airspace the aircraft may be vectored around unidentified traffic. Information will be given by use of the 12 hour clock, 12 o'clock being straight ahead, three o'clock over the pilot's right shoulder, and so on. The distance and relative direction of movement is also given, together with any information on speed, type of aircraft if known, etc. Typical traffic information is passed in this form: 'ABC123 unknown traffic 10 o'clock, five miles crossing left to right, fast moving.'

If the pilot does not have the traffic in sight he may request avoiding action. This may, in any case, be initiated by the controller if he considers it necessary. Sometimes rapid action is required to avert the risk of collision: 'ABC123 avoiding action turn left immediately heading 110'. At locations with no radar, procedural methods are used. The same applies when radar is normally available but unserviceable or seriously affected by weather clutter, or if the pilot wishes to carry out a procedural approach for training purposes. On transfer from the ACC, the first call will go something like this:

Aircraft: Ostend Approach OTM descending to 3,500 ft, estimating ONO at 42.
ATC: OTM cleared for beacon approach Runway 26 descend to altitude 2,500 ft QNH 1021. Report beacon outbound.

Subsequent reports will be made when 'base turn complete' and, if the beacon is several miles out on final approach, a 'beacon inbound call' will be made as well. These standard calls help the tower controller to plan his traffic, bearing in mind that there may be no radar to give him ranges from touchdown.

Where the airport is equipped with ILS, permission to make a procedural approach is given thus: 'FGM cleared for ILS approach Runway 27, report beacon outbound QNH 1008'. Subsequent exchanges would be:
Aircraft: FGM beacon outbound.
ATC: GMB report established inbound. (The phrase 'report procedure turn complete' may be substituted.)
Aircraft: FGM established ILS inbound.
ATC: FGM report outer marker or Report 4 DME.
Aircraft: FGM outer marker (or 4 DME).
ATC: FGM contact Tower 118.1.

In good weather, by day or night, even though nominally flying IFR, a pilot may request permission to make a visual approach. This will be granted subject to certain provisos, the most important of which is that the pilot must have visual reference to the surface, i.e. the ground or water, and a reasonable assurance exists that he will be able to complete the landing visually. Standard separation continues to be applied between this aircraft and other arriving and departing traffic unless the pilot states that he can see an aircraft ahead in the approach sequence and follow it down to the runway. During daylight hours only, IFR flights may be cleared to approach maintaining VMC and their own separation, if reports indicate that this is possible.

Busy airports with complex airspace often have a Departure Controller who, as his name implies, deals only with departing traffic, separating it from inbounds before handing it over to Area. An Approach unit may also

Off-set holding procedures based on a VOR/DME, as explained in the accompanying text.

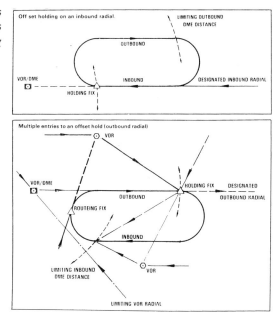

have responsibility for one or more subsidiary airfields whose close proximity makes overall control desirable. An example is Paris/Charles de Gaulle Approach which is responsible also for arriving and departing traffic at Le Bourget and Creil.

Holding Patterns and STARs

The most efficient way of delaying terminal traffic until it can be sequenced on to final approach has always been the holding pattern based on a radio beacon. Modern navigational aids make it possible to hold over an imaginary point, of which more later. The standard hold is an oval or racetrack pattern with Rate One turns, i.e. 3° per second, taking four minutes to complete. The turns are normally to the right but some change above a particular flight level. A holding pattern is contained within what is known as a holding area, which allows for a certain amount of inaccuracy caused by wind effect, turning errors, and other variables. It also ensures that aircraft in adjacent patterns do not conflict. Generally speaking, the higher the holding level, the less accurate the indications from a radio beacon, which is why some holding patterns change direction above a certain level to avoid possible confliction.

In recent times there has been increased use of offset VOR/DME procedures. An offset VOR/DME pattern can be established either along an inbound radial to a VOR/DME or along an outbound radial. In both instances, a holding fix is located at a specified range along the designated VOR radial from the co-located DME. To hold on an inbound radial, the pilot flies towards the beacon on the designated inbound radial and on reaching the holding fix position carries out a procedure turn on to the reciprocal outbound track. This outbound track is flown either for the appropriate period of time or until the limiting DME distance is attained. At the end of the outbound track, the pilot turns the aircraft to intercept the VOR radial back to the holding fix position.

Holding on an outbound radial involves the pilot leaving the VOR on a designated radial until reaching the holding fix as shown by a specified DME distance. He then continues and turns on to the reciprocal track. So-called multiple entry procedures are used when routeing to an offset holding pattern from more than one direction. Standard Terminal Arrival Routes (STARs) are designed either towards or away from suitable VORs. The arrival tracks join the pattern at a holding fix, an intersection of the outbound track with the limiting DME distance, or at another designated position known as the routeing fix. The holding and routeing fix positions are usually given five-letter identifying designators as described on pages 43-44. A typical STAR designator is the BLUFI Four Arrival at Miami. To guard against the possibility of ground equipment failure at a VOR/DME installation, a standby procedure is published. Where possible this procedure will be established in the same geographical area but will be based on an alternative VOR/DME. It will be identified by a different name and published as a separate STAR. Levels in holding patterns are assigned so as to permit aircraft to approach in their correct order. Normally, the first aircraft to arrive over a holding facility should be at the lowest level with following aircraft at successively higher levels. The first aircraft will descend from the lowest level of the holding stack and commence its approach when instructed. The second aircraft in the approach sequence may be told to descend to the level previously occupied by the first, after the latter has reported vacating it. If, however, severe turbulence is known to exist, permission will be withheld until the first aircraft has reported at least 1,000 ft below the vacated level.

Traffic may also need to hold en route, perhaps because an adjacent ACC is not able to accept the flight immediately because of congestion. Except where otherwise instructed by ATC, holding en route is carried out on tracks parallel to the centreline of the airway, turning right at the reporting point. Whenever possible, pilots will be given a specific time at which to leave the reporting point and are expected to adjust the pattern accordingly.

Chapter 9

Oceanic Control

The control of traffic over the world's oceans requires special techniques, both to take advantage of tailwinds and also to apply the increased separations required because of the impracticability of fixed navigational aids. For the same reason Polar routes between Europe and Alaska are treated as oceanic airspace. The North Atlantic is now an extremely busy piece of airspace and the Pacific, hitherto relatively quiet in terms of long-range aircraft, seems set to follow its example as the boom in Pacific Rim economies continues. The mid-Atlantic routes are also becoming more congested.

Separations

Vertical separation is standard but lateral separation is very large. For example, the airspace between 27,500 ft and 40,000 ft over most of the North Atlantic is known as MNPS (Minimum Navigation Performance Specification) airspace. Aircraft flying within it are required to carry a certain scale of navigation equipment so that they can be flown accurately within the parameters of the ATC clearance. Any deviation in this congested area could be dangerous.

Aircraft which do not meet MNPS requirements are separated laterally by 120 nm, which is reduced to 90 nm in certain designated airspace. A spacing of 60 nm is permitted for aircraft which meet MNPS. The same applies to supersonic operations at or above FL 275. The rules for longitudinal spacing are too complicated to detail here but range from 15 down to 10 minutes and sometimes less. It all depends upon speed which is expressed as a Mach Number.

HF communications

VHF radio is useless for long range communications because it is virtually line-of-sight. Therefore over long stretches of ocean or sparsely populated areas such as Africa, HF, often referred to as short wave, is used instead. HF transmissions 'bounce off' the ionizing layers which lie above the earth but, since the layers are affected by day and night conditions, a suitable range of daytime frequencies might suffer severe interference at night and vice versa. To circumvent these effects, HF stations use blocks of radio frequencies consisting of one or more primary frequencies backed up by one or more secondaries. All signals are single side band (SSB, which is explained in Chapter 12).

Over the oceans, position reports are passed in a similar fashion to those on VHF, i.e. the present position and a forward estimate for the next one. The positions are given in terms of latitude and longitude, 56 North 10 West being an example, or as a reporting point or beacon when nearing a coastline.

SELCAL

Unfortunately HF lacks the clarity of VHF channels and the atmospheric noises and constant chatter make it very tiring for crews to maintain a constant listening watch. The answer is SELCAL, short for Selective Calling. Using this method, crews need not monitor the frequency but when the ground station wishes to communicate with them a tone is sent and decoded by the cockpit equipment. A 'bing-bong' sound can be heard on the radio and, on the flight deck, a chime or light signal alerts the pilots to respond by R/T. Each aircraft with SELCAL capability is allocated a four-letter code by ARINC (Aeronautical Radio Inc), an American company which, since the introduction of SELCAL in 1957, acts as worldwide agent to ICAO to perform this function.

On first contact with the controller, the SELCAL will normally be checked, and here is where the interest lies for aircraft registration collectors. The SELCAL code remains with the aircraft as long as the 'box' does, despite changes of ownership. ARINC refuses to make public the registration/SELCAL tie-ups but painstaking detective work by enthusiasts has tracked most of them down. The Aviation Society in Manchester publishes an extensive list in *High in the Sky*, which is available from them or specialist bookshops. The Society's magazine, and also that of LAAS International, details new allocations.

SELCAL codes comprise two sequential tone pulses with each pulse containing two simultaneously transmitted tones. These pulses are used to modulate the ground station transmitter on the selected R/T voice channel. The tones are generated in the ground station coder and are received by a decoder connected to the audio output of the airborne receiver. Each SELCAL code consists of a four-letter alpha group, e.g. AB-CD, where each letter represents a specific frequency from 312.6 Hz to 1479.1 Hz. The assigned SELCAL code is normally included in the aircraft's flight plan. Following a successful check of the equipment with the ground station, the crew can reduce the volume on the radio receiver and thereafter be alerted by the visual and/or audible signal when a call is initiated by a ground station.

The SELCAL system was based originally on 12-tone codes which provided for a total of 2,970 individual aircraft assignments. While this number was adequate in the beginning, ARINC encountered a growing problem in the early 1980s when the requests for code assignments from aircraft operators exceeded the number of unassigned codes available. This shortcoming was resolved in 1985 when a 16-tone code system was introduced to increase the number of codes available.

At the present time, all of the possible 2,970 12-tone codes have been assigned and 2,859 of these have already been given to more than one operator. (They are carefully allocated so that aircraft flying in the same hemisphere are very unlikely to be carrying the same SELCAL.) ARINC is increasingly concerned that it may soon be impossible to provide exclusive SELCAL assignments from the expanded 16-tone group. Of the total 7,950 16-tone codes made available since 1 September 1985, 5,422 have already been assigned for use on a worldwide basis. ARINC estimates that at the present rate of assignment it will become necessary to assign multiple users on 16-tone codes by 1997.

Another problem, apparent from years of operational experience with the current system, is that aircraft SELCAL decoders can occasionally respond erroneously to signals where different but similar repeated tone pulses are used. For example, AB-CD followed by EF-GH can activate a unit assigned code CD-EF.

A number of short and long-term solutions are available to resolve the shortage of SELCAL codes, or at least to reduce its impact. One is to assign temporary SELCAL codes for short-term use, another is to assign SELCAL codes for worldwide use only where necessary. To facilitate future sharing of 16-tone codes, ARINC will begin screening applications for SELCAL codes with a view to limiting worldwide assignments to cases which cannot be accommodated on a more restricted regional basis. This, of course, permits multiple assignment of a single SELCAL code to users operating exclusively in the different regions without the problem of multiple SELCAL activations. ARINC is making more use of short-term assignment of codes which can subsequently be reassigned to other operators with similar short-term requirements.

Long-term solutions could include the authorization of a new tone group or the introduction of a new addressing technology altogether. Either option would require the retrofitting of existing equipment or complete renewal, and international agreement would have to be reached first. A further and even more important consideration is the anticipated increased use of satellite VHF communications in place of HF. Whatever the outcome, the task of matching SELCAL to aircraft registration is likely to become more difficult during the next few years!

Chapter 10

Emergencies and Interceptions

One of the subsidiary responsibilities of all ATS units is the provision of an alerting service. In other words, to ensure the aerodrome rescue and fire-fighting services are on standby or responding in accordance with local procedures when an aircraft reports that it is in difficulties or is seen to – or is suspected to – have crashed. Where an aircraft has come down in the sea or has crashed or force-landed in mountains, desert, bush, or similar inhospitable terrain, the Search and Rescue (SAR) authorities are also informed. Many states have one or more Rescue Co-ordination Centres (RCC), usually military-operated, which organize and direct the search and any subsequent rescue operations. Canada, for example, has four: Victoria, Edmonton, Trenton, and Halifax. The satellite-based COSPAS-SARSAT system gives global coverage in detecting emergency locator transmitters and in locating aviation distress sites.

Apart from assisting ATC in handling a particular flight, the Flight Plan serves also to alert them in the event of the aircraft's non-arrival at destination. This is particularly true of VFR flights, for which there is often no requirement to contact any station whilst en route. After an aircraft lands safely the pilot is required to 'close' the Flight Plan by reporting his arrival to the nearest appropriate ATC unit. In the more sophisticated ATC systems the destination aerodrome will do this automatically. When an aircraft is operating on a Flight Plan and fails to turn up within 30 minutes of its ETA, or no communication is received within 30 minutes of an expected radio call, the controller or operator at the destination is required to confirm the ATD (actual time of departure) from the departure airfield. The Uncertainty Phase (INCERFA in teleprinter language) now begins. After one hour, or sooner in certain cases, the Alert Phase (ALERFA) comes into effect, during which continued attempts are made to contact the aircraft and further information is sought. The Distress Phase (DETRESFA) is deemed to exist when more widespread unsuccessful enquiries point to the probability that the aircraft is in distress, or when the fuel on board is considered to be exhausted or to be insufficient to enable the aircraft to reach safety. Other factors include information received that a forced landing is likely because of technical problems or fuel shortage, or that a forced landing or crash has already occurred. Full Overdue Action is taken by the parent ACC and a search is launched for the missing aircraft, responsibility for further action being transferred to the SAR organization.

It is easy to see why many countries with extensive wilderness areas, and perhaps limited resources for searching, make Flight Plans compulsory for *all* flights. The details give some indication of where the missing aircraft may be found, working from its intended route and fuel endurance. If no Flight Plan has been filed, no overdue action will be taken until people start asking about the whereabouts of a particular aircraft. By this time it may be too late to render aid to any survivors.

A pilot requiring immediate assistance is expected to transmit a distress message using the prefix *Mayday, Mayday, Mayday* (from the French *m'aidez*, 'help me'). Normally it is sent out on the frequency already in use but in some situations the pilot may decide to use 121.5 MHz, the VHF International Distress Frequency. The information passed in a *Mayday* message is aircraft callsign, type, position or estimated position and time, heading and indicated airspeed, altitude or flight level, and pilot's intentions, e.g. bailing out, ditching, crash-landing, etc. If carried, the transponder is set to the Emergency Code 7700. If the situation is urgent but not actual distress – lost or short of fuel, for example – the prefix *Pan, Pan, Pan* is used, based on the French *la panne* ('breakdown'). During trans-oceanic flights and over certain inhospitable parts of the world, crews are required to monitor 121.5 MHz, commonly known as the 'Guard frequency'.

In the USA there is a formal 'Minimum Fuel Advisory' which the pilot can declare when fuel has reached a state which precludes the acceptance of undue delay upon reaching destination. It is not an emergency situation but is used to indicate to ATC that one may arise if significant delay is incurred. Traffic priority is not required at this stage but if the fuel state reduces to the level where priority handling is necessary to ensure a safe landing, a further category is available to the pilot: the 'Emergency Account Low Fuel'. ATC then confirms the remaining endurance and handles the aircraft accordingly.

Radio failure

In the event of radio failure there are published procedures to which the pilot is expected to adhere. If SSR is available, a transponder code setting of 7600 will alert ATC to his problem. Quite often the failure is of the transmitter only, and the controller will instruct the aircraft to make one or more turns to check if the pilot is complying. If it becomes obvious that the receiver is working, normal radar service will be resumed. Sometimes the aircraft radio will transmit a carrier wave without speech and this can be used to acknowledge instructions by pressing the transmit button a certain number of times as specified by the controller.

If there is no indication that the aircraft can either send or receive signals, separation from other traffic will be maintained on the assumption that in VMC the aircraft will land at the nearest suitable aerodrome. In IMC it must proceed according to the current Flight Plan to the navigation aid serving the destination aerodrome and commence descent at, or as close as possible to, the expected approach time last received and acknowledged, holding if necessary to comply with the time. If no EAT has been received, descent must commence as close as possible to the Flight Plan ETA and a landing completed within 30 minutes. In the meantime, ATC will transmit blind for the benefit of the radio failure aircraft the weather conditions at destination, on all available frequencies and on radio beacon voice channels if available. Other pertinent information may include weather conditions favourable to a cloud-breaking procedure in areas of less congested traffic. Continuous liaison will be maintained with the destination and flight-planned alternate as well as other en-route ATC units. Such a situation, rare these days, causes much disruption of traffic and it is vital that it be resolved as soon as possible. Where it is suspected that the aircraft is completely lost because of the failure of navaids as well as radio, a shepherd aircraft may be dispatched to lead it to a safe landing. This may well be a military fighter with all-weather capability.

Air Defence Identification Zones (ADIZ)
To differentiate between commercial flights or friendly military aircraft going about their lawful business and potential aggressors, many countries have an ADIZ around their borders. Best known is the one round the USA which is divided into Domestic (along international land boundaries) and Coastal. Over the coastal waters of Alaska it is known as the Distant Early Warning IZ. The defence authorities are aware of all flight plan information and any stranger will be intercepted by fighters on permanent standby. With reduced international tension the main function of the Coastal ADIZ is as a net to catch drug-running aircraft from Central America. Iceland also has an ADIZ, as have the Philippines, Cuba, Finland, Libya, Guam, Hawaii, India (including separate ones around Bombay, Delhi and Calcutta), Japan, Korea, Myanmar, Okinawa, Pakistan, Panama, Peru, Taiwan, and Thailand.

In the cramped airspace of Western Europe an ADIZ is not feasible but NATO air forces have long operated a series of Buffer Zones designed to prevent friendly aircraft wandering into hostile airspace and provoking an incident. Since the re-unification of Germany the original border is now the centre-line of a Deconfliction Zone extending from ground level up to infinity. NATO aircraft are prohibited from entering the zone without specific authority from the respective air defence commands.

Unfortunately, in many parts of the world strayed or unidentified aircraft are still perceived as a threat and are liable to be shot down without any real attempt to establish their bona fides. Several tragic incidents in the distant past resulted in an international agreement to standardize interception procedures. Of course they have not always been successful (the Korean 747 shot down over the North Pacific, for example), but a number of potentially dangerous situations have been resolved with little more than diplomatic embarrassment.

ICAO defines a strayed aircraft as one which has deviated significantly from its intended track or which reports that it is lost. As soon as an ATC unit becomes aware of a strayed or lost aircraft, it is expected to take all possible steps to assist it. Locally agreed procedures will include the passing of its flight details to the appropriate military authorities and adjacent ATC units. ICAO lays down basic procedures for interception, as detailed below, but certain states publish additional or slightly amended rules. In Israel, for example, the intercepted aircraft is to contact Ben Gurion Approach. Over the former Yugoslavia the penultimate action by the interceptor is to fire two short bursts from a position to the left and level with the subject aircraft and flash navigation lights. This means: 'Follow me. This is the final warning. Your safety is not guaranteed'. The intercepted aircraft must respond by rocking its wings to indicate 'Understood. Will comply'.

In all cases the intercepted aircraft must follow instructions, if possible notifying the ATC unit with which it is in contact and *squawk* the 7700 Emergency Code unless told otherwise. It must also attempt to contact the interceptor on 121.5, repeating the call on the UHF Emergency Frequency of 243.0 if carried. If radio contact between the two aircraft is established but communication in a common language is not possible, the following phrases are used to convey instructions and obtain acknowledgements:

Intercepting aircraft

Phrase	*Meaning*
Callsign	What is your callsign?
Follow	Follow me
Descend	Descend for landing
You Land	Land at this aerodrome
Proceed	You may proceed

Intercepted aircraft

Phrase	*Meaning*
Callsign	My callsign is . . .
Wilco	Understood will comply
Cannot	Unable to comply
Repeat	Repeat your instruction
Am Lost	Position unknown
Mayday	Mayday
Hijack	I have been hijacked
Land (place name)	I request to land at (place name)
Descent	I require descent

In 1972 the US and Soviet governments agreed additional procedures to defuse potentially dangerous violations or near-violations of each other's airspace by military aircraft. A list of phonetic Russian and English short phrases was devised so that both sides could communicate on certain frequencies in order to resolve the situation before it escalated to war alert status.

In time of war or defence emergency the SCATANA rules come into force, an acronym for Security Control of Air Traffic and Air Navigation Aids. The aim is to clear the relevant airspace of civilian aircraft, either by instructing them to land as soon as possible or changing course to avoid or leave it immediately. Once clear, most, if not all, ground navigation aids will be shut down. More details can be found in the section on Saudi Arabia.

Hijack

In the event of a hijack (or 'unlawful interference' as it is known officially) aircrew will attempt to set the dedicated SSR code 7500. As with the Emergency and Radio Failure codes, it activates an alarm system at any ground station within range which is equipped with SSR. To determine that its use is not accidental, the ATC unit will ask: 'Confirm you are squawking assigned code?' If the answer is in the negative, no reference will be made to the circumstances but the controller will pass on the information to the appropriate authorities who will respond with agreed procedures. In the meantime the flight's progress is monitored and normal instructions are issued whether or not a reply is received from the aircraft. Because of the unpredictable behaviour of such aircraft, considerable co-ordination will be necessary to keep other traffic well clear.

Chapter 11

Weather and Air Traffic Control

Accurate forecasts and the constant updating of existing weather reports are essential to aviation. The basic report, normally from a half-hourly observation and in no circumstances at greater than one hour intervals, follows a standard format. First comes the wind speed and direction, usually in knots but in some parts of the world in kmph or metres per second, then the visibility in increments of 100 m when 5,000 m or less, and in whole km when greater than 5,000 m. The distance is determined from the known range of conspicuous landmarks visible in the locality. Note that the unit of measurement in the USA is statute miles and fractions thereof.

The next item is the weather, e.g. rain, fog, mist, etc. Cloud base is measured by means of a cloud base recorder which scans the sky overhead with a laser beam. At less well-equipped airfields, cloud base is found by estimation, with experience a surprisingly accurate method. Pilot reports can be requested to confirm the base. At night estimation is difficult so a vertical searchlight is often used. The angle of the 'spot' on the cloud can then be found by sighting with a simple instrument known as an alidade. Simple pre-calculated trigonometry enables the height to be read off a table.

Cloud amount is measured in oktas, i.e. eighths, and height in feet: 1–4 oktas is passed to aircraft as *scattered*, 5–7 as *broken* and 8 as *overcast*. Not more than three layers are reported, the exception being when cumulonimbus cloud, known as Cb or Charlie Bravo, is present. This information is passed as a fourth group, as its turbulence and lightning discharges are an obvious hazard to aircraft.

Air temperature is given in degrees Celsius, except in the USA, Canada and a few other places, where Fahrenheit is still the norm. The dew point temperature is also noted because if the two figures are close together fog may be about to form. The QNH and QFE are passed in millibars in the UK and certain other parts of the world but the new term hectopascals is now in widespread use, particularly in continental Europe. The USA and

Canada still use inches of mercury as the value for altimeter settings, as do several other countries.

Automated and semi-automated surface weather reporting systems have been in use since the 1960s and the latest ones are able to process the data and transmit it on VHF radio, using computer-generated voice. The quality of information is constantly self-checked automatically, and it seems likely that this equipment will one day virtually replace the human observer method.

Where the weather conditions meet particular criteria – visibility of 10 km or more, no precipitation, no thunderstorm or shallow fog, no cloud below a level of 5,000 ft above aerodrome elevation (or highest minimum sector altitude in some parts of the world) and no Cb at any level – the visibility and cloud groups are omitted and the word 'CAVOK' (pronounced 'Cav OK') is passed. It is derived from the phrase Ceiling and Visibility OK. A variation in the USA is CAVU – Ceiling And Visibility Unlimited.

At many busy airports the current meteorological observation is transmitted continuously on a separate VHF radio channel or the appropriate terminal VOR frequency by means of a continuous loop tape. The facility is known as ATIS (Automatic Terminal Information Service), pronounced Ay-Tiss. As well as the weather report it may also include useful information such as type of approach to be expected, any holding delays, and equipment unserviceabilities. Some airports may have a second ATIS channel for departure information, others combine both as an arrival and departure ATIS. Each broadcast has an identifying letter which a pilot must pass to ATC on first contact to ensure that he has received the current details. (A typical example is *American 55 for start with Bravo*.) In the USA, TWEBs (Transcribed Weather Broadcast Route Forecasts) are transmitted continuously on certain NDB and VOR frequencies and updated every eight hours.

In foggy conditions, Runway Visual Range, or RVR as it is normally referred to, offers a more localized assessment of how far the pilot is likely to be able to see along the runway. Measurement only begins when the official meteorological report gives a general visibility of 1,500 m or less, and it is essential to enable the pilot to decide whether or not it is within the limits of what are known as 'company minima' for landing or take-off.

RVR is calculated by either the human observer method or by means of electronic equipment. The former requires a person, usually an airport fireman, to stand on a vehicle adjacent to the runway threshold at a specified height to simulate pilot eye-level. He then counts the number of lights or, at some locations, marker boards, that he can see down one side of the runway. The total is passed by radio to the tower and the RVR read off a pre-computed table. The Instrumented RVR system, called IRVR, measures the opacity of the atmosphere and gives a constant read-out in the tower of the RVR at three fixed points along the runway, referred to as touchdown, mid-point, and stop end.

The term *sigmet* is sometimes heard on R/T, this being a warning of such hazardous phenomena as thunderstorms, severe turbulence, severe airframe icing, and volcanic ash clouds. Another jargon word is *nosig*, short for no significant change. The term *trend* is employed to indicate the way the weather is likely to go, codes like *tempo* for a temporary change being added as appropriate. In the USA, Centre Weather Advisories are broadcast over ARTCC frequencies when conditions are likely to threaten IFR operations. They are sent out at 30 minute intervals at 15 minutes and 45 minutes past the hour. Another American facility is EFAS, the En Route Flight Advisory Service provided by Flight Service Stations. On pilot request, it provides timely weather information pertinent to his type of flight, route, and altitude.

Wind shear is a hazard which has caused a number of serious accidents in the past 20 years. Briefly, it is a change of wind speed and/or direction between two points in the atmosphere. By such a definition it is almost always present and normally does not cause undue difficulty to the pilot. However, on take-off or landing what amounts to an instantaneous change in headwind can be dangerous. The pilot will be faced with a rapid change in airspeed which could cause the aircraft to stall or undershoot the runway.

Since wind shear is obviously invisible much experimental work has been carried out with acoustic Dopplers, Doppler radar, and lasers to try to detect and measure it. Certain weather criteria are used to assess its possible presence and this is backed up by pilot reports. The alert message is inserted in the ATIS broadcast or passed by R/T. In the USA, Terminal Doppler Weather Radar (TDWR) is coming into use to detect weather and measure wind velocity within a 50-mile radius and, within a six-mile radius, to detect the presence and onset of wind shear with updates at one minute intervals.

Another major hazard to aircraft is fortunately easier to measure. This is braking action when the runway is icy, or if snow or slush is present. The original method of measuring it was a simple decelerometer carried in a vehicle but this has largely been replaced by the Mu Meter which is towed by a vehicle. It provides a continuous automatic print-out of the mean coefficient of friction along the runway, the higher the figure the better the braking action (0.25, for example, would be very poor, 0.85 a dry surface).

The word *Snowtam* refers to an ingenious system of describing and tabulating runway conditions under snow, slush, or ice and the degree to which they are cleared or about to be cleared. Braking action as determined above is also included. A series of letters and figures, each referring to a specific detail, can easily be decoded on receipt by telex.

Strategically located stations throughout the world transmit continuous Volmet broadcasts, the 'Vol' part of the title being derived from the French word for flight. VHF Volmet broadcasts current aerodrome reports with trends where available. Those on HF, many of which can be monitored in the UK, also include aerodrome forecasts if required by regional air navigation agreements, as well as any current Sigmets. Over the North Atlantic during the next few years, datalink will automate the Volmet broadcasts to produce specific written reports directly in the cockpit on request.

WAFS (World Area Forecast System) is a global method of providing en route meteorological forecasts in standardized formats. They are the responsibility of 15 regional centres located in Brasilia, Buenos Aires, Cairo, Dakar, Frankfurt, Las Palmas, London, Melbourne, Moscow, Nairobi, New Delhi, Paris, Tokyo, Washington, and Wellington. ICAO plans to reduce them to two centres, each up-linking its data to an international satellite system for dissemination to national centres for processing and distribution.

To add to the input of data, pilots are expected to report any unexpected phenomena they encounter, such as severe turbulence and severe icing, indeed any condition which they consider may affect the safety or efficiency of other aircraft operations. In certain airspace, particularly oceanic, pilots may be required to file AIREPS, a name derived from the air reporting form. For example, a random selection of aircraft about to make an Atlantic crossing may have the phrase 'Send Met' appended to their oceanic clearance. They are then expected to include an AIREP with each en route position report. The PIREP (Pilot Report, pronounced Pie-Rep) is a US Air Force procedure equivalent to the AIREP. They can often be heard on GHFS frequencies when on a telephone patch to a Metro (Mee-tro) weather station.

Chapter 12

Air Band Radios, Charts and Documents

Modern electronics have brought us pocket-sized receivers, better known as scanners, capable of monitoring the entire spectrum of radio frequencies. More specifically, the aviation enthusiast can listen to messages between aircraft and air traffic control, civil and military, as well as a whole range of other aviation communications from airline operations to military air-to-air conversations. For the beginner there is a bewildering array of suitable radios, varying in price from about £15 up to well over £900. If you want mobility, forget about the desk models (base stations), which are generally more expensive and usually dependent upon a mains electricity supply.

An annoying drawback with all the cheaper receivers is that they are impossible to tune accurately, so you are never quite sure what station you have selected until you have listened for a while. Some radios cover the entire air band with a one-inch scale and if, say, 124.2 MHz is tuned in, transmissions on the adjacent frequencies of 124.0, 124.05, 124.10 and 124.15, and 124.25, 124.30, 124.35 and so on, may be picked up as well. They are not usually as loud as the primary frequency being monitored, but are annoying and confusing, particularly when a powerful transmission from a nearer source swamps the aircraft in which you are interested. A longer scale makes tuning easier but has no effect on the lack of discrimination.

Despite these shortcomings, a basic radio will perform quite well at or close to your local airport simply because the aircraft and ground trans-missions are near enough for strong signals. Remember that Very High Frequency (VHF) waves are virtually line-of-sight – if the horizon gets in the way you will not hear anything, no matter how sophisticated the receiver, except in very rare, freak atmospheric conditions.

The so-called VHF air band runs from 108 to 137 MHz, although up to 118 is reserved for navigation beacons and Instrument Landing System (ILS) Localizer beams. The upper section of the band is where all the ATC messages can be found. This leads to a further warning – some of the cheaper radios on sale have a scale ending at 135 and some even stop at

130! Ultra High Frequency (UHF) air band (approximately 225 to 400 Mhz) is used exclusively by military aircraft, many of the first-line combat aircraft having no VHF capability. Transport and training aircraft likely to use the civil air route ('airways') system are also VHF-equipped. If you wish to monitor military air band as well, the only answer is to invest in a synthesized receiver, controlled by a micro-processor and colloquially known as a scanner. There are, to the writer's knowledge, no cheap dial-tuneable UHF portables.

With a scanner's pin-point tuning, frequency overlap is almost completely eliminated but we are now considering costs in the vicinity of £300. (However, for a set restricted to VHF air band, the price can be as low as £130.) The more expensive sets are advertised as communications receivers because they are able to monitor far more than merely aviation messages. It all depends on whether you wish to listen to bus and taxi drivers and the countless other users of the public service bands, as well as marine and other bands. The ideal set for the aviation enthusiast receives 108 to 137 MHz and 225 to 400 MHz, both audio-modulated (AM). Some sets *claim* to do this but have gaps, so it is essential to make a careful study of the radio's frequency ranges before deciding which one to purchase. Advice from existing owners is also an advantage, as all sets have their own little peculiarities.

There are, theoretically, 760 channels in the communications (COM) section of the air band between 118.0 and 136.975 inclusive. In parts of the world with relatively light traffic the spacings tend to be 50 kHz, i.e. 118.10, 118.15, etc. In Europe and the USA many of the intervening 25 kHz frequencies – e.g. 118.125, 118.175, and 118.225 – have been allocated, and a change to 8.33 kHz spacing has been agreed at some future date. Many en route airways control frequencies are transmitted from up to four remote locations to render the coverage as wide as possible. To eliminate the characteristic screech, known as a heterodyne, when more than one station transmits simultaneously, an offset carrier system is used. The offsets are ±5 kHz for a two-carrier system, ±7.5 kHz and 0 kHz for a three-carrier, and ±7.5 kHz and ±2.5 kHz for a four-carrier system. Therefore, when the sensitivity of the receiver allows, reception may be improved by tuning the set slightly higher or lower than the published frequency. Note that you cannot do this accurately with some scanners.

All scanners share a similar mode of operation, although some are not very user-friendly, particularly if the instructions are written in Japanese-English! The desired frequency is keyed in and displayed on a liquid crystal display (LCD) which resembles that of a pocket calculator. Specific frequencies can be stored in a memory (up to 1,000 separate channels on some sets), and in scanning mode the radio scans through them continuously, stopping when a transmission is received and resuming the scan when it ceases. A 'delay' facility can be keyed-in so that the reply can be heard as well and continuous transmissions such as weather broadcasts can be 'locked out' of the scanning sequence. Some sets have a 'hold' as well so that any transmission is locked on to until the 'scan' button is pressed again.

In search mode, the radio searches between pre-set upper and lower frequencies and again locks on to any transmissions. In practice, search is difficult because the scanner stops at intervals at 'noises' generated by its own internal circuitry and external interference, familiarly known as 'birdies'. They can be locked out individually at the press of a button, a somewhat tedious process. Memories are usually divided into banks so that, for example, civil ATC frequencies, military channels, and airline operations can be scanned individually.

Obviously, a scanner is a considerable investment, and although one can be bought from a high street outlet it is a much better idea to obtain one from a specialist dealer who will have a wide range available. They all advertise in the aviation and radio enthusiast magazines and most readers in the UK will be within reach of at least one. If a personal visit is impractical a mail order service is generally offered.

Since most dealers are enthusiasts as well they will sell you what you want rather than what will give them the maximum profit. Many people tend to 'trade up' with radios and a satisfied customer will always come back. The sets taken in part-exchange can be good buys as well. A specialist dealer will stock all the necessary back-up material, from high performance aerials and other accessories to navigation charts and air band guide books.

On the subject of aerials, several different types are obtainable, including some for loft or outside mounting. Generally speaking, the higher the aerial the better the reception. As most air band listening will probably be done at home, it is useful to discover the best position for reception by moving the set around the house. Radio waves behave in a very peculiar fashion and marked differences will be found even in the same room. If the usual telescopic aerial or rubber antenna supplied with the radio proves inadequate, a remote antenna can be purchased.

A further method of improving performance is a pre-amplifier (usually abbreviated to 'pre-amp') which fits between the antenna and the receiver on a hand-held model or inside the case of a base station. The device boosts the received signals and feeds them into the receiver. Results can vary but it may be possible to receive, say, the ground transmissions from a distant airport which were not previously audible, except as noise, from the same location.

At this point the reader may ask: 'But is air band listening legal?' The answer, under the Wireless Telegraphy Acts in the UK and the various legal codes of other countries, is: 'Definitely not!' It is also a myth that one can listen but not divulge the content to anyone else. However, VHF air band monitoring has been a popular pastime since at least 1965 and the UK authorities have never sought to regulate it. Perhaps it has been tolerated up to now because it is an essentially harmless activity. In parts of the USA it seems to be encouraged, as shown by Miami International Airport's information sheet which includes the following: 'Aviation enthusiasts with an aircraft band radio may listen in on airport communications. Miami tower controllers broadcast instructions to pilots on 118.3 MHz or 123.9. Ground controllers use 121.8 for taxying aircraft. Pilots get flight plan clearance on 135.35. Automatic terminal information service broadcasts are made on 112.0.'

However, in certain countries, and some states in the USA, scanners are illegal. Enquiries are necessary before taking one overseas and it may be wiser to revert to a cheap tuneable radio and a personal earphone in order to allay suspicion. Apart from the paranoia of certain governments, the reason for prohibition is that most scanners are capable of picking up police and emergency service messages and listening to these is severely discouraged, particularly in the UK. There have been cases where fines were imposed and scanners confiscated, even though it was obvious that the information was not being used for criminal purposes. Having police frequencies stored in the scanner memory is considered evidence of guilt in Britain, even if the radio is not in use at the time. You have been warned!

Some scanners are now able to monitor HF air band (short wave) transmissions but, unfortunately, in my experience the performance is nowhere near as good as a dedicated HF receiver, even one of the cheaper ones costing around £130. To get comparable reception right across the radio spectrum in one small hand-held package is almost impossible, but no doubt the manufacturers are working on it!

HF is used for transatlantic operations and, indeed, for any long overwater flights, as well as over much of Africa. There is also a lot more of aviation interest on this band, and many people prefer it to VHF air band. The main advantage is the long range reception of both aircraft and ground controller, even as far away as the Pacific if conditions are favourable. There is, however, a drawback: HF listening can be hard work as stations fade in and out or are swamped by atmospherics. Unlike VHF radio waves, which travel straight out into space, HF signals are reflected by the ionosphere and can thus 'bend' around the curvature of the earth, giving an effective range of several thousand miles. Unfortunately, the behaviour of the ionosphere cannot be predicted with any accuracy as its height and density vary considerably under the influence of the sun. This is why ground stations are allocated several alternative frequencies for day and night use in order to minimize interference.

Virtually all HF aircraft communications use Single Side Band (SSB) signals. Without going into too many technicalities, the AM (Audio Modulation) method employed by HF transmissions is built up of three components: a lower side band, a carrier, and an upper side band. By removing the carrier and one of the side bands, the power of the signal is compressed into a smaller band width which boosts reception at long range and reduces interference. However, an ordinary short wave receiver which may have the necessary frequency bands (2–28 MHz) will pick up SSB in something which has been described as 'sounding like Donald Duck'. To make the signal intelligible, the carrier has to be reintroduced and this can only be done if a Beat Frequency Oscillator (BFO) or crystal controlled carrier oscillator is fitted. Beware of short wave sets which receive only broadcast bands or else have no SSB capability. Advertisements are often misleading on these vital points, implying that the product will receive everything.

Charts and related documents

Almost as important as an air band radio itself is the acquisition of a set of radio navigation charts. They are essential to build up an overall picture of the international airways system and the positions of its beacons and reporting points. The aviation authority for each state is responsible for producing charts but of course not all have the resources to do so.

En route charts are published by a number of commercial and official organizations, the most readily obtainable in Britain being those by British Airways Aerad, the Royal Air Force, and Jeppesen Sanderson. The US Department of Defense produces its own worldwide charts but these are more difficult to obtain. Obviously the information on the different charts is fundamentally the same, but the presentation differs quite considerably. There is also some variation in scales and the areas covered. Some charts combine high and low level airspace information, others have a separate sheet for each.

Aerad also produces a wide range of other related documentation, including Standard Instrument Departure charts, Standard Arrival Route charts, and airport and apron layouts. Aerad's other important publications, much prized by enthusiasts, are a set of four volumes which cover the entire world. They are the *Europe and Middle East Supplement*, *Western Hemisphere Supplement*, *Africa Supplement*, and *Asia, Australasia and Pacific Supplement*. Soft-backed and compact, they are absolutely packed with information on airports, including their aids, runway lengths and radio frequencies.

The other chart publisher, Jeppesen Sanderson Inc, is an American firm whose main distributor in the UK is CSE Aviation at Oxford Airport. The company also produces a wide variety of associated data, the most important of which are airport approach charts.

At first sight, radio navigation charts are a perplexing welter of intersecting lines, symbols, and figures, but as with any other map there is a key, and with a few minutes' study they become logical. The radio beacons are identified by name and a three or two-letter abbreviation. Frankfurt VOR, for example, may be referred to by ATC and aircraft as Frankfurt or Foxtrot Foxtrot Mike. The frequency of 114.2 MHz on which the beacon radiates will be adjacent to its name on the chart. Also shown on the chart are airways and advisory routes, their bearings in both directions, the distances in nautical miles between reporting points, the heights of their bases, and upper limits and the lowest available cruising levels.

Many of the charts are stocked by air band radio suppliers but they can also be purchased direct from the publishers or their agents at the addresses listed below. Out-of-date charts are sometimes advertised in the aviation press at reasonably low prices. Provided that they are not too old – say more than 12 months – they can still be useful. For comprehensive frequency information, most enthusiasts will settle for one of the numerous unofficial frequency lists on the market. They often include unpublished confidential military frequencies so, again, discretion is required.

Each country in ICAO is required to publish an Aeronautical Information Publication (AIP) and the organization provides detailed guidance for its compilation. It can run to several volumes for complex airspace and ATC systems but many AIPs, in Africa for example, are quite slim documents. Whatever the size, the format is identical, consisting of the following sections:

GEN – general information including differences from ICAO standards, recommended practices and procedures;

AGA – aerodromes and ground aids;

COM – communications such as radio and navaid frequencies;

MET – provision of weather information;

RAC – Rules of the Air and ATC procedures, including types of airspace, details of air routes, and approach procedures;

FAL – facilitation, including provisions for handling international passengers and cargo, associated fees and charges, and customs and health regulations;

SAR – a brief outline of the state's search and rescue organization;

MAP – description of available aeronautical charts.

AIPs are updated or amended by NOTAMs, which 'contain information concerning the establishment, condition or change in any aeronautical facility, service, procedure or hazard, the timely knowledge of which is essential to personnel concerned with flight operations.' Class I NOTAMs are distributed by teleprinter; Class II, which are of a much less urgent nature, are sent out by post.

UK suppliers of Airways Charts, Flight Guides and related material

British Airways, Aerad Customer Services, Aerad House, PO Box 10, Heathrow Airport, Hounslow, Middlesex, TW6 2JA.

CSE Aviation Ltd (Jeppesen Agents), Oxford Airport, Kidlington, Oxford, OX5 1RA.

Royal Air Force, No 1 Aeronautical Documents Unit, RAF Northolt, West End Road, Ruislip, Middlesex, HA4 6NG.

Civil Aviation Authority, Printing and Publishing, Greville House, 37 Gratton Road, Cheltenham, Gloucestershire, GL50 2BN.

Air Supply, 83B High Street, Yeadon, Leeds, LS19 7TA.

Interproducts, 8 Abbot Street, Perth, PH2 0EB.

Pooleys, Elstree Aerodrome, Elstree, Hertfordshire, WD6 3AW; Wycombe Airpark (Booker), Marlow, Buckinghamshire, SL7 3DR; 16 New Quebec Street, London W1.

Transair, West Entrance, Fairoaks Airport, Chobham, Nr Woking, Surrey, GU24 8HX; 50a Cambridge Street, London, SW1V 4QQ.

Visitors to the USA will find that the American Aircraft Owners and Pilots Association publish a very useful directory of small US aerodromes and airstrips, complete with radio frequencies. It is inexpensive and available at fly-ins, etc.

Principal air band and hobby suppliers in the UK

Air Supply, 83b High Street, Yeadon, Leeds, LS19 7TA. *Telephone 0113 2509581.*

World Radio Centre, Adam Bede High Tech Centre, Derby Road, Wirksworth, Derbyshire, DE4 4BG. *Telephone 01629 825926.*

The Aviation Hobby Centre, 1st Floor, Main Terminal Building, Birmingham Airport, Birmingham, B26 3QJ. *Telephone 0121 782 2112/6560.*

The Aviation Hobby Shop, Horton Parade, Horton Road, West Drayton, Middlesex, UB7 8EA. *Telephone 01895 442123.*

The Aviation Shop, Spectator Terraces, Manchester Airport, M22 5SZ. *Telephone 0161 499 0303.*

BUCHair Shop, Spectators Terrace, Gatwick Airport.

Flightdeck, The Airband Shop, 192 Wilmslow Road, Heald Green, Cheadle, Cheshire, SK8 3BH. *Telephone 0161 499 9350.*

Haydon Communications, 132 High Street, Edgware, Middlesex, HA8 7EL. *Telephone 0181 951 5782.*

Javiation, Carlton Works, Carlton Street, Bradford, West Yorkshire, BD7 1DA. *Telephone 01274 732146.*

Lowe Electronics Ltd, Chesterfield Road, Matlock, Derbyshire, DE4 5LE. *Telephone 01629 580800*; 152 High Street, Chesterton, Cambridge, CB4 1NL. *Telephone 01223 311230*; Communications House, Chatham Road, Sandling, Maidstone, Kent, ME14 3AY. *Telephone 01622 692773*; 3 Weaver's Walk, Northbrook Street, Newbury, RG13 1AL. *Telephone 01635 522133*; 117 Beaumont Road, St Judes, Plymouth, PL1 4PQ. *Telephone 01752 257224*; 79/81 Gloucester Road, Patchway, Bristol, BS12 5QJ. *Telephone 0117 9315263*; 34 New Briggate, Leeds. *Telephone 0113 2452657*; Cumbernauld Airport, Falkirk, G68 0HH. *Telephone 01236 721004*; Mitford House, Newcastle Airport, E20 9DF. *Telephone 01661 860418.*

Mach III, Spectators Terrace Gift Shop, Terminal 2 Rooftop, Heathrow Airport, Hounslow, Middlesex, TW6 1LS. *Telephone 0181 897 2747.*

Martin Lynch, 140–142 Northfield Avenue, Ealing, London, W13 9SB. *Telephone 0181 566 1120.*

Nevada Communications, Mail Order, 189 London Road, North End, Portsmouth, Hants, PO2 9AE. *Telephone 01705 662145*; Showrooms, 1A Munster Road, Portsmouth, PO2 9BS.

Raycom Communications Systems Ltd, International House, 963 Wolverhampton Road, Oldbury, Warley, West Midlands, B69 4RJ. *Telephone 0121 552 0073.*

The Short Wave Centre, 95 Colindeep Lane, Sprowston, Norwich, NR7 8EQ. *Telephone 01603 788281.*

SRP Trading – Mail Order: Unit 20, Nash Works, Forge Lane, Belbroughton, Nr Stourbridge, Worcs. *Telephone 01562 730672*; Shop: 1686 Bristol Road South, Rednall, Birmingham, B45 9TZ. *Telephone 0121 460 1581.*

Stewart Aviation, PO Box 7, Market Harborough, Leics, LE16 8FP. *Telephone 01536 770962.*

Touchdown Aviation Shops, 4 Tavistock Road, West Drayton, Middlesex, UB7 7QT. *Telephone 01895 434510*; 5A Mill Street, Mildenhall, Suffolk, IP28 7DN. *Telephone 01638 515971.*

Transair Pilot Shop, West Entrance, Fairoaks Airport, Chobham, Nr Woking, Surrey, GU24 8HX. *Telephone 01276 858533.*

Waters & Stanton Electronics, Warren House, 22 Main Road, Hockley, Essex, SS5 4QS. *Telephone 01702 206835*; 12 North Street, Hornchurch, Essex, RM11 1QX. *Telephone 017084 44765.*

Chapter 13

Future Developments in Air Traffic Control

Air Traffic Control and Air Traffic Management are likely to see many major changes over the next few years. Inevitably, the use of voice communications will decrease and, with it, listening possibilities. Fortunately, this will not mean the end of our hobby; there are still many situations where there can be no substitute for direct speech between pilot and controller or pilot and ground operations. Apart from the North Atlantic, where VHF via satellite will take over, HF communications will still be the norm over much of the world's oceans and wilderness areas.

Mode S datalink will, in the foreseeable future, remove many of the routine message exchanges from radio communications. They include enroute climb or descent instructions, re-routeings, or approval of existing pre-planned routes, together with level and speed allocation. Indeed, North Atlantic oceanic clearances are already passed by datalink where the aircraft is suitably equipped. The messages appear on a display screen on the flight deck and are acknowledged by the touch of a button. A miniprinter produces a hard copy of all messages. Tactical instructions such as immediate heading changes, temporary level instructions, or rate of climb or descent requests will continue to be made by voice communications. However, it is expected that computer predicted and assisted 'flight trajectories' will one day become so accurate that there will be little need for radar vectoring and virtually no need for voice exchanges. The role of controllers will mainly be to monitor the overall situation.

In the meantime, the use of digital voice (vocoders) may be the answer to the frequency congestion described in Chapter 5. Human speech can be translated into a digital stream and reconstructed at the receiving end, one second of speech taking about a quarter of a second to transmit. It would also be possible for two voice channels to operate on the same radio frequency. This could mean that two ATC sectors located in the same Area Control Centre could use the frequency without interfering with one another. However, it is sometimes vital to convey emotion, for example urgency or emergency, beyond the phraseology being used, which is why ICAO includes the use of conventional R/T as a back-up in any future systems.

ICAO's FANS (Future Air Navigation Systems) philosophy has evolved to become known as the ICAO CNS/ATM concept (Communications, Navigation, Surveillance/Air Traffic Management). The communications system will provide global air/ground coverage using datalink. Voice communication will be used mainly as a stand-by. Worldwide area navigation (RNAV) capability will exist, depending on the required navigational performance for a particular piece of airspace. Initially, a choice of navigation systems will continue to be available, but there will be a reduced need to overfly ground-based navaids.

At a much later date, the Global Navigation Satellite System (GNSS) is expected to meet all requirements for navigation whether it be en-route, in terminal control areas, non-precision approaches and eventually, using differential GPS (see page 40), for precision approaches. A gradual phase-in of satellite systems for navigation is planned, first for use as a supplement to conventional ground aids and ultimately as a 'sole means' system. At this point, theoretically, ground-based navaids could be withdrawn from use. However, there are fears in some quarters that satellite signals are too easily jammed, either deliberately or inadvertently. These and a number of other considerations will have to be addressed and solved before SatNav comes into universal use.

Automatic Dependent Surveillance (ADS) will complement SSR more and more. Over the oceans where radar cover is impracticable it will be of great benefit in reducing the current separations between aircraft, which are so wasteful of airspace.

In the near future a doubling of capacity over the North Atlantic will be accomplished by reducing the 2,000 ft vertical separation between aircraft operating between FL 290 and FL 410 inclusive. This has been made possible by analysing a mass of data, including precision radar monitoring and aircraft flight data recordings, to establish that height-keeping accuracy is acceptable. A further doubling of airspace capacity over the Atlantic will be possible (target date 2000) with proposed application of 30 nm lateral and longitudinal spacing between aircraft flying at the same level. It will require RNAV-derived distance information, ADS, and direct pilot-controller communications via datalink. Carriage of TCAS would provide an additional safeguard to any inadvertent deviation from track. Using a combination of modern FMS, GPS and datalink, an aircraft's position will be known with pinpoint accuracy, enabling its arrival time at any future position to be predicted within one minute.

SatNav has the potential to offer the same service to pilots in remote areas of the world, such as African deserts and sub-arctic Canada and Russia, as in more populated regions. If the point of landing has been surveyed accurately, it should be possible to devise and have approval for an instrument approach procedure without any equipment on the ground.

Still under test is a concept known as synthetic or enhanced vision, using a blend of radar and infra-red sensors in the aircraft to penetrate fog. An artificial image of the runway is created on a 'head-up' display on the windscreen, together with certain flight instrument and navigational information. It enables the pilot to fly an instrument approach with his head and eyes in the same position needed to perform a visual approach. Thus the transition from instruments to the visual phase of the approach is easily accomplished.

A computer-based procedure for traffic-stream sequencing is under development by Eurocontrol. It will achieve the most efficient arrival-rate at an airport by regulating the speed of aircraft in the en-route phase so that they can come straight on to the approach. This so-called 'linear holding' will, in theory, remove the need for holding patterns. A US procedure likely to be adopted in Europe is reduced separation on final approach. A minimum separation of 2.5 nm is permitted between succeeding aircraft on final, compared with the ICAO standard of 3 nm.

As a foretaste of things to come, the following is taken from a presentation given before an air traffic controllers' convention in the USA:

'On the flight deck, the crew are going through their pre-flight checks. The airways clearance has already been downloaded into their Flight Management System from ATC together with the digital ATIS information. No flight plan is required as the flight is part of the National Airspace System and the fuel efficient "wind" route has already been determined and integrated with their clearance. Once start-up clearance is given, an automatic taxi clearance is received and shows on one of the FMS VDUs. This information is downloaded from the tower's ASDE (Airport Surface Detection Equipment) radar and provides the aircrew with a graphical map and their taxi route to the runway. The Traffic Management system has already computed the en-route times for this aircraft the moment it left the gate.

'As all other aircraft movements are subject to this control, there will be no delay at the holding point. After departure, the aircraft is flown in accordance with instructions sent up by ground based systems interfacing with the aircraft's Mode S and FMS equipment. One assumes that with all this automation and control there is no need for TCAS, but we've left it on just in case . . . The en-route weather is often extremely important in the

'States, where Cbs can climb to over 60,000 ft; an en-route weather map is displayed via the FMS, showing colour-coded intensity. A Flow Management message is received offering the pilot three options to avoid delay at the arrival airport – speed control, en-route hold or a re-route. We decide on speed control. At 250 miles from destination the FMS receives Arrival ATIS information, including the type of approach for the runway-in-use. Descent clearance is subsequently given for a straight-in descent approach for the curved Cat 3c MLS approach.

'The FMS is able to provide us with a presentation of the integrated radar picture (compiled from SatNav and ground-based systems) showing other traffic in our vicinity. We are told to remain five miles behind the B767 ahead and are cleared to land. We check the progress of the aircraft as we taxi from the runway to the stand, using the map display on the FMS. The visibility outside is 75 metres and the ground sensors alert us to our position as we taxi to the gate.'

Fact or fiction? The truth is that all this technology is either available now or likely to be perfected over the next few years! Anyway, I leave you with these thoughts for the future heard over the air waves recently:

Aircraft: London, 946, any chance of a straight-in on 08 Right?
ATC: I'm afraid not 946, you're about number 12 to land.
Aircraft: That's ridiculous London; what's going to happen in 10 years when the traffic's doubled?
ATC: You'll be number 24 . . .

ATC: How long does it take you to fly to Sydney direct, sir?
Bored voice of A340 pilot: 27 computer inputs . . .

Chapter 14

World Air Traffic Control Systems

This section has been laid out roughly according to ICAO Regions, with a few anomalies for convenience. For example, although the CIS stretches to the Far East, it has been confined to the European section for ease of reference. The following abbreviations are used to identify VHF radio frequencies:

A: Approach Control (includes Radar)
ACC: Area Control Centre
A/G: Air/Ground Service
AFIS: Aerodrome Flight Information Service
AT: Automatic Terminal Information Service
D: Clearance Delivery
DEP: Departure Control
FIS: Flight Information Service
G: Ground Movement Control
Ops: Operations
T: Tower

Europe and Eurocontrol

Eurocontrol was set up in the 1960s with the aim of unifying all ATC operations in the upper airspace of the signatory states. Initially, Eurocontrol's Maastricht Centre co-ordinated traffic over Holland, West Germany, Belgium, and Luxembourg. It was hoped that the organization would in due course be responsible for the whole of Western Europe's airspace. Unfortunately, this ambitious concept was thwarted by concerns over national sovereignty. Convinced that its time would come, Eurocontrol began a programme of integrating the Area Control Centres at Maastricht, Amsterdam, Brussels, Dusseldorf, and Bremen, together with certain co-located military ACCs. The aim was to show what could be achieved by a unified system, even when confined to a small area of Europe. Congestion and delays on the Mediterranean holiday routes, meanwhile, became worse and worse during the 1980s, until in 1989 the problem hit the headlines and politicians called for action. The obvious answer to the problem was Eurocontrol, which had been waiting so long for just such an opportunity to prove itself.

Progress has been slow, however, and in 1992 it was said that Europe's 52 ACCs operated 31 different systems with computer hardware from 18 suppliers, running 20 operating systems with 70 different programming languages! In contrast, a mere 20 centres in the USA handle airspace twice the size of Europe's with almost double the traffic. Eurocontrol currently has 18 member states which comprise most of Western Europe together with Hungary, Greece, Cyprus, and Turkey. Several former Eastern Bloc countries will join in the near future, as well as the Scandinavian countries.

The European Civil Aviation Conference (ECAC) is an inter-governmental organization set up as long ago as 1955. In 1990 EATCHIP, the European Air Traffic Control Harmonisation and Integration Programme, was launched under the auspices of ECAC. It is planned that the programme will culminate in the creation of a comprehensive European Air Traffic Management System, (EATMS) in 2000. Amongst its objectives are common standards, specifications, and procedures throughout the region, especially at the interfaces between the national systems. They include universal SSR coverage, standardized communications and data exchange between ACCs, and the introduction of Mode S datalink. The progressive integration of national ATC structures will one day lead to a seamless system, which is the only way the predicted increases in European traffic can be handled.

A step in the right direction is a new European Air Traffic Trunk Route Network above Flight Level 330, which is coming into service in planned phases, based on extensive use of Area Navigation (RNAV). It will serve the major high demand traffic flows. Direct routeings are used as often as possible and turning points are not necessarily based on ground beacons. A new RNAV designator has been allocated to each Trunk Route for its entire length. In practice the new network will integrate with the existing upper airways system rather than replace it. When segments of the new Trunk Routes are superimposed on conventional airways, states are to maintain a 'double designator' – the new RNAV and the conventional designator. This will allow the utilization of these segments by both RNAV and non-RNAV equipped aircraft. Although the new network is confined to the airspace above FL 330, it will eventually be extended in phases to lower levels as an ongoing process.

Also part of EATCHIP is the idea of the flexible use of airspace, which should no longer be designated as either purely civil or military, as in some states, but rather considered as one and allocated according to user requirements. Any necessary airspace segregation will be temporary, based on real-time usage within a specific time period. This will enable the permanent air route network to be complemented by Conditional Routes allocated for specified durations. The chief benefits will be an increase in ATC capacity, reduction in delays, and enhanced civil/military co-ordination.

Meanwhile, seven countries have linked together to consider an ATC centre to provide similar services in mid-Europe to those which Maastricht UAC provides in Western Europe. They are Austria, Croatia, the Czech Republic, Hungary, Italy, Slovakia, and Slovenia. The plan is fraught with difficulties, among them where to build the centre and who would be responsible for its management.

Austria
Graz – T:118.2; A:119.3, 123.025; AT: 126.125. Innsbruck – T:120.1; A:119.275; AT:126.025. Klagenfurt – T:118.1; A:119.45; AT:124.075. Linz – T:118.8; A:129.625; AT:128.125. Salzburg – T:118.1; A:123.725, 124.975; AT:125.725. Vienna – T:119.4, 121.2; G:121.6; D:122.125; A:128.2, 119.8, 124.55; AT:122.95.

Despite being one of Europe's smaller countries, Austria has one of the largest and most advanced ACCs. Vienna ACC controls the entire airspace except for TMAs around Linz, Salzburg, Graz, Klagenfurt, and Innsbruck. On the two routes linking Germany with Italy, near Innsbruck, control is delegated to Munich ACC and in a similar agreement some Hungarian airspace near Vienna is delegated to Austria. A useful innovation to reduce co-ordination between controllers is that each Austrian TMA adjoins its neighbour. This avoids the need for domestic low level flights to be handled by the ACC over most of their routes. Until recently, major international air routes across Austria were generally north-south from Germany into Yugoslavia. However, the war in that country has caused an enormous increase in east-west traffic over Austria. RNAV routes have been established in the Vienna and Budapest FIRs to improve the flow of traffic. Austria is a committed member of Eurocontrol and continues to provide a great deal of assistance to east European states so that they can integrate with their western ATC counterparts. In the future Austria will ensure that new or replacement long-range radars will be sited to benefit neighbouring ACCs as well as the state's own system.

Belgium
Antwerp – T:121.4, 119.7; G:121.8. Brussels – T:118.6, 120.775; G:121.875; D:121.95; A:118.25, 120.1, 122.5; AT:114.6, 110.6, 132.475. Liege – T:129.25, 119.7; G:122.1; A:129.25, 122.5, 123.05. Ostend – T:118.7; G:121.9; A:120.6.

A founder member of Eurocontrol, Belgium recognizes that the future lies with integration between adjacent ATC systems. With this aim in mind, it opened CANAC (the Computer Assisted National ATC Centre) in 1993. Located at Brussels Airport, it controls traffic in the lower airspace (i.e. below FL 245) and provides approach control for Brussels, Antwerp, and Chiévres, in similar fashion to the US Tracon and UK Central Control Function concepts. Airspace above FL 245 is the responsibility of Maastricht ACC. CANAC is expected to handle some 275,000 movements a year and has a capacity in excess of 500,000.

Bulgaria
Burgas – T:118.0, 119.9; A:125.1, 119.65; AT:120.95. Plovdiv – T:119.6. Sofia – T:118.1; A:123.7, 119.5, 120.2; AT;118.9. Varna – T.118.9; A:124.6; AT:121.2.

As a member of ECAC, Bulgaria has an obligation to ensure that its ATC system becomes part of the future European harmonized one. To this end, it has already reorganized its airspace and air routes in close co-ordination with ICAO and European air navigation bodies. The war in Yugoslavia has brought an enormous increase in overflying traffic from Western Europe to the Aegean islands and beyond. It is a tribute to Bulgarian ATC that all this extra traffic is handled competently with limited resources. Modern radars will soon replace outdated equipment and the country is likely to join Eurocontrol in the near future. Airspace is divided into two FIRs, Sofia and Varna, with ACCs at these two cities' airports.

Commonwealth of Independent States
Armenia
Yerevan – T:128.0; G:119.0; A:126.0, 123.7, 120.9, 128.0; AT:128.7.
Azerbaijan
Baku – T:119.2; G:121.7; A:129.3, 120.8; AT: 126.4.
Belarus
Minsk 2 – T:118.3; G:121.7; A:125.9, 120.8; AT:127.2.
Georgia
Tbilis – T:128.0; G:119.0; A:125.3, 129.0; AT:132.8.
Kazakhstan
Alma Ata – T:119.4; G:121.7; A:124.8; AT:135.1.
Kyrgyzstan
Bishkek – T:118.1; G:121.7; A:124.6, 122.3; AT:127.9.
Moldova
Kishinau – T:118.1; G:121.8; A:125.9, 127.8, 120.6; AT:133.725.

Russian Federation
Irkutsk – T:118.1; G:121.7; A:125.2, 126.1, 119.3; AT:124.8. Khabarovsk – T:119.3; G:121.8; A:125.2, 126.1, 119.3; AT:124.8. Moscow (Sheremetievo) – T:120.7; G:119.0, 121.8; A:119.3, 123.7, 131.5, 118.1. Moscow (Vnukovo) – T:118.3; G:119.0; A:122.3, 126.0; AT:125.875. Novosibirsk – T:118.5, 128.0; G:121.7; A:133.8, 128.5, 127.1, 122.0.

St Petersburg – T:118.7, 118.1; G:121.7, 121.9; A:129.8, 120.3, 125.2, 128.0; AT:127.4.
Tajikistan
Dushanbe – T:118.1; G:121.7; A:127.1, 121.2; AT:126.2.
Turkmenistan
Ashkhabad – T:120.0; G:121.7; A:123.7, 118.7.
Ukraine
Kiev (Borispol) – T:119.3, 119.2; G:119.0; A:130.6, 127.9, 124.6, 132.6, 121.2; AT:126.7.
Kiev (Zhulyany) – T:122.5; G:119.0; A:120.0. Lvov – T:128.0; G:119.0; A:126.0;
AT:128.7.

Russia covers 75 per cent of the territory of the former Soviet Union and its
ATC system is badly in need of modernization. A contract called *Raduga*
(Russian for rainbow) has been signed with a consortium of several major
Western radar and ATM companies, normally fierce competitors, for a 15-
year replacement project. As long ago as 1975, an automated radar system
known as *Start* was brought into service at many airports. It combined
radar and flight data processing and was subsequently developed to cover
a large range of useful ATC functions.

Russia's airspace is divided into nine air zones which are sub-divided
into 100 FIRs, one of which, Irkutsk, covers an area as large as France. There
are now 142 ACCs, including a chief centre, eight zonal centres, 70 regional centres, and 63 assistant ones, covering some 239,903 km of air routes. A
long-term plan will reduce the number of ACCs to about 30. Russian aviation officials admit that many of the centres are in urgent need of renova-
tion, and priority is being given to Moscow ACC which serves 20 airports
in the area. Moscow's TCA extends over about 200 km, divided into a number of sectors and one-way departure and arrival corridors, each up to 8 km
wide. Many of the so-called Area Control Centres in Siberia and the
Russian Far East are literally wooden huts with one VHF frequency. Even
on the important Trans-Siberian air routes there are gaps in radar coverage
of up to 700 km. However, although HF frequencies are available, good
VHF coverage means that they are rarely used.

Advisory service was never provided in the USSR; ATC was mandatory
in its entirety, including low-level operations. Another anomaly is the use
of the metric system for altitude readings. This results in odd-numbered
flight levels such as 116 (FL 290). Careful handling of aircraft altitude is necessary when crossing boundaries where flight levels are based on foot values. For example, between the Khabarovsk and Tokyo FIRs flight level
changes should be commenced at a point not less than 45 nm prior to and
completed by not less than 15 nm from the boundary. Airways in the CIS
are, incidentally, 5.4 nm (10 km) wide, a legacy from the Soviet era when
overflights were very strictly regulated. For state security reasons such

important information as airport ground co-ordinates for INS checks were not published! As a standard procedure, all ILS approaches are monitored by PAR.

A Flow Management Unit has recently been established in Moscow with links to St Petersburg, Rostov, Chita, Khabarovsk, Yekaterinburg, and Novosibirsk. The density of air traffic is currently well below capacity but the infrastructure will be there to handle anticipated growth, particularly long distance flights from Europe to Asia across Siberia. There are also four Siberian routes between North America and Asia (Siberia 1–4) which save up to 1,000 km compared with the traditional route over the North Pacific.

One of the ex-Soviet republics, Ukraine, is similar in area and population to France. It is divided into five FIRs, each having an associated ACC. Lvov is responsible for western Ukraine, Kiev the centre, Odessa the south, Kharkov the east, and Simferopol has responsibility for the Crimea. There is a fairly extensive airways structure but non-Ukrainian aircraft are limited to a few routes designated as international. Primary means of navigation is still the NDB but VOR/DMEs will soon be installed at strategic locations.

Croatia
Dubrovnik – T:118.5; A:123.6. Pula – T:120.0; A:118.4, 124.0. Zagreb – T:118.3; A:118.5, 125.175, 120.7; AT:120.8.

Before the outbreak of war, Yugoslavia's airspace was divided into two FIRs – Belgrade (Serbia) in the east and Zagreb (Croatia) in the west. The Zagreb ACC was forced to close in September 1991 and did not reopen until well into 1992. The Zagreb FIR was reactivated, now covering Croatia and Bosnia-Herzegovina. Much of the airport and ATC equipment had been destroyed and it has been a long struggle to restore the basic system in operation today. Once a permanent peace settlement has been achieved and confidence restored, it is hoped that the tourists will return in force.

Cyprus
Akrotiri – T:122.1; A:123.3. Larnaca – T:119.4; A:121.2; AT 112.8. Nicosia – ACC:126.3, 125.5. Paphos – T:119.9; A:120.8.

To handle its ever-increasing tourist traffic, Cyprus is upgrading its area radar systems to incorporate multi-radar tracking and automatic flight data processing. Strained relations with Turkey mean that all airspace over Cyprus and its territorial waters is prohibited unless within established air routes and control zones. No contact is maintained between Ankara and Nicosia ACCs and IATA publishes special procedures which effectively mean that aircrew co-ordinate their own flights by contacting the other ACC at least 10 minutes before entering its airspace. Only north and southbound flights are handled in this way: east and westbounds are unaffected.

Czech Republic
Prague – T:118.1; G:121.9; A:121.4, 119.7, 119.0, 126.1, 124.1; AT:122.15.

Area control in the Prague FIR/UIR has four sectors. An upper sector controls the entire airspace above FL 245 while the lower airspace is split into North, West, and East Sectors. Flight data is transferred automatically between Prague ACC and the Vienna and Bratislava ACCs. Prague approach control consists of two sectors: one is responsible for the TMA from FL 60 up to FL 125, the other – the Director – handles traffic below FL 60.

Denmark
Aalborg – T:118.3; A:123.875, 120.7, 120.775. Billund – T:119.0; A:127.575, 119.25; AT:118.775. Copenhagen (Kastrup) – T:118.1, 119.9, 118.575; G:121.9, 121.6; A:120.2, 119.8, 120.25, 124.975; AT: 122.75, 122.85. Copenhagen (Roskilde) – T:118.9; A:131.0; AT:123.8.

In 1989 Denmark decided to reorganize its airspace for the benefit of all users, whether civil or military. It is now an integrated system and all area functions are performed from a single ACC. All controllers, including those in the towers of military airfields, are civilians. Danish airspace is thus based on an 'area' concept and not constructed around fixed air routes. Military training can be accommodated for the duration of a mission but it is still possible for civil aircraft to penetrate the area, traffic permitting, because control comes under the same ATC facility.

Estonia
Tallinn – T:120.6; A:127.9, 122.9, 120.6; AT:124.875; ACC:132.5, 125.3.

Based on obsolete Soviet equipment, the ATC system is badly in need of modernization.

Finland
Helsinki (Malmi) – T:118.9; G:121.6; AT:122.7. Helsinki (Vantaa) – T:118.6; G:121.8; A:119.1, 119.7, 119.9, 129.85; AT:135.075.

Finland is currently embarking on an integration programme to modernize its ATC system. It is centred on the Tampere FIR, which covers the southern half of the country. The Great Circle route between Western Europe and the Far East passes over it and offers the most direct, and therefore cheapest, routeing. To accommodate the rapidly increasing flow of traffic, Tampere ACC will soon have an ATM service which is claimed to be the most advanced in Europe. The system will process data from 25 radars and will include Short Term Conflict Alert and Minimum Safe Altitude Warning functions. The future introduction of Mode S datalink is also feasible. Traffic in the Rovaniemi FIR in northern Finland is mainly domestic with a single airway, A22/UA22, running north to Kirkenes in Norway.

France
Beauvais – T:121.4; A:119.9. Bordeaux (Merignac) – T:118.3, 118.1; G:121.9, 121.725; A:118.6, 121.2, 125.475; AT:131.15. Brest – T:120.1; A:121.125; AT:120.375. Caen – T/A:124.425. Calais-Dunkerque – T:118.1. Cannes – T/A:118.3; G:121.8; AT:127.475. Cherbourg – T/A:119.35. Dinard – T:121.1; A:120.15, 119.7; AT:124.575. Le Touquet – T:118.45; G:125.3. Lyon (Bron) – T:118.1; G:121.85; A:119.45; AT:126.125. Lyon (Satolas) – T:120.0; G:121.8; A:119.25, 127.575; AT:131.2, 121.7. Marseille – T:119.5; G:121.7; A:120.2, 123.725; AT:125.35. Nice – T:118.7; G:123.15; A:124.175, 134.475, 125.575; AT:129.6, 121.7. Paris (Le Bourget) – T:119.1, 118.925; G:121.9; AT:120.0, 118.4. Paris (Charles-de-Gaulle) – T:119.25, 120.65, 125.325; G:121.6, 121.8; A:118.15, 119.85, 121.15, 125.825, 126.575, 124.35, 133.375; AT:128.0. Paris (Orly) – T;118.7, 135.0; G:121.7, 120.5, 121.05; A:118.85, 127.75, 124.45, 120.85; AT:126.5. Perpignan – T:118.3, 121.9; A:120.75; AT:127.875. Pontoise – T:121.2; A:118.8; AT:124.125. Strasbourg – T:118.7; G:121.8; A:120.7, 119.575; AT:126.925. Toulouse (Blagnac) – T:118.1; G:121.9; A:129.3, 125.175, 123.925, 121.1; AT:118.025, 121.7. Toussus le Noble – T:119.3; G:121.3; A:120.75, 119.7; AT:127.475. Villacoublay (Velizy) – T:122.3; G:121.875; A:119.425, 120.8.

Unusually, France's area control has recently been decentralized, with four sectors transferred from Paris ACC to Reims, Brest, and Bordeaux ACCs. The centres (the fifth of which is Marseille) currently handle over 1.6 million flights per year, a figure representing 40 per cent of total European traffic. Although each ACC has its associated FIR, all airspace above FL 195 is known as the France UIR. The Paris TMA is one of the most complex in Europe with De Gaulle Approach also controlling arriving and departing traffic at Le Bourget and Creil, and Orly being responsible for that at Toussus and Velizy.

Air Inter Airbus at Paris-Orly. (Ian Doyle)

A procedure unique to France is the Indirect Approach, a circling procedure published for some airfields where prescribed tracks are flown to establish an approach to the runway-in-use after an instrument approach to another runway. It is similar to circling minima but more precise. Another anomaly is the use of the term 'stopping point' on a taxiway instead of 'holding point.'

Since French is used at all small aerodromes, British private pilots planning an aerial visit may find the following standard R/T phraseology useful. French is also employed for traffic broadcasts when operating at uncontrolled aerodromes. On these occasions the 'club' or common frequency for all light aircraft is 123.45.

Au sol	*On ground*
A/C - Jodel VM bonjour, demande roulage (vol local ou navigation)	Request taxi (local flight or navigation)
A/C – FZG demande à traverser piste 20	Request cross Runway 20
Twr - FZG maintenez position	Hold position
A/C – FZG je maintiens position	
Twr - FZG accélérez le roulage si possible	Can you expedite taxi?
Twr - FZG laissez passer le Jodel	Give way to the Jodel
Twr - FVM alignez vous	Line up
A/C - FVM je m'aligne	
Twr - FVM autorisé au décollage	Clear to take off
A/C - FVM je décolle	

En vol	*In flight*
A/C - TB20 ZG au point Echo 1500 ft pour atterrissage	At Point Echo 1500 ft for landing
Twr - FZG entrez en vent arrière piste 03 . . . faites une approche direct . . . attendez verticale . . .	Join downwind Runway 03 . . . make straight-in approach . . . hold
Twr - FZG faites une approche courte	Make a short approach
Twr - FZG allongez le vent arrière	Extend downwind
Twr - Rappelez en finale	Report final
Twr - FZG autorisé à l'atterrissage	Clear to land
A/C - FZG j'atterris	I'm landing
Twr - FZG rappelez piste dégagée	Report runway vacated
A/C - FZG demande toucher	Request touch and go

Standard phrases	
Accusez réception	Acknowledge
Annulez	Cancel
Approuvé	Approved
Collationnez	Read back
Comment recevez-vous?	How do you read?
Confirmez	Confirm
Circuit à gauche	Left hand circuit
Dèpassez	Overtake
Demande heure exacte	Request time check
Laissez passer	Give way

Maintenez position	Hold position
Rappelez après décollage	Report airborne
Remettez les gaz	Go around

Germany

Berlin (Schoenefeld) – T:120.025, 127.875; G:121.6, 121.8; A:121.3, 119.7, 119.5; AT:126.125. Berlin (Tegel) – T:124.525; G:121.925; AT:123.775, 112.3, 113.3. Berlin (Tempelhof) – T:119.575, 118.1; G:121.9; AT:126.025. Bremen – T:118.5, 118.575, 118.3; G:121.75; A:125.65, 119.45; AT:117.45. Cologne-Bonn – T:120.5, 124.975; G:121.85; A:120.25, 126.325, 120.9; AT:119.025, 112.15. Dusseldorf – T:118.3; G:121.9; A:119.4, 128.85, 120.05; AT:123.775. Frankfurt – T:119.9, 124.85; G:121.9, 121.7, 121.8; A:120.15, 118.5, 124.2; AT:118.025, 114.2. Hamburg – T:126.85, 121.275; G:121.8, 121.7; A:120.6, 124.225, 118.2; AT:123.125, 108.0. Hanover – T:120.175, 123.55; G:121.95; A:118.05, 118.15, 119.6; AT:121.85. Leipzig – T:121.1; G:121.6; A:124.175, 119.7; AT:120.525. Munich – T:118.7, 120.2, 120.5; G:121.975, 121.825, 121.775; A:132.55, 128.025, 128.25, 123.9, 120.775, 127.95; AT:123.125. Saarbrucken – T:118.35, 118.55; A:129.475, 129.05; AT:113.85. Stuttgart – T:118.8, 119.05; G:121.9; A:125.05, 119.85, 119.2; AT:126.125.

German airspace is divided into three UIRs. In the north Hanover UIR is controlled by the Eurocontrol ACC at Maastricht. The former German Democratic Republic upper airspace is controlled from Berlin and the southern Rhein UIR by Karlsruhe (south-west) and Munich (south-east). There are five lower FIRs, Berlin, Bremen, Dusseldorf, Frankfurt, and Hanover, each controlled by an ACC and 10 local air navigation services units – equivalent to terminal control units. A major re-equipment project is seen as a giant step towards a common European ATC system as foreseen by the Eurocontrol EATCHIP/EATMS programmes. Frankfurt ACC is the busiest in Germany, handling more than 3,000 flights on peak days. With the re-unification of Germany, Frankfurt took over a large part of ex-DDR

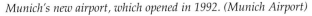

Munich's new airport, which opened in 1992. (Munich Airport)

airspace and new sectors were introduced to deal with it. There is automatic data exchange of flight information with other German ACCs, as well as Maastricht, Zurich, and Prague. ATC problems in the Frankfurt area are some of Europe's most complex and a new ACC at Langen, near Frankfurt, is scheduled to be operational by the end of 1996. All major airports use controlled VFR procedures to improve safety in airspace with a high density mixture of IFR and VFR traffic. VFR flights in specified airspace are separated by ATC from both IFR and other CVFR flights by clearances or instructions in respect of route and altitude.

Gibraltar
Gibraltar – T:123.3; A:122.8, 130.4. Seville Control – 132.925.

The airport is under the administrative and operational control of the Royal Air Force and, apart from the physical constraints of the adjacent Rock, it is almost surrounded by Spanish prohibited or restricted airspace. There is an agreement allowing civilian aircraft on approach and climb-out to fly through the restricted area but all military flights have to remain clear. Therefore, with the exception of the civil approach to Runway 27, all approaches are offset from the runway centreline with a radar talk-down relating the aircraft's position to the 'recommended track' as opposed to 'centreline'. Because of the Rock every aircraft must be visual with the runway at three miles (visual decision point) and, if not, execute a missed approach procedure. Gibraltar is located in the Madrid FIR with a parent ACC at Seville which issues all clearances and releases for aircraft departing via airways. Tangier is the normal diversion airfield for military aircraft operating from Gibraltar due to the present restrictions which forbid aircraft to fly to and from Gibraltar over Spanish territory. Civil operators use Malaga as a diversion.

Greece
Athens – T:118.1; G:121.7; D:122.4; A:119.1, 121.4, 129.55, 118.3; AT:123.4. Chania/Souda – T:121.1; A:122.0, 121.1. Heraklion – T:120.85; A:119.85; AT:127.55. Kerkyra (Corfu) – T:120.85; A:122.35; AT:126.35. Kos – T:121.05; A:119.95; AT:126.95. Mikonos – T/A:118.75. Rhodes – T:118.2; A:120.6, 119.7; AT:126.35. Santorini – T/A:118.05. Skiathos – AFIS:123.25. Thessaloniki – T:118.1; G:121.7; A:120.8; AT:127.55. Zakinthos – T:125.425.

Apart from the complex Athens TCA, there are other TCAs around some of the most popular tourist islands, such as Crete and Rhodes. Smaller island airports like Karpathos have Control Zones and a number of airports are used jointly by the Greek Air Force. Greek is normally used by controllers and domestic flights. The continuing dispute with Turkey means that co-ordination between controllers in each country is often less than adequate and sometimes non-existent. The situation results also in flights over Greek

Kos, a typical Greek island airport where the busiest summer peaks are Wednesdays and Thursdays, when the package holiday passengers arrive and depart! (Author)

territory not being permitted outside airways, advisory routes, or permitted flying routes. New long-range radar has been promised, but in the meantime the country's ATC system struggles gamely to accommodate all its holiday flights, using out-dated procedural methods. Throughout Greek airspace a radar advisory service, collective callsign TUGRIT, is available. It is an acronym for Turkey, Greece and Italy and is provided by air defence radars which are predominantly American-manned. Originally, its most important function was to prevent aircraft straying over hostile borders but, with the easing of East-West relations, this is no longer so necessary. Its frequency over Greece is 129.8.

Hungary
Budapest – T:118.1; G:121.9; A:129.7, 119.5; AT:117.3, 124.65; ACC:128.1, 128.35(West), 126.5(East), 133.2(South); FIS:133.0 (E of Danube), 125.5 (W of Danube).

Hungary's airport and ATC infrastructure has benefited from a liberal foreign trade policy which existed long before the collapse of communist eastern Europe. Full radar coverage with modern equipment has enabled the system to accommodate with ease the vast increase in traffic avoiding Yugoslavian airspace. The weak link has been the lack of radar cover on the interface between the Budapest and Arad ACCs in neighbouring Romania. Now that Arad has new radar, data exchange has been implemented in both directions with excellent results. Hungary is the first ex-Soviet Bloc country to join Eurocontrol.

Ireland
Baldonnel (Casement) – T:123.5; G:123.1; A:122.8, 122.0, 122.3, 129.7. Connaught – T:130.7; G:121.9. Cork – T:119.3; G:121.8; A:118.8, 119.9; AT:120.925. Donegal – T:129.8. Dublin – T:118.6; G:121.8; A:121.1, 119.55, 118.5; AT:124.525; ACC:124.65, 129.175, 124.65, 119.55. Galway (Carnmore) – T:122.5. Kerry (Farranfore) – T:124.1; G:121.6. Shannon – T:118.7; G:121.8; A:121.4, 120.2; D:121.7; AT:130.95; ACC:131.15

(Cork Sector), 135.6, 135.225 (SOTA), 134.275, 124.7 (Shannon/SOTA), 132.15 (BABAN/DEVOL Sector), 127.5 (As directed). Sligo – T:122.1. Waterford – T:129.85. Weston – A/G:122.4.

Irish airspace is contained entirely within the Shannon FIR/UIR and controlled from Shannon ACC; Dublin ACC, however, is responsible for the Dublin TMA and the air routes to the east until they reach the Shannon/London FIR boundary. It has a fully integrated flight data processing system, with radar tracking using information from several sites. Shannon ACC handles 75 per cent of transatlantic movements, the peak period beginning at dawn when as many as 100 aircraft are overflying bound for Northern Europe from the USA. Using a transmitter site on Mount Gabriel, near Cork, radar coverage extends 200 miles out over the Atlantic. This has enabled delegation of airspace known as the Shannon Oceanic Transition Area (SOTA) from the Oceanic ACC at Prestwick to Shannon ACC. Further Atlantic coverage will be provided when a radar is installed on the west coast in Mayo.

The degree of sectorization of Shannon's airspace depends directly on the daily orientation of the North Atlantic Track System (See page 168). Currently, it is divided horizontally into eight upper sectors which can be further split vertically if required. Built-in flexibility allows Shannon to cope with the twice-daily changes in the orientation of the North Atlantic flows. Operational procedures are among the most advanced in Europe, with controllers passing information electronically between adjacent ACCs in France, London, and Scotland. Complying with the common standard set by Eurocontrol, automatic radar handover is carried out 'on screen' without the need for constant voice communications, a system known as OLDI (On-Line Data Interchange). Radar data comes from three sites – Mount Gabriel, Woodcock Hill near Shannon, and Dublin Airport. Traffic density will increase when North Atlantic vertical separation is reduced to 1,000 ft at some future date. As a further challenge Shannon controllers will have to re-establish 2,000 ft vertical separation as the traffic transitions into European domestic airspace. In the lower sectors Shannon has two sectors: Cork and Shannon Approach.

Italy
Genoa – T:118.6; A:119.6. Milan (Linate) – T:118.1, 119.25; G:121.8; A:132.7, 126.3, 126.75; AT:116.0. Milan (Malpensa) – T:119.0, 128.35; G:121.9; A:132.7, 126.3, 126.75. Naples – T:118.5; G:121.9; A:124.35, 120.95; AT:135.975. Rimini – T:119.1, 122.1; D:121.6; A:118.15, 118.575, 124.85. Rome (Ciampino) – T:120.5; G:121.75; A:119.2. Rome (Fiumicino) – T:118.7, 119.3; G:121.9; D:121.8; A:119.2; AT:114.9, 121.7. Rome (Urbe) – T:123.8; G:122.7. Turin – T:118.5; A:121.1, 120.15. Turin (Aeritalia) – AFIS:119.15. Venice – T:120.2; G:121.7; A:120.4, 121.15, 118.9. Venice (San Nicolo) – AFIS:120.0.

Airspace is divided into three FIR/UIRs: Milan, Rome, and Brindisi, with four ACCs – Milan, Padova, Rome, and Brindisi. Some Swiss airspace is delegated to Milan ACC. Complete radar cover for en-route traffic is not yet provided, resulting in a combined procedural and radar-controlled environment in some areas and solely procedural in others. The concept of controlled VFR is in use (see entry for Germany). A network of advisory routes over the sea between the mainland, Sardinia, and Sicily is administered by Rome ACC, using the callsign *Roma Advisory*.

Latvia
Riga – T:118.1; A:127.3, 121.2, 130.0; AT:121.2; ACC:120.8, 135.1 128.0.

Since gaining independence, Latvia has begun a complete modernization of its ATC system to meet Eurocontrol specifications.

Lithuania
Vilnius – T:118.2; G:119.0; A;120.7, 128.0; AT:132.8; ACC:135.2 (West Sector), 133.3 (East Sector).

Since this small state on the Baltic broke away from the former Soviet Union, its radar coverage has been upgraded to increase traffic capacity in the Vilnius FIR. With a new automated ATC system Vilnius ACC is now one of the most modern in the world.

Luxembourg
Luxembourg – T:118.1; A:118.45; AT:112.25.

This small country lies within the Brussels FIR/UIR and was a founder member of Eurocontrol.

Malta
Luqa – T:118.9; A:121.0, 127.1. Malta – ACC:128.7, 129.1.

Malta is a member of Eurocontrol and its ACC is responsible for a number of routes connecting Europe with North Africa, as well as feeders bringing in its own considerable tourist traffic.

Monaco
Monaco Heliport – T:118.2, 118.325.

The Principality lies within the Marseille FIR. The heliport is the sole aviation facility.

Netherlands
Amsterdam – T:118.1; G:121.7, 121.8; D:121.975; A:121.2, 131.15, 119.05, 118.8 (SUGOL Arrival), 120.55, 129.3 (NARSO Arrival), 130.95 (RIVER Arrival); AT:132.975, 108.4, 122.2. Den Helder (De Kooy) – T:123.25; A:119.1. Eelde – T:118.7; G:121.7; A:120.3, 134.625; AT:112.4. Eindhoven – T:131.0; A:123.175, 124.525, 122.45;

Amsterdam, one of Europe's main hub airports. (Amsterdam Airport)

AT:126.025. Maastricht (Beek) – T:119.475, 119.7; G:121.825; A:123.975; AT:124.575. Rotterdam – T:118.2, 119.7; G:122.175; A:127.025; AT:110.4.

Because of considerable military traffic the Amsterdam FIR has a unique airspace management system. It is shared between the Royal Netherlands Air Force, with a control centre at Nieuw Milligen (callsign *Dutch Mil*), and the Amsterdam ACC. At FL 300 and above the Eurocontrol ACC at Maastricht is responsible for all airways traffic. All airspace above 1,500 ft over land and FL 55 over the sea is controlled. W-prefixed airways are reserved for domestic traffic. Amsterdam ACC is divided into five sectors, one of them solely for the complex traffic where the east/west and north/south airways cross at the Spijkerboor VOR, just north of Amsterdam. The vertical boundary between Amsterdam Approach and area control is at FL 90. Amsterdam Schiphol, with five runways, is one of Europe's most complex airports. The new tower was necessary for full vision of the many taxiways and, at 102 m, is currently the highest in the world. To date unique in Europe, Amsterdam uses a Converging Runway Display Aid developed in the USA. It assists controllers in spacing aircraft on simultaneous approaches to converging runways, using a technique called 'ghosting' to project the radar image of aircraft on approach to one runway on to the approach of the converging runway.

Norway

Bergen (Flesland) – T:119.1; A:125.0, 121.0, 118.85; AT:125.25. Oslo (Fornebu) – T:118.1, 119.775; G:121.7; D:121.95; A:120.45, 118.225, 131.35, 119.65; AT:126.125. Oslo (Gardermoen) – T:120.1, 118.3; A:120.1; AT:127.15. Stavanger (Sola) – T:118.35; G:121.75; A:119.6, 119.4; AT:126.0.

Although not yet a member of Eurocontrol, Norway conforms to its operational requirements and planning criteria. Air traffic management will, over the next few years, be based increasingly on RNAV. Norwegian airspace is divided into four FIRs: Bodo, Oslo, Stavanger, and Trondheim. In addition Bodo has an Oceanic FIR. Each has an ACC and the one at Oslo will soon be replaced by an entirely new facility (built inside a mountain!) which will provide not only area control but also approach control services within the area. Norway has 54 airports handling scheduled traffic, and few people realize that from Oslo to the northern tip of the country is the same distance as from Oslo to Rome. Just above 78°N, Longyearbyen has the distinction of being the most northerly airport in the world. The control tower is an oddity in that it is a combined maritime/aviation facility. Dual qualified staff provide an information service to both aircraft and shipping. Bodo Oceanic is responsible for three of the routes in the Polar Track Structure (see pages 171-172) until they cross the Reykjavik boundary around 80°N.

Poland
Gdansk – T:132.2. Krakow – T:121.075, 129.0; A:120.6. Warsaw – T:121.6; G:121.9; A:128.8, 120.3; AT:120.45.
The Warsaw FIR comprises the entire airspace. A major ATC redevelopment programme is based on ECAC strategy and is expected to be completed by about 1996. Area Control is divided into three sectors which will soon have full radar coverage. Construction of a new ACC is also being considered.

Portugal
Faro – T:118.2; A:119.4. Funchal (Madeira) – T:118.1; A:119.2; ACC:132.25. Lisbon – T:118.1; G:121.75; A:119.1. Oporto – T:118.1; A:121.1.

The Lisbon FIR/UIR covers the whole country with a narrow extension to the south-west to include the Portuguese island of Madeira. The overall authority is Lisbon ACC, using three radar heads at Lisbon, Faro in the south, and Oporto in the north. An associated Oceanic Control Centre is now responsible for the Santa Maria FIR/UIR. It was formerly controlled from the Azores but new technology and automation have made it possible to centralize ATC in the Portuguese capital. Further details of the Santa Maria OCC can be found in the North Atlantic section.

Romania
Bucharest (Baneasa) – T:120.8; G:129.95; A:120.6, 125.2. Bucharest (Otopeni) – T:120.9, 121.85; G:121.7; A:120.6, 128.0; AT:118.5. Timisoara – T/A:120.1.

Until the 1989 revolution, Romania's ATC system relied heavily on procedural methods, supported by some very outdated Russian approach radars. An ICAO report predicted that, whilst facilities were satisfactory at that time, the expected growth in traffic would soon overload the system. The government's intention was to become part of Eurocontrol in the reasonably near future. International finance was obtained to support a capital investment programme which included new navigational aids and modern en route radars. Fortunately, much of this infrastructure was in place when civil operators were forced to re-route their flights to avoid the airspace of former Yugoslavia. Within the Bucharest FIR are four ACCs: Arad, Bacau, Cluj, and Constanta. Problems with the lack of radar cover on the interface with the Budapest and Arad ACCs were solved by a Eurocontrol technical team which arranged for both the Arad and Cluj ACCs to receive radar cover from Hungary. Now that new radar has been installed at Arad, permanent radar data exchange has been implemented in both directions.

Slovakia
Bratislava (Ivanka) – T:118.3; A:120.9, 120.0, 119.7; AT:128.65.

Equipment at Bratislava ACC processes data from a new monopulse SSR radar, as well as from a similar radar in the neighbouring Czech Republic and a radar site near Vienna.

Slovenia
Ljubljana – T:118.0; A:118.75; ACC:128.875.

After Slovenia seceded from Yugoslavia in June 1991, the latter's government closed its airspace, which had been controlled from the Zagreb ACC in what was now Croatia. Before the war in the region, Slovenia lay under a European air route system which connected central and south-eastern Europe and, further on, the Middle and Far East. Before the airspace closure, the number of overflights was 700 to 800 per day with peaks reaching up to 1,200 per day. Unfortunately, Slovenia and neighbouring Croatia's new sense of independence extends to ATC separatism, in contrast to the rest of Europe which is moving towards a unified system. Slovenia, however, aspires to join Eurocontrol and a new ACC at Ljubljana has a modern en route radar with equipment allowing data transfer to all adjoining ACCs. Control of the north eastern Mura Sector above FL 125 has been delegated to Vienna ACC to save pilots having to contact a third ACC for a few minutes whilst flying between Graz and Croatia.

Spain (See also Canaries in Africa Section)
Alicante – T:118.15; G:121.7; A:118.8. Barcelona – T:118.1; G:121.7; D:121.8; A:119.1, 124.7; AT:118.65. Bilbao – T:118.5; G:121.7; A:120.7. Ibiza – T:118.5; G:121.8; A:119.8. Madrid (Barajas) – T:118.15, 120.15; G:121.7; D:121.95; A:119.9, 120.9, 127.1, 128.7;

AT:118.25. Malaga – T:118.15; G:121.7; A:123.95, 118.45; AT:118.05. Minorca – T:119.65; G:121.75. Palma – T:118.3; G:121.7, 121.9; A:118.95, 119.15, 119.4; AT:119.25. Santiago – T:118.75; G:121.7; A:118.2, 120.2. Seville – T:118.1; G:121.7; A:128.5, 120.0, 120.8. Valencia – T:118.55; G:121.7; A:120.1, 120.4, 124.75.

Spanish airspace, as well as that of Andorra and Gibraltar, is divided into the Madrid and Barcelona FIR/UIRs, Majorca and Minorca lying within the latter. In the past the ATC system was often unable to cope as tourist traffic increased, and delays were frequent. However, it has now been modernized and traffic flows are greatly improved. There are three ACCs: Madrid, Seville, and Barcelona. They use satellite fixed links as a backup to ground communication lines in order to transmit radar data from the remote antenna to the ATC units concerned. The result is high quality data which can be shared with neighbouring states, such as Portugal and its Lisbon ACC.

Sweden
Gothenburg (Landvetter) – T:118.6; G:121.9; A:124.675; AT:118.375. Malmo (Sturup) – T:118.8, 121.7; A:135.9, 120.9; AT:113.0. Stockholm (Arlanda) – T:118.5 (Rwy 01/19 and VFR traffic), 125.125 (Rwy 08/26); G:121.95; D:121.7; A:126.65; AT:119.0, 121.9. Stockholm (Bromma) – T:119.4, 118.1; G:121.6; A:120.15; AT:122.45. Stockholm (Skavsta) – T:127.7.

Currently, Sweden has three ACCs – Stockholm, Malmo, and Sundsvall – but there are plans to reduce them to two. First step will be the replacement of the existing Stockholm ACC with a completely new facility in 1997. Sweden is not yet a member of Eurocontrol but is being urged to join.

Switzerland
Basle – T:118.3, 119.7; G:121.6; A:119.35, 121.25; AT:127.875. Berne – T:118.9; A:127.325; AT:125.125. Geneva – T:118.7; G:121.9, 121.75; A:131.325, 120.3, 119.525 121.3; AT:125.725. Lugano – T:118.25, 122.55; G:121.775; AT:121.175. Zurich – T:118.1; G:121.9; A:118.0, 120.75, 119.7, 127.75, 125.95; D:121.8; AT:128.525.

The country is split into two FIRs, Geneva and Zurich, with a single UIR, known as Switzerland, above. Geneva ACC's major responsibility is the big crossing point at St Prex VOR where eight airways meet. An unusual vertical sectorization is in use by Geneva Control with four separate frequencies for specified height bands between FL 200 and FL 340 and above. Such is the system's flexibility that the creation of a sector of one flight level is possible. This is usually flight level 330, the busiest and therefore most difficult to handle. A reduced vertical separation of 1,000 ft above FL 290 was suggested to solve the problem of congestion and may have been implemented by now. Swiss airspace makes extensive use of RNAV routes. The airways are designed in such a way that there is a difference in their use by RNAV and by more traditionally equipped aircraft using VOR and even NDB navigation. The RNAV routes are offset from the VOR/NDB centrelines, giving an immediate indication of whether an aircraft is on RNAV or conventional navigation. As a bonus, RNAV-equipped aircraft separate themselves from the others by flying parallel to the centreline by 5 nm. In this way Zurich ACC creates what is, in fact, a triple airway configuration. The three streams of traffic increase capacity enormously. At Zurich Airport, if wind conditions permit, two runways (14 and 16) are used for landing. Since they are crossing, not parallel, traffic is fed in simultaneously from the north and the south, one after the other, crossing each other's tracks with about 5 nm separation. Zurich is so far unique in Europe in utilizing the American Separate Access Landing System for its Runway 28. It provides a discrete approach path and missed approach procedure for commuter aircraft, taking advantage of their ability to make steep approaches and short landings.

Turkey
Ankara (Esenboga) – T:118.1; G:121.9; A:119.1, 119.6, 122.1; AT:123.6. Ankara (Etimesgut) – T:122.1. Dalaman – T:118.5; G:121.9; A:129.5. Istanbul – T:118.1, 121.8; G:121.9, 121.7; A:121.1, 120.5; AT:128.2; ACC:119.3, 126.5, 129.3. Izmir (Menderes) – T:118.1; G:121.9, 121.7; A:120.1, 132.9; AT:129.2.

As a result of an extensive modernization programme initiated in 1988, virtually all of Turkey's air route system is under radar control. The two FIRs, Istanbul and Ankara, are administered from ACCs at Ataturk and Esenboga airports respectively. Each is fully automated and equipped with radar and flight data processing systems. Both centres are also integrated with the country's military defence network. Turkey is a member of Eurocontrol and her ATC organization is now more than adequate to handle the continuing rapid growth in tourism. Current plans include developing Istanbul airport into a connecting hub between Europe, the Middle East, and the Turkic republics of the former Soviet Union. An unusual feature of Turkish airspace is the use of the US-style Victor prefix to the airway designator to denote a VOR route (e.g. VR32 between Izmir and Ankara).

United Kingdom
See *Air Band Radio Handbook* 5th edition.

Yugoslavia
Belgrade – T:118.1; A:119.1. Skopje – T:118.5; A:120.3.

All flights are to be carried out in airways or authorized routes.

Middle East

The rich oil states have sophisticated ATC systems to deal with terminal traffic to the many major airports in the region, as well as the busy air routes between Europe and the Far East. Improved relations with Israel have meant the opening of several airways previously 'blocked' at boundaries with neighbouring states. However, there is still a lack of overall regional planning, with fears that the present system will not be able to support forecast traffic growth.

Bahrain
Bahrain – T:118.5; G:121.85; A:122.3, 124.3; AT:115.3. Bahrain (Sheikh Isa) – T:124.45; G:125.95; A:125.65.

The Bahrain FIR/UIR also includes Qatar and part of Saudi Arabia.

Iran
Shiraz – T:118.1; G:121.9; A:119.0, 131.4, 134.1. Tabriz – T:124.1; A;122.0, 123.4, 122.85. Tehran (Mehrabad) – T:118.1; G:121.9; A:119.7, 125.1, 123.4.

Since the war with neighbouring Iraq, the area remains highly sensitive and segments of Airways W5, G55, G202 and B51 over the borders are closed to all traffic. The Royal Air Force flight planning document notes: 'The lateral limits of the Tehran FIR as published by Iran do not agree with those published by Iraq'. The entry goes on to say: 'All aircraft entering Iranian territorial airspace should be at FL 150 or above. Aircraft unable to do so shall obtain prior permission. FIR boundary estimates are required to be made good within ±5 minutes. Foreign aircraft must enter Iranian airspace via the established ATS routes only. Aircraft not complying with these regulations will be subject to air interception.' Tehran ACC has delegated its authority to Bahrain ACC to provide air traffic services to flights operating in the southern portion of the Tehran FIR which lies over the Persian Gulf.

Iraq
Baghdad (Saddam) – T:118.7; G:121.7; A:119.4, 120.4; AT:112.9. Basrah – T:118.7; A:119.4.

At the time of writing, civil aviation in Iraq was completely paralysed as a result of UN Security Council Resolutions. Needless to say, Iraq considers the air embargo unjustified!

Israel
Eilat – T:118.6, 119.0; A:132.55. Jerusalem – T:118.8, 127.4. Tel Aviv (Ben Gurion) – T:118.3; G:121.8; A:120.5; AT:132.5.

The Tel Aviv FIR is also a control area. The country's main airport, Ben

Gurion, is within the TCA of the same name. Flights outside controlled airspace are prohibited and positive control is applied to all VFR flights, which must use designated routes. Isolated from most of its Arab neighbours, Israel has its own route network using the J and H prefixes which identify airways not forming part of a regional system. To the west and south west they link with the existing international routes.

Jordan
Amman (Marka) – T:118.1; G:121.7; A:128.9. Amman (Queen Alia) – T:119.8; G:121.9; A:128.9, 128.3, 119.6; AT:127.6. Aqaba – T:118.1; G:121.7; A:119.2.

There are only two airways over this small country; R52, which connects Amman with Egypt and Saudi Arabia, and A52 north-east into Syria.

Kuwait
Kuwait – T:118.3; G:121.7, 121.9; A:121.3, 124.8.

Most of the country is contained within the Kuwait CTA. Although badly damaged during the Iraqi occupation, the airport was back in full operation within months.

Lebanon
Beirut – T:118.9, 121.9; A:119.3, 120.3.

Owing to its geographical position, Lebanon has always been a junction between Africa, Asia, and Europe, not least in aviation. With the ending of the civil war, the country has regained authority over most of its territory and airspace, and the badly damaged Beirut International has been rehabilitated. The Beirut FIR is relatively small and Beirut Control also performs the approach function for the main airport on the same area frequencies. An HF net is in use for longer range communications.

Oman
Muscat (Seeb) – T:118.4; G:121.8; A:121.2, 119.8; AT:126.8. Salalah – T:118.2; A:119.1, 125.1.

Muscat ACC is responsible for a complex system of overflying and domestic air routes.

Qatar
Bahrain – T:118.5; G:121.85; A:122.3, 124.3; AT:115.3. Doha – T:118.9; A:121.1; AT:112.4.

Qatar is within the Bahrain FIR and responsibility for airways control is delegated to Bahrain ACC.

Saudi Arabia
Dharan – T:118.7, 118.4; G:121.7; D:126.3; A:120.3, 125.8; AT:117.2. Jeddah – T:124.3,

Part of an Area Control Centre in the Middle East. (Via Leo Marriott)

118.2; G:121.6, 121.8; A:124.0, 119.1, 123.8; AT:114.9. Riyadh (King Khalid) – T:118.6, 118.8; G:121.7, 121.6; D:121.8; A:126.0, 120.0; AT:113.3.

Saudi airspace is divided between Bahrain and Jeddah FIRs and Kuwait TCA. International tension in the area means that flying outside the airways system is prohibited without special permission. Frequency 122.8 is designated for aircraft operating within 40 nm of an uncontrolled aerodrome for exchange of traffic information. In time of war or defence emergency the SCATANA Plan will be put into operation (Security Control of Air Traffic and Air Navigation Aids). All Saudi ATC units will broadcast on all available frequencies a message to this effect. Aircraft are then required to comply with SCATANA instructions to change course, altitude, or to land at the nearest suitable aerodrome. The aim is to clear the skies of civilian aircraft so that ground-based navaids can be shut down as soon as possible.

Syria
Aleppo – T:118.1, 119.1. Damascus – T:118.5; G:121.9; ACC:120.3, 121.3.

The country is contained within the Damascus FIR and Airway R55 is the primary route for overflights.

United Arab Emirates
Abu Dhabi – T:119.2; G:121.75; A:124.4, 127.5, 125.9, 128.1; AT:113.0. Abu Dhabi (Bateen) – T:119.9; G:121.9. Al Ain – T:119.85; A:126.1, 129.15. Dubai – T:118.75; G:118.35; A:124.9, 127.9; AT:115.7. Fujirah – T:124.6; G:119.45; A:124.6; AT:114.7. Ras Al Khaimah – T:118.25; G:121.6; A:124.0. Sharjah – T:118.6; AT:112.3.

The UAE lies within the Emirates FIR and a new ACC has just become operational at Abu Dhabi.

Yemen
Aden – T:118.7; G:121.9; A:119.7. Sana'a – T:118.9; G:121.6; A:125.3.

The newly-opened Al Ain Airport in the United Arab Emirates. (Abu Dhabi DCA)

The north-west portion of the country, until 1990 the Yemen Arab Republic, is within the Jeddah FIR and most of its airways control is the responsibility of Sana'a Airport's approach unit. The former South Yemen is located in the Aden FIR. Above FL 300 air traffic services are provided by Jeddah ACC/FIC.

Africa and Indian Ocean

It is fortunate for Africa that low levels of traffic and generally good weather partially compensate for the shortcomings of its ATC systems and navigational aids. Many African states have no money to spare for improving the situation and, for want of technical expertise, navaids are frequently out of service for long periods. The equipment is often old or even obsolete and spares may be difficult to obtain. HF radio is the only way to maintain communications over huge wilderness areas and a limited number of crowded frequencies are shared with ground stations as far away as India. In some parts of the continent, for all practical purposes, the airspace might as well be oceanic. Often unable to contact any Area Control or Flight Information Centre, aircrew maintain the planned flight level and trust to low traffic density and good lookout for collision avoidance, using TIBA as detailed below.

Few international airports are equipped with anything more than Category 1 ILS and at many, aids consist of an NDB and a windsock. Often, the destination only expects a flight because it is on a published schedule. The Flight Plan sent via the land-based teletype AFTN may well arrive some time after the flight itself. In this environment satellite navigation and communications will one day transform the system. ICAO's AFI Planning and Implementation Regional Group has a long-term vision that much of Africa will go from procedural control based on HF radio to SatCom and VHF datalink-aided Automatic Dependent Surveillance (ADS). The AFTN will be upgraded with the backing of fixed SatComs which will permit seamless handovers from one ACC to the next.

A basis for this grand plan is already in existence: the organization known as ASECNA. The word is an acronym for the French title which, in translation, means 'Agency for the Security of Aerial Navigation in Africa'. The African equivalent of Eurocontrol, it manages five FIRs in an integrated airspace which covers one and a half times the surface area of Europe. It is composed of 14 West African states, plus the island of Madagascar, which were all French colonies or protectorates prior to independence. France herself is also a member. A policy of co-operation with adjacent non-member states has resulted in a satellite communications network being set up with Nigeria and Ghana. ASECNA calibrates navaids on behalf of non-member states as far afield as the Indian Ocean and the Caribbean. It also runs an ATC school which offers instruction in English, as well as French, to cater for nationals from former British colonies.

Traffic Information Broadcasts by Aircraft (TIBA)

These are intended to permit position reports and relevant information to be transmitted by pilots on VHF frequencies to alert other aircraft in the vicinity to their presence and intentions. Sanctioned by ICAO only as a temporary measure where there is a disruption of normal air traffic services, or outside controlled airspace, TIBA is, however, in constant use over much of Africa because of the often inadequate or non-existent area control systems. Indeed, it is regularized with the title IATA In-Flight Broadcast Procedure, IATA being the International Air Transport Association. Apart from Africa, the procedure is used over much of Brazil, the airspace to the west of the Central and South American coasts, and within the Kunming FIR in western China.

All pilots should maintain a listening watch on the designated frequency (normally 126.9) and broadcast such information as estimated time at a reporting point, intended change of level, etc. A typical example is: *All stations. Windair 671 Flight Level 350 north-west bound direct from Punta Saga to Pampa. Position 5040 South 2010 East at 2358 estimating crossing Route Lima 31 at 4930 South 1920 East at 0012. Windair 671 Flight Level 350 north-west bound. Out.*

Cruising level changes should not be made unless considered necessary to avoid traffic conflictions, for weather avoidance, and other relevant operational reasons. All available aircraft lighting should be used to improve visual sighting by other traffic when changing level or to resolve other conflictions. Pilots can communicate with each other on the TIBA frequency and agree a course of action.

Algeria
Algiers – T:118.7; G:121.8; A:121.4, 119.7. Annaba – T:118.7; A:119.0. Constantine – T:118.3; A:120.1, 119.7. Oran – T:118.1; A:128.2, 121.1.

Several important north-south air routes cross Algeria into the interior of Africa. An extensive TCA protects the airspace around the airports of the coastal cities.

Angola
Luanda – T:118.1; A:119.1.

All air routes within the country are currently advisory or flight information only. A minor part of south-western Zaire lies within and is serviced by Luanda FIC.

ASECNA States
Benin
Cotonou – T/A:125.9.

Benin's airspace lies within the Accra and Niamey FIRs.

Burkina-Faso
Ouagadougou – T:120.3.

The airspace of Burkina is divided between Dakar and Niamey FIRs.

Central African Republic
Bangui – T:119.7.

Airspace is divided between the Brazzaville and Ndjamena FIRs.

Chad
Ndjamena – T:118.1; A:119.7.

Much of the country is desert and HF frequencies in the AFI3/4 net have to be used over the great distances involved.

Congo
Brazzaville – T:118.7. Point Noire – T:124.3.

The Brazzaville FIR also covers a number of neighbouring states as a result of ASECNA agreements.

Gabon
Franceville (Mvengue) – T/A:118.2. Libreville – T:118.7; AT:112.1. Port Gentil – T:118.3.

Another state whose airspace falls within the Brazzaville FIR.

Ivory Coast
Abidjan – T:118.1, 121.1.

Lies within the Dakar and Roberts FIRs.

Madagascar
Antananarivo (Ivato) – T:118.1.

Unique to Madagascar is the use of smoke signals on airfields without VHF radio equipment. They indicate that a regular commercial flight is in the vicinity and has priority. Pilots must then conform to the radio procedures for unattended aerodromes, using 118.1 to broadcast intentions.

Mali
Bamako (Senou) – T:118.3; A:119.1.

Lies within the Dakar and Niamey FIRs.

Mauritania
Nouadhibou – T:120.8. Nouakchott – T:118.5.

Administered by the Dakar FIR.

Niger
Agades – T:118.1. Niamey – T:119.7. Zinder – T:118.3.

As well as Niger, Niamey FIR covers the north-eastern part of Mali, the eastern and northern parts of Burkina Faso, and the north of Benin, all delegated by ASECNA. Niger airspace has two TCAs and 23 international airways. Common FIR boundaries are shared with Algeria and Libya to the north, Senegal to the west, Ghana and Nigeria to the south, and Chad to the east. All except Libya and Nigeria are connected by satellite telephone.

Senegal
Dakar – T:118.1; ACC:120.5.

Its geographical position makes Senegal a cross-roads of international air routes and a terminus for internal African flights. The headquarters of ASECNA, as well as the regional offices of ICAO and IATA, are situated in the capital, Dakar. Airspace is made up of the Dakar FIR with its sub-FIR, Abidjan, and the Dakar Oceanic Control Area.

Togo
Lome – T:120.7.

As in some other parts of Africa, advisory routes over Togo are normally 50 nm wide.

Botswana
Francistown – T:118.1. Gaborone – T:118.3; G:121.9; A:128.2, 119.2; ACC:126.1 (East), 127.1 (West).

Until 1991 Botswana's airspace was administered from Johannesburg in South Africa, with just a small northern sector controlled from Windhoek in neighbouring Namibia. With an improving economy the country was able to set up its own ATC system. Surrounded by five states and under the direct line of flight between Europe and South Africa, Botswana experiences traffic surges at peak periods which are handled by the modern ACC at Gaborone. A new FIR was created along with new air routes and modern navigation aids. There are many uncontrolled airstrips and pilots flying within 20 miles of them are expected to make position reports and broadcast intentions on 125.5, as well as maintaining a listening watch.

Burundi
Bujumbura – T:118.1; G:121.9; A:119.7.

Between 0400 and 1600 UTC daily Bujumbura Tower has total responsibility for FIS in the Bujumbura Sub-FIR up to FL 245. Outside these limits the whole area reverts to the Dar Es Salaam FIR.

Cameroon
Douala – T:119.7; ACC:129.5, 125.1. Garoua – T:118.3, 120.0.

The country's airspace is divided between the Brazzaville and Ndjamena FIRs in neighbouring Congo and Chad respectively, an indication of the high degree of co-operation between the ASECNA states.

Canary Islands
Gran Canaria (Las Palmas) – T:118.3, 131.3; G:121.7; A:124.3, 120.9, 121.3; AT:118.6.

New tower at Gaborone, Botswana.
(Siemens)

Fuerteventura – T:118.5; G:121.7. Lanzarote – T:120.7; G:121.8; A:129.1. Tenerife (Norte) – T:118.7; G:121.7; A:119.7. Tenerife Sur – T:120.3, 119.0; G:121.9; A:120.3.

The islands are surrounded by a very large TCA within the Canarias FIR. Some years ago, when Spanish airspace was becoming very congested, aircraft flying to the Canaries from Northern Europe avoided it by flying west over the Atlantic within the Shanwick OCA. These unofficial detours were recognized and designated as UT8, UT9, and T9, and all user aircraft were expected to be equipped to MNPS. (See page 80).

Cape Verde
Sal (Amilcar Cabral) – T/A:119.7.

This island group off West Africa lies within the Sal Oceanic FIR/UIR beneath several major routes from Europe to South America.

Comores
Moroni (Hahaia) – A:119.7. Moroni (Iconi) – T:119.7.

These islands in the Indian Ocean lie within the Antananarivo FIR but have their own airspace, designated the Comores Flight Information Sector.

Djibouti
Djibouti – T:122.1; A:121.1.

The country lies within the Addis Ababa FIR. There is no en route control; a listening watch only is provided for such traffic.

Egypt
Cairo – T:118.1; G:121.9, 120.1; A:119.05, 119.55, 120.7. Luxor – T:119.9; G:121.9; A:124.3.

Egypt will soon possess the most advanced ATC system in North Africa. Complete radar coverage of the Cairo FIR has now been achieved, and satellite systems are being installed to consolidate communications and convey radar data.

Equatorial Guinea
Bata – T:118.3. Malabo – T:128.3.

This relatively small country lies within the Libreville Sub-FIR.

Ethiopia
Addis Ababa (Bole Intl) – T:118.1; G:121.9; A:119.7. Addis Ababa (Liddetta) – T:119.1.

Addis Ababa ACC is a main communications centre on the AFI3 HF network. Its associated FIR also covers Djibouti and part of Sudan. There is no en route control but all IFR flights must maintain a listening watch on the appropriate frequency.

Gambia
Banjul – T:118.3; A:121.3.

Gambia is one of several West African states located within the Dakar FIR/UIR. An ACC at Banjul operates an entirely HF service on the AF1 network.

Ghana
Accra – T:118.6; A:118.6, 119.5. Takoradi – T:122.8. Tamale – T:118.1; A:119.1.

Ghana is currently engaged on a long term plan to create a comprehensive procedural control system supported by a reliable VHF/HF communications system. At present the routes over much of the country are advisory only. It is hoped that access to SatCom will eventually reduce the use of unreliable HF communications.

Guinea Bissau
Bissau – T:124.3; A:123.9.

The country lies within the Dakar FIR/UIR. Bissau ACC uses HF frequencies in the AFI1 net to communicate with aircraft on several long distance trunk routes across its airspace.

Guinea
Conakry – T:118.7; A:119.7.

Guinea's airspace lies within the Dakar and Roberts FIRs. A special warning on the charts reads: 'Aircraft operating within Guinea territory

Control Tower at Kotoka International, Accra, Ghana. (Siemens)

must contact Conakry APP 119.7 when within TMA and contact Conakry Tower on 5680 Khz when outside TMA. Aircraft failing to make contact are liable to be fired upon.'

Kenya
Nairobi – T:118.7; G:121.6; A:119.7, 121.3, 124.7. Mombasa – T:118.6; G:121.6; A:120.3, 122.7, 121.7. Nairobi (Eastleigh) – T:124.3; A:124.8. Nairobi (Wilson) – T:118.1.

The Nairobi FIR includes the territory of Kenya and parts of the Indian Ocean out towards the Seychelles. The main airport is Jomo Kenyatta International which is very well equipped with modern navigational aids, in contrast to the airstrips which serve game parks, farms, and settlements all over the country. There are well over 100 of them, mostly uncontrolled and relying on good airmanship and standard procedures for safe operation. Pilots must broadcast their intentions when approaching, leaving, or moving on the ground on a common frequency of 118.2. At peak tourist times strips like Keekorok in the Mara Game Reserve can have three or four aircraft in the vicinity, very possibly landing and taking off in opposite directions because of the ground slope.

Lesotho
Maseru – T:118.5; G:121.7; A:120.7.

Lesotho lies within South Africa's Bloemfontein FIR and, like most African states, has a large number of unpaved airstrips.

Liberia
Monrovia (Roberts) – T:118.3; G:121.9; A:124.5. Monrovia (Spriggs Payne) – T:118.7.

At the time of writing the country was still suffering from its recent civil war. Roberts International Airport and its associated facilities were completely destroyed and Roberts FIC had to be relocated temporarily to Freetown, Sierra Leone. Great efforts are being made to rebuild and a new communications centre has just been opened. In due course it will be self-financed from fees paid by airlines operating in this heavily-travelled region.

Libya
Benghazi (Benina) – T/A:121.3, 118.1; G:121.9. Tripoli – T:118.1; G:120.1; A:124.0.
Libya is currently denied international air transport. The Tripoli FIR also takes in parts of Chad and Niger.

Malawi
Blantyre (Chileka) – T:118.1; A:124.9. Lilongwe – T:118.7; G:121.9; A:128.0, 124.7.

Malawi services and constitutes the major part of the Lilongwe FIR. Zambia is responsible for the portion of Malawi above FL 145 contained in the Lusaka FIR. At unmanned airfields, 118.1 is used as a Unicom frequency.

Mauritius and Réunion
Mauritius – T:118.1; A:119.1. St Denis (Gilot) – T:118.4; G:121.9; A:119.4, 123.1; AT:126.8.

The islands are an aerial crossroads of the Indian Ocean as well as tourist destinations in their own right. Mauritius FIC administers a number of flight information routes using HF frequencies in the INO1 net.

Morocco
Agadir – T:119.5; A:120.9. Casablanca (Mohamed V) – T:118.5, 119.9; A:121.3. Marrakech – T:118.7; A:119.7. Rabat (Sale) – T:118.3, 119.7; A:118.9. Tangier – T:119.5; A:121.2.

Although an area radar system is being installed as a long term project, ATC is still done procedurally in Morocco. A further responsibility is the oceanic airspace between Spain and the Canary Islands. The airways system is aligned north-east/south-west, connecting Europe with West Africa, and there is a TCA around Casablanca.

Mozambique
Beira – T:118.1; G:121.7, 121.9; A:130.9; ACC:118.5. Maputo – T:118.1; A:121.3; FIS:127.3.

Most of the country lies within the Beira FIR. A network of advisory routes connects the TMAs around the main airports.

Namibia
Windhoek – T:118.1; G:121.9; A:124.7. Windhoek (Eros) – T:118.7.

The Namibia FIR is serviced by the Republic of South Africa.

Nigeria
Kano – T:118.1; A:124.9. Lagos – T:118.1; G:120.9, 121.7; A:124.3; AT:123.8.

Airspace is divided into Kano FIR and the Lagos Sub-FIR, with 13 TMAs surrounding the most important international and domestic airports. Outside the TMAs all ATS routes are advisory only.

Rwanda
Kigali – T:118.3; G:121.7; A:124.3.

This state has some unusual rules in that flight below FL 170 must be in accordance with VFR and flight at night is not permitted, apart from scheduled international services to and from Kigali.

São Tomé and Principe
São Tomé – T:118.9.

These islands off the coast of Gabon come partly within the Libreville Sub-FIR and the Accra FIR and are connected to the mainland by several advisory routes across the Gulf of Guinea. São Tomé is one of the stations in the AFI4 HF net.

Seychelles
Seychelles Intl – T:118.3; G:121.9; A:119.7.

In response to the islands' increasing popularity as a holiday destination, an ongoing programme of improvements is under way. Until very recently the air routes within the Seychelles FIR (excluding the TMA and CTZ) were subject to advisory service only but a full ATC service has now been introduced. Apart from Mahé, Praslin is the only other island with a controlled aerodrome. Neighbouring FIRs are Kenya, Tanzania, Madagascar, India, Somalia, and Mauritius, and direct controller to controller satellite telephone links exist with most of them.

Sierra Leone
Freetown – T:118.1; G:121.9; A:119.1.

The entire country lies within the Roberts FIR, which is administered by an FIC at Roberts Field in neighbouring Liberia. Magnificent coastal scenery and other attractions have great tourist potential and the single international airport is being improved accordingly.

Somalia
Mogadishu – T:118.1; G:120.9; A:122.5.

At the time of writing there was no government in Somalia and the UN has had to perform its functions. ATC services are provided, using basic equipment brought in to replace that destroyed in the civil war.

South Africa
Cape Town (D.F. Malan) – T:118.1; G:121.9, 122.65; A:119.7; AT:115.7. Durban (Louis Botha) – T:118.7; G:122.65, 133.45; A:119.1; AT:112.0, 112.5.
Durban (Virginia) – T:120.6. Johannesburg (Jan Smuts) – T:118.1; G:121.9, 122.65; D:121.7; A:134.4, 124.5, 123.7; AT:115.2. Johannesburg (Rand) – T:118.7. Lanseria – T:124.0; G:121.65.

South Africa is well advanced with a long-term plan aimed at updating all ACCs, providing VOR/DME coverage along all airways and extending VHF coverage to replace the HF communications which are often necessary. The country is divided into six FIRs: Bloemfontein, Cape Town, Durban, Johannesburg, Port Elizabeth, and Windhoek. South Africa also provides ATC services for neighbouring states, including Lesotho and Swaziland. The use of TIBA procedures (see pages 127-128) is mandatory for all aircraft operating at or below 1,500 ft outside controlled airspace. The frequency is 124.8, and 130.35 is also available as a common frequency for general communications other than essential traffic information broadcasts. Peculiar to South Africa are published General Flying Areas using 124.4 as a common frequency. Pilot Activated Lighting (PAL) is used at some airfields, Johannesburg (Rand) and Lanseria, for example. The pilot keys his microphone several times on a specific frequency (118.9 at Rand) and the carrier wave switches on the runway lights automatically. PAL is common in the USA, Australia, and some other parts of the world, such as Nadzab in Papua New Guinea.

Sudan
Khartoum – T/A:120.3, 120.9.

Most of Sudan is within the Khartoum FIR but its eastern portion is serviced by Addis Ababa FIR. En route services are provided by Khartoum ACC/FIC to aircraft on the trunk routes over Sudan. However, because of poor HF communications, all aircraft are advised to listen out and transmit blind position reports and intentions on 126.9 for possible relay to Khartoum ACC. Standard R/T procedure at unmanned aerodromes is to transmit position and intentions on 124.1.

Swaziland
Matsapha (Manzini) – T:118.3; G:121.9; A:124.9.

Air traffic services are provided by South Africa, except for departing/arriving traffic at Matsapha. Aircraft entering Swaziland, including landing at unattended strips, must contact Matsapha Tower before landing.

Tanzania
Dar Es Salaam – T:118.3, 121.8; A:119.6, 120.0. Kilimanjaro – T:119.9; A:120.1, 120.5.

The Dar Es Salaam FIR covers the whole territory, as well as neighbouring Burundi and Rwanda. There are many uncontrolled airfields and a common frequency of 118.2 is used by aircraft approaching, leaving, or taxying.

Tunisia
Carthage – T:118.1; G:121.9; A:121.2. Monastir – T:118.3; A:119.3. Tunis – ACC:132.55, 129.3.

Most traffic is concentrated in the northern sector of the Tunis FIR serving the popular holiday destinations. Full VHF coverage is provided but the AFI2 HF network is available if necessary.

Uganda
Entebbe – T:118.1; A:119.1; ACC:128.5.

ATC service in the Entebbe FIR is advisory only, apart from the Entebbe TMA.

Zaire
Kinshasa – T:118.1; G:121.9; A:119.7.

Kinshasa is the centre of a web of advisory and flight information routes. There are 220 airfields and airstrips in Zaire, most of them uncontrolled.

Zambia
Lusaka City – T:118.3. Lusaka Intl – T:118.1; A:121.3, 120.1; AT:113.5.

The Lusaka FIR services the FIR of the same name as well as part of neighbouring Malawi.

Zimbabwe
Bulawayo – T:118.3. Harare – T:118.1; A:119.1; AT:113.1. Harare (Charles Prince) – T:118.7, 118.9. Victoria Falls – T/A:121.1.

The country has three international and five national airports (most of the latter are very small) and in 1992 handled an average of 650 overflights a week in both upper and lower airspace. In addition, there are over 170 airstrips, mostly uncontrolled, although many have paved runways.

Far East
A main feature of the booming economies in this part of the world is the number of new airports under construction. In China and the Russian Far East (see Europe/CIS section) the very basic ATC systems are being modernized to handle the expected upsurge in traffic. Western radar and ATM suppliers are competing strongly for shares of an enormous market. However, officials warn of the lack of a regional plan, which is likely to produce the very problems which Europe's Eurocontrol was set up to solve. There is no overall flow management unit and no prospect of one in the short term. Severe delays will be the inevitable result of a non-integrated ATC system. Japan has an ambitious plan to establish a satellite system for navigation and communications in the Asia/Pacific region which will cover all oceanic and remote land areas.

Bangladesh
Chittagong – T:126.5; G:121.8. Dhaka – T:118.3; G:121.8; A:121.3, 126.7.

The country has one FIR, Dhaka, but Calcutta ACC in India is responsible for its southern portion. On ATS routes below FL 150 only FIS is provided. At and above FL 150 an advisory service only is provided.

Bhutan
Paro – T:122.7.

Totally land-locked and mountainous, Bhutan is bordered by China and NE India. The national airline, Druk Air, connects the capital with Bangkok, Kathmandu, and several Indian cities.

Brunei
Brunei – T:118.7; G:121.9; A:121.3, 119.2, 127.7.

Entirely within the Kota Kinabalu FIR, Brunei lies at the junction of several air routes crossing the South China Sea.

China
Beijing – T:118.1; A:129.0; AT:127.6; ACC:125.9, 128.3. Guangzhou (Canton) – T:118.1; G:121.8; ACC:132.4, 123.9. Shanghai – T:118.1; A:119.7; ACC:133.25, 125.95, 134.3.

Prior to 1990, ATC in China was provided by the military, emphasis being on the protection of national security rather than on accommodating civil aviation requirements. The country's economic growth has revealed the shortcomings of this policy and great efforts are being made to improve the situation. Much of China's ATC is still procedural, with up to 15 minutes between aircraft on the same route at the same level, but radar control has been introduced between Beijing, Guangzhou, and Shanghai, as well as in most of the upper airspace in the south-east of the country. A major incompatibility with the ATC infrastructure of its neighbours has always been the use of the metric system for aircraft levels. As a compromise, China has now adopted the ICAO-style flight level system but retains metric height measurements. Of China's 120 airports, 60 have been selected for development. There are also plans to build a large ACC in Sanya to serve flights over the South China Sea.

Hong Kong and Macao
Hong Kong – T:118.7; G:121.6; D:124.65; A:119.1, 126.3, 119.5; AT:128.2.

As is well known, Hong Kong's airport is close to the city and surrounded by high ground and man-made obstructions. Air navigation charts include various warnings such as: 'Runway 31 Instrument Departure: the take-off path is located in a densely built-up area. Numerous obstructions exist either side of the take-off path and this should be taken into consideration whenever aircraft are unable to achieve the radius of turn required to adhere to the nominal track. There is also rapidly rising ground to the north of this area.' Since Hong Kong operates a non-ICAO separation procedure, another note reads: 'Aircraft separation is based on the accurate flying of a VOR radial and any deviation from the cleared radial involves loss of separation. Hence ATC must be informed immediately, so that different separation standards can be applied.' Hong Kong is beneath the busy main north-south routes across the South China Sea, between Bangkok, Taipei, and Tokyo, and China's routes to South Asia. When the new airport at Chek Lap Kok is opened in 1997 it will have a new ACC. In the meantime, radar and flight data processing at Hong Kong is being upgraded to handle forecast traffic demands. In neighbouring Macao another entirely new airport is being built on reclaimed land.

India
Bombay – T:118.1; G:121.9; A:127.9, 119.3, 119.5; AT:126.4. Calcutta – T:118.1; G:121.9; A:127.9, 119.3; AT:126.4. Delhi – T:118.1; G:121.9; A:127.9, 125.3, 119.5.

The sub-continent, which handles more than 700 overflights a day, is well advanced with a programme of ATC improvement. Many important air routes are now better defined by new VOR/DME equipment. An unusual feature of Indian airspace is that airways prefixed 'Whiskey' are reserved exclusively for domestic operators. The country is divided into three FIRs – Bombay, Madras, and Calcutta – each with its own Flight Information Centre. India is the first country, other than the USA, to adopt the FAA's

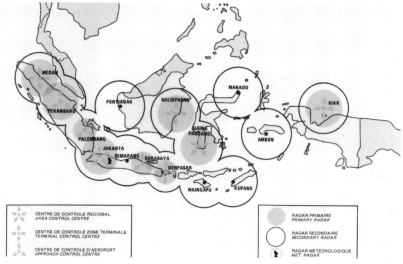

Indonesian ATC network, showing radar coverage. (Via Leo Marriott)

SSR Mode-S system and there will soon be complete radar coverage over the northern part of the country.

Indonesia
Bali – T:118.1; A:119.7; AT:126.2. Jakarta (Halim) – T:118.3; A:120.0, 119.7; AT:128.8. Jakarta (Soekarno-Hatta) – T:118.2, 118.75; G:121.75; D:121.95; A:135.9, 125.45, 119.75, 127.95; AT:126.85. Medan (Polonia) – T:118.1; A:119.7; AT:120.6.

Under an Air Navigation Plan instituted in 1983, Indonesia is upgrading its area radar system and navigational facilities at all main airports. The long-term goal is to develop integrated radar coverage for the whole country, as well as a satellite communication system. A major air route, A576 between Singapore and Australia, passes overhead Bali.

Japan
Fukuoka – T:118.4, 126.2; G:121.7; D:119.7; A:119.1, 127.9, 120.7; AT:127.2. Kansai – T:118.2; G:121.6; D:121.9. Nagoya – T:118.7, 126.2, 122.7; G:121.7; A:120.3, 120.7, 134.1, 119.9; AT:126.4. Osaka – T:118.1, 126.2, 127.5, G:121.7; D:118.8; A:124.7, 126.2, 119.5, 125.3; AT:128.6. Tokyo (Narita) – T:118.2; G:121.8, 121.6; D:121.9; A:125.8, 124.4, 127.7. Tokyo (Haneda) – T:118.1, 118.8; G:121.7; D:121.8; A:119.1, 126.0, 119.5, 125.3, 119.7.

The entire country is contained within the Tokyo FIR. To the east and south is the Tokyo OCA, which is controlled via HF frequencies in the NP3 and CWP1 networks. There are four ACCs – Fukuoka in the west, Tokyo in the east, Sapporo for the northern part of the islands, and Naha for the airspace to the south-west, including Okinawa. Domestic air routes are designated, American-style, as Victor Airways, while international ones follow normal practice. (A1, which begins in Scotland, ends in the Tokyo CTA!) To the north-east are Oceanic Transition Routes which lead into the North Pacific Composite Route System (see page 147). Japan's chronic problem is, of course, lack of spare land, and constraints on major airports already at

Kansai, built on an artificial island in Osaka Bay, is designed to handle up to 31 million passengers and 160,000 aircraft movements a year. (Kansai Airport)

capacity make expansion impossible. In an effort to solve the problem, Kansai Airport opened in 1994 on an artificial island offshore from Osaka, the first of several similar projects. Its controllers handle terminal area control for Kansai, as well as approach control for nearby Osaka and Yao. Throughout Japan a radar advisory service operates primarily for air defence purposes, using the collective callsign *Star Gazer*. Frequencies are 121.5 or 243.0 UHF. The recent opening of Asia's first Flow Management Unit at Fukuoka ACC is a significant step as traffic in Japan is expected to double over the next 10 years.

Kampuchea
Phnom-Penh – T:118.1; ACC:123.8, 127.9, 132.4.

At FL 195 and above airways control is delegated to Bangkok ACC by regional agreement.

Korea, North
Pyongyang – T:133.0; G:121.8; A:130.0; ACC:120.9.

The country has only two air routes, one into Russia's Vladivostok FIR, the other into China. Pyongyang Control has a single VHF frequency but also makes use of several HF channels.

Korea, Republic of
Cheju – T:118.1, 126.2; G:121.65; A:119.0, 121.2, 124.05; AT:126.8. Pusan (Kimhae) – T:118.1, 126.2; G:121.9; A:119.22, 135.7, 134.4; AT:126.6. Seoul (Kimpo) – T:118.1; G:121.9; A:119.1, 123.8, 125.5, 119.9, 124.8; D:122.6; AT:126.4.

As well as the three major international airports, Korea has 62 other civil airports. An ongoing project is a mammoth new airport 52 km from Seoul to handle more than 40 million passengers per year. It is designed as a major air transport hub for Asia and the first phase is due for completion in 1997.

Lao People's Democratic Republic
Vientiane – T:118.1; A:119.7.

A land-locked mountainous country, it relies primarily on civil aviation as road and river routes are not passable at all times of the year. The Vientiane FIR is administered from an FIC via a single VHF frequency and two HF channels in the SEA3 network. Much of the navigation and communications equipment is obsolete and a programme is under way to replace it, despite limited resources.

Malaysia
Kota Kinabalu – T/A:129.1; G:118.3; AT:127.4. Kuala Lumpur – T:118.2, 124.2; G:121.9; A:125.1; AT:127.6. Kuala Lumpur (Simpang) – T:126.5. Kuching – T/A:118.1. Penang – T:121.1; G:121.6; AT:126.4.

Malaysia has embarked on a programme to upgrade its ATC system in line with that of neighbouring Singapore. An entirely new airport, Sepang International, is due to open in 1997 in anticipation of a huge growth in Asia/Pacific air traffic.

Maldives
Gan – T:119.1. Male – T:118.1; A:119.7.

These islands in the Indian Ocean have long been a useful refuelling stop and site for en route navigational aids but they are now being developed for tourism. The Male FIR borders on Bombay to the west and north and the Perth FIR to the south east.

Myanmar
Yangon (Mingaladon) – T:118.1; G:121.9; A:119.7; AT:128.4.

Formerly known as Burma, Myanmar lies between India and Thailand under a series of connecting air routes. An ADIZ surrounds its borders and territorial waters.

Nepal
Kathmundu – T:118.1; G:121.9; AT:121.3; ACC:126.5, 124.7.

Two-thirds of Nepal's territory is mountainous and includes Everest. There are 43 airports, ranging from an altitude of 230 feet up to 12,297 feet. The Kathmundu FIR has eight control zones, one TCA, and four international airways. Kathmundu's single runway is surrounded by high ground and classified C (special procedures) by most airlines. It has no ILS or radar and VOR/DME approach procedures are used.

Pakistan
Islamabad – T:123.7, 119.7; A:125.5; AT:129.6. Karachi – T;118.3, 121.8; A:121.3, 118.4, 123.7; AT:126.7. Lahore – T:118.1; A:121.3; AT:126.3. Peshawar – T:122.5; A:122.9.

Control is restricted mainly to terminal areas. Advisory service is provided on all ATS routes above FL 150 but below FL 150 only flight information is available. American-style Jet Route designators are used with F or D suffixes indicating FIS or advisory service respectively. Conventional designators are also in use for international routes crossing the country, sometimes resulting in very confusing dual and sometimes triple designators for the same airway!

Philippines
Manila – T:118.1; G:121.9, 121.7; D:125.1; A:121.1, 119.7; AT:126.4.

A complex airways system includes major routes linking mainland Asia with Australia. An ADIZ surrounds the islands.

Singapore
Seletar – T:118.45, 130.2; G:121.6. Singapore (Changi) – T:118.6; G:124.3; D:121.65; A:119.3, 120.3, 124.6; AT:128.6. Singapore (Paya Lebar) – T:118.05; A:119.9, 127.7, 120.95. Tengah – T:122.0; A:123.0.

In 1991 the Singapore FIR handled 170,000 aircraft movements, an annual figure expected to double by the end of the decade. A new long-range radar system is capable of handling 400 aircraft simultaneously and will greatly reduce separation distances and allow the use of RNAV. It is expected that ADS for oceanic control will be operational within the next few years, using Singapore's own aeronautical satellite station.

Sri Lanka
Colombo Intl – T:118.7; A:119.1, 120.9, 132.4. Colombo (Ratmalana) – T:118.1. Trincomalee (China Bay) – T:118.1; A:126.18, 119.7.

This very large island is situated at the western extremity of the Colombo FIR and borders on the Madras FIR. The latter's south-east corner is the delegated responsibility of Colombo. A primary radar has been sited in the central hills in order to extend coverage out to the east where Indian Ocean ATS routes intersect. The FIR's eastern boundary is with the Jakarta FIR, about 800 miles to the east and HF is used for most of this oceanic airspace.

Surinam
Paramaribo (Pengel) – T:118.1; A:120.0; AG:123.9.

Surinam has three airways across its territory and a TCA around its major airport.

Taiwan
Kaohsiung – T:118.7; G:121.9; A:121.1, 124.7, 119.5; AT:127.8. Taipei (Chiang Kai Shek) – T:118.7; G:121.7; D:121.8; A:119.6, 119.7; AT:127.6. Taipei (Sungshan) – T:118.1; G:121.9; A:119.7; AT:127.4.

Taiwan's FIR boundary is also an ADIZ which abuts on the east with Japan's outer ADIZ and on the south with that of the Philippines. Major air routes between Hong Kong and Japan run NE/SW and there is only one airway connection (W6) with mainland China.

Thailand
Bangkok – T:118.1; G:121.9; D:121.8; A:119.1, 126.2, 125.5; AT:126.4. Chiang Mai – T:118.1; G:121.9; A:129.6; AT:127.2. Phuket – T:118.1; G:121.9; A:126.7; AT:116.9.

Bangkok is the focal point for a large number of airways and its FIR covers the entire country, as well as part of the South China Sea. Unique to Thailand, but similar to Purple Airways in the UK, are Pink Airways. They are special, temporary airways established for VIP flights within Bangkok FIR.

Vietnam
Hanoi (Noibai) – T:118.1; A:121.0; ACC:125.9. Ho Chi Minh (Ton Son Nhut) –
T:118.7, 130.0; A:125.5, 134.1.

Vietnam has upgraded its ATC system as the national economy has developed and tourism expanded. Primary radar and SSR have been installed to handle approach control at Ho Chi Minh, as well as en route control for parts of the Ho Chi Minh FIR, formerly the Saigon FIR. When the Saigon regime collapsed in 1975, ICAO delegated some parts of the Saigon FIR to Hong Kong, Singapore, and Thailand so that air traffic services could be maintained. Vietnam's ATC facilities are now more than adequate and it is currently regaining responsibility for its airspace.

Australasia

Australia
Adelaide – T:120.5; G:121.7; D:126.1; A:124.2, 118.2; AT:116.4, 134.5. Adelaide (Parafield) – T:118.7, 124.6; G:119.9; AT:120.9. Brisbane – T:120.5; G:121.7; D:118.6; A:124.7, 125.6; AT:113.2, 125.5. Brisbane (Archerfield) – T:118.1, 123.6; G:119.9. Cairns – T:124.9; G:121.7; A:118.4; AT:113.0, 131.1. Darwin – T:133.1; G:121.7; D:126.8; A:134.1, 126.2, 123.0; AT:112.4. Melbourne – T:120.5; G:121.7; D:127.2; A:124.7, 118.9, 129.4; AT:114.1, 132.7. Melbourne (Essendon) – T:125.1; G:121.9; A:124.7, 118.9; AT:119.8. Melbourne (Moorabbin) – T:118.1; G:119.9; AT:120.9. Perth – T:120.5; G:121.7; D:128.1, 133.0; A:118.7, 123.7; AT:113.7, 123.8. Perth (Jandakot) – T:118.1, 119.4; G:119.9; AT:120.9. Sydney Intl – T:120.5; G:121.7, 122.3; D:127.5; A:126.1, 124.4, 125.3, 123.0; AT:115.4, 127.6. Sydney (Bankstown) – T:118.1; G:121.9; AT:120.9.

Poor land communications mean a heavy reliance on air transport. The country's fleet of aircraft, particularly the lighter types, is disproportionately large and logs an extraordinary number of flights from remote, unattended landing strips. Australia is at present replacing its seven FIRs with one equivalent in size to Europe (which has more than 20). A very advanced ATC structure now provides radar coverage for 80 per cent of traffic, mainly on the eastern seaboard and around Perth in the south-west. It is unusual in combining oceanic and continental traffic management operations. Radar data, flight plans, or ADS all update the flight data processing and generate tracks on the controller's display. He can see immediately what the source is, and thereby determine the accuracy, by the shape of the aircraft position symbol. The Australian CAA was, in fact, instrumental in developing ADS for use in oceanic and other environments. More details can be found in the Pacific section. Satellite communications have extended VHF coverage nationwide and virtually eliminated the use of HF radio for aircraft flying above 19,000 ft. The existing HF network will, however, be retained for the foreseeable future, as GA aircraft flying at low altitudes will often be beyond line-of-sight contact with the ground-to-satellite sites, especially in the north and centre of the country.

Geographically isolated, Australia's ATC has tended to develop its own procedures, some of which are rather different from ICAO recommendations. For example, it is unique in declaring meteorological minima and ATC is authorized to prohibit an approach to land (except in an emergency) or a take-off when weather conditions are below minima. The R/T phraseology is: 'The aerodrome is closed to take-off [or landing]'. Australia provides full positive control to all aircraft in controlled airspace, whether they be IFR or VFR. GPS is approved as an en-route supplementary navaid, subject to a number of conditions, including the monitoring of the normal ground-based aids throughout the flight. The aim is to gain operational experience in using GPS. So far, Australia is the only country in the world with approved RNAV separation standards. Sydney's Kingsford Smith Airport has recently opened a third runway and parallel IFR approaches will become routine in the near future.

New Zealand
Ardmore – T:118.1; A:124.3, 120.5; AT:121.0. Auckland Intl – T:118.7; G:121.9; D:123.0; A:124.3, 129.6, 120.5; AT:127.8, 127.0. Christchurch – T:118.3; G:121.9; A:120.9, 125.0. Wellington – T:118.8, 120.0; G:121.9; A:122.3, 119.3, 126.5, 121.1; AT:126.9.

The New Zealand ATC system is one of the few in the world to be run commercially. Privatization took place in 1986 and the original four ACCs were reduced to three – Auckland, Ohakea, and Christchurch. The New Zealand FIR covers the whole area and is surrounded by the Auckland Oceanic FIR. Auckland VOR is the hub of 15 international airways. Unusually, domestic airways have no designators and are mainly direct tracks using published VOR radials. SSR cover is provided, although there are some gaps in the lower levels caused by mountainous terrain.

Milford Sound on the South Island is claimed to be the world's busiest short airstrip, with as many as 70 sight-seeing aircraft movements an hour on sunny days. Christchurch is the gateway for flights servicing the US Antarctic Programme at McMurdo.

Papua New Guinea
Port Moresby (Jacksons) – T:118.1; G:121.7; A:125.8; AT:117.0, 128.0.

Its mountainous terrain and island-archipelago geography make Papua New Guinea heavily dependent on aviation. There are no roads between the capital, Port Moresby, and the main provincial towns, and even agricultural produce has to be flown from remote mountain villages to regional centres. A long-term upgrade of ATC facilities was under way to provide either ground-based or satellite linked VHF coverage throughout the Port Moresby FIR. An FIS via HF or VHF will be available in uncontrolled air-

Jacksons Airport, Port Moresby, Papua New Guinea, with its parallel runways. (Paul Howard)

space and a traffic advisory service will be provided when radar has been installed. However, at the time of writing lack of finance was causing some ATC services to be withdrawn. A TMA surrounds the capital's Jacksons International Airport. Before independence in 1975, the country was an Australian-controlled territory and, although all ATC duties are now carried out by Papua New Guinea nationals, ATC procedures are still modelled on those of Australia.

Pacific Islands

Traffic between the US mainland and Hawaii is controlled by OACCs at Oakland, California, and Honolulu, using a Composite Route System. There are six parallel Romeo-prefixed airways, three for westbound traffic and three for eastbound. Separation is applied at and above FL 290 and is achieved by management of route and altitude assignments so that there is at least 50 nm lateral spacing and 1,000 ft vertical separation for traffic flying in the same or opposite directions. Position reports are made every 5° of longitude (10° if the time taken is 1 hr 20 min or less). Aircraft with slow ground speeds may be required to report every 2.5°). Reduced separation is used in the vicinity of Hawaii and other islands, depending upon the range of radar and land-based navaids. A similar

Composite Route System in the North Pacific (NoPac) between Anchorage, Alaska, and Tokyo uses five one-way routes – two westbound and three eastbound. Nine ATS routes feed traffic into the NoPac system from the US/Canadian mainland, three being selected each day and published by NOTAM.

In August 1990, four international routes were established between Nome, Alaska, and the Russian Far East, connecting the national airspace systems of the USA and what was then the USSR. They are designated Kamchatka 1, 2, 3 and 4.

Aircraft operating on routes within the Oakland FIR between the US West Coast and Hawaii, and southern routes towards Tahiti, will be under the radio guard of the ARINC Honolulu or San Francisco communications centres, using the Central East Pacific (CEP) family of HF frequencies. Honolulu is responsible also for aircraft within the Oakland FIR in the South Pacific (SP), Central West Pacific (CWP), and North Pacific (NP) regions, as well as on routes between Anchorage and Tokyo, using the associated HF nets. ARINC, by the way, dates back to 1929 and the scheduled airlines of the USA are the principal customers and stockholders. Its non-profit making services, however, extend to all aircraft, US or foreign, with charges based on 'cost in proportion to use'. ARINC also operates a domestic air/ground service in the USA through which aircraft communicate with their operations offices.

The sheer vastness of the Pacific Ocean is difficult to imagine. From Auckland, New Zealand, to Singapore (considered a near neighbour!) is 5,231 miles. Auckland to Los Angeles is about 13 hours' flying, a similar time to that from London to Bangkok. The huge gaps in radar coverage will soon be eliminated by the Automatic Dependent Surveillance System (ADS) promoted by the ICAO FANS Committee. Extensive trials are being held involving a number of Australian, Japanese, and American airlines and five Area Control Centres in the South Pacific. Aircraft have been equipped to send periodic ADS position reports over a satellite datalink. The reports are processed by ground computers and displayed as aircraft position symbols on a situation display which provides controllers with an easily interpreted traffic picture. The trials have been so successful that it is hoped by 1996 that the present procedural system control techniques will be replaced by this 'pseudo-radar environment'.

In a separate trial begun a few years ago, the US FAA agreed with the Fijian authorities to use their airspace as a test site to develop air traffic management techniques, using GPS as the sole navigational aid. Pilots and controllers devised a system of en-route navigation and descent until clear of cloud, using conventional navaids as a safety back-up.

The trials were so successful that in 1994 Fiji became the first country in the world to authorize GPS as the primary navaid in domestic airspace.

A so-called 'In Trail Climb Procedure' is now approved over US-controlled stretches of the Pacific. It solves the problem of an aircraft becoming 'trapped' behind traffic at a higher level and being unable to climb above it to a more fuel-efficient altitude. The aircraft ahead is identified on the TCAS equipment (see pages 38-39) by the simple expedient of asking the pilot to switch off his transponder. If the symbol on the TCAS display disappears, it must be there! Climb clearance is then requested and granted by the controller subject to certain conditions.

Cook Islands
Rarotonga – T/A:118.

Surrounded by a TMA within the Cook Sector of the Auckland Oceanic FIR.

Fiji
Nadi – T:119.1; G:121.9; AT:112.5. Nadi Centre – 126.7. Naurori (Suva) – T:119.7.

Fiji is literally a crossroads of the South Pacific over which many major air routes converge. The area for which its Nadi ACC is responsible is enormous and sectors of it are delegated to Port Vila in Vanuatu and Noumea in New Caledonia. The FIR above FL 95 is designated as an OCA and in the long term Fiji plans to use radar for all terminal and area control in its domestic airspace and automatic data processing for oceanic coverage.

French Oceania
Hao – T:118.3; A:119.1. Noumea (La Tontouta) – T:118.1; A:119.7. Tahiti (Faaa) – T:118.1; G:121.9; A:121.3.

A new ACC at Faaa is also the Rescue Co-Ordination Centre for the region.

Hawaii
Hickham AFB – T:133.6. Honolulu – T:118.1, 123.9; D:121.4; G:121.9, 121.8, 132.2; A:118.3; AT:127.9.

Surrounded by an octagonal ADIZ, Hawaii has an ATC system which conforms to US practice. As noted above, an organized route system is in operation between the islands and the US mainland.

Micronesia
Guam (Agana) – T:118.1; G:121.9; A:119.8. Guam (Anderson) – T:126.2; G:121.7; A:119.8. Koror (Airai) – A/G:123.6. Majuro – A/G:123.6. Saipan – A/G:123.6.

Agana Airport, Guam, Micronesia, with a B-52 on approach. (Paul Howard)

Nauru
Nauru – A/G:118.1.

A small island with its own Flight Information Centre covering a number of air routes which cross or terminate in its airspace.

Niue
Niue (Hanan) – A/G:118.1.

A New Zealand territory within the Nadi FIR.

Samoa (American)
Pago Pago – T:118.3; G:121.9; A:126.9.

Lies within the Pago Pago TMA which services a very busy air route intersection.

Samoa (Western)
Apia (Faleolo) – T:118.1; A:118.5.

Also within the Pago Pago TMA.

Solomon Islands
Honiara – T:118.1; A:119.1.

With Japanese assistance, Honiara's Henderson International Airport has been upgraded to Boeing 767 standard. At present, Honiara FIR provides only an FIS but it is hoped in the long-term to provide a full ATC service. The plan has begun with the establishment of aerodrome control at Honiara. Currently, FIS is provided during daylight hours only, and when communications units are closed responsibility for flight watch etc is delegated to Sydney ACC.

Tonga
Fua' Amotu – A/G:118.1, 118.5.

Tonga currently provides only FIS but hopes in future to be able to offer full ATC. The islands are located within the Nadi FIR.

Tuvalu
Funafuti – A/G:118.1.

An island group within the Nadi FIR.

Vanuatu
Port Vila – T/A:120.0. Santo – T:118.1; G:121.9.

Many of the 40 islands in the archipelago have grass airstrips. Considerable use is made of HF frequencies, particularly over the oceanic areas for which Vila is responsible.

North America
Alaska
Anchorage Intl – T:118.3; G:121.9; D:119.4, 128.65; A:118.6, 119.1, 123.8, 124.6, 126.4; AT:118.4. Elmendorf – T:127.2; G:121.8; A:118.6, 119.1; AT:124.3. Fairbanks – T:118.3; G:121.9; D:127.6; A:118.1, 126.6; AT:124.4

Alaska conforms to the ATC procedures of the rest of the USA, including a Victor Airways system. North Pacific procedures in the Anchorage Oceanic FIR are described on page 147. Anchorage International is a busy refuelling point for Polar flights between Europe and the Far East and has an unusual sectorized approach control system using five separate frequencies.

Canada
Calgary – T:118.4; G:121.9; D:121.3; A:128.7, 133.3, 125.9, 123.85; DEP:119.8; AT:114.8, 127.2. Edmonton – T:118.3; G:121.7; A:120.5; AT:128.0. Gander – T:118.1; G:121.9; A:128.5; AT:124.8. Goose – T:119.1; G:121.9; A:119.5; AT:128.1. Montreal (Dorval) – T:119.9; G:121.9; D:125.6; A:125.15, 125.4; DEP:124.65; AT:128.0, 127.5. Montreal (Mirabel) – T:119.1; G:121.8, 122.4; D:121.8; A:125.15; DEP:124.65; AT:125.7, 126.1. Ottawa – T:118.8; G:121.9, 121.6, 122.4; D:119.4; A:135.15; DEP:128.175; AT:121.15, 124.8. Quebec – T:120.3; G:121.9; A:127.85; AT:119.8, 128.3. Toronto – T:118.7, 118.35; G:121.9, 121.65; D:121.3; A:125.4, 124.475; DEP:128.8, 127.575; AT:114.8, 113.3, 120.825, 133.1. Vancouver – T:118.7, 124.0, 128.6; G:121.7; D:121.4; A:120.8; DEP:120.5; AT:124.6, 114.8. Winnipeg – T:118.3, 125.4; G:121.9; D:121.3; A:119.5; DEP:119.9; AT:114.8, 120.2.

Canada is currently implementing a massive airspace management plan, the core of which is the Canadian Automated Air Traffic System. The aim is to re-equip all seven ACCs with modern radar, data processing equipment and display systems, as well as upgrading major tower and terminal control units. The ACCs and associated FIRs are: Vancouver, Edmonton, Winnipeg, Toronto, Montreal, Moncton, and Gander. Montreal is probably the busiest ACC because it is responsible for much domestic traffic as well as funnelling the bulk of North Atlantic traffic in and out of the interior of North America. In accordance with the Canadian constitution it also offers a bilingual service in English or French. Montreal, along with Winnipeg and Edmonton ACCs uses the Northern Area Control System which is a precursor of global ADS (Automatic Dependent Surveillance System). It handles traffic far beyond the range of radar on the northern great circle routes between Europe and North America. Using aircraft-derived data via satellite, NACS displays the estimated position of each aircraft on a plan view of the vast northern airspace and is an invaluable aid to procedural controllers.

Canadian airspace is divided into Southern and Northern Domestic roughly along the 60°N meridian. The Southern Control Area, 18,000 ft and above, stretches to 60°N, the Northern CA, FL 230 and above, ends about 75°N, and beyond is the Arctic CA, FL 280 and above. A similar system of Victor, Jet, and High Level Routes to that of the USA is in use (See page 154). An oddity is the Company Route, which is defined as a route exclusive of an airway, approved by Transport Canada for the specific use of an operator or number of operators. Associated with it is the Company Instrument Approach Procedure, which again has to be approved.

North of the North American routes are two Track Systems: the Northern, which links with North Atlantic random route traffic operating between Europe and Western North American (Los Angeles, San Francisco, etc); and an Arctic Route System that interfaces with the Polar Track System between Europe and Alaska. More details can be found on pages 171-172. The tracks also interact with the Canadian domestic airways systems. The four Northern Tracks are designated Alpha to Delta, the five primary Arctic Tracks Oscar to Sierra.

The Canadian Arctic comprises the Yukon Territory to the west, bordering Alaska, and the immense North-West Territory. The area is rich in mineral resources and is almost completely dependent on aviation to supply its needs. There are few control tower facilities at its numerous airfields, airstrips, and seaplane bases. Most rely on an American-style Flight Service Station to handle radio communications on both VHF and HF. Others have a Unicom Aerodrome Traffic Frequency on which pilots broadcast their intentions. The proximity of the Magnetic Pole makes compasses unreliable so headings are always expressed in degrees true, using true as a suffix to the instruction. For the same reason runway headings are given in degrees true rather than the customary magnetic.

Canadian R/T phraseology and procedures are based on ICAO's, although some follow US practice. For example, QNH is referred to as 'the altimeter' and passed in inches, back-course ILSs are approved, and 'one thousand on top' clearances may be issued in certain airspace, i.e. 1,000 ft above a cloud layer. US phraseology in use includes 'cleared for the option' (see page 161). Provisional landing and take-off clearances are permitted on the assumption that the preceding aircraft will be either clear of the runway or airborne by the time the landing aircraft crosses the threshold or the departing commences its take-off roll. Typical phraseology is: 'Air Canada 841 cleared to land, 737 exiting to the right at the far end.' There are built-in safeguards to the procedure and it relies heavily on the controller's discretion.

The US 'land and hold short' procedure is in use at some large airports to facilitate dual intersecting runway operations. Phraseology examples are, for landing aircraft: 'Cleared to land Runway 25, hold short of Runway 32, 7,000 ft available to the intersection, traffic a Dash 8 landing/departing 32.' 'Cleared to land Runway 32, traffic Boeing 737 landing 25 will hold short of 32.' For departing aircraft: 'Traffic (type) landing 25 will hold short of 32, cleared for take-off Runway 32.' Stopping distance information need not be issued with each landing clearance if an ATIS message containing the information has been acknowledged by the aircraft, or an agreement has been negotiated with a local operator. The runway to be used by the restricted aircraft must be dry with no tailwind component unless the pilot agrees otherwise.

Canada's bilingual status extends to ATC and there are supplementary procedures for the use of French when required. A pilot is entitled to choose either language for communications but, as the Canadian AIP notes: 'Random switching from one language to the other may result in confusion and cannot be permitted under normal operating conditions.' The rules are strict and there are a number of checks intended to eliminate misunderstandings caused by inadvertent use of the wrong language by either pilot or controller. Because of the controversy raging between the US and ICAO over the implementation of MLS, Canada is delaying its MLS programme.

United States of America
Atlanta – T:119.1, 119.5; G:121.75; D:121.65; A:118.35, 127.9, 127.25; DEP:125.0, 125.7; AT:119.65, 125.55. Baltimore – T:119.4, 123.75; G:121.9; D:118.05; A:119.7, 119.0, 128.7, 124.55; DEP:125.3, 128.7, 124.55, 133.75; AT:115.1, 127.8. Bangor Intl – T:120.7; G:121.9; D:135.9; A:124.5, 125.3; AT:127.75. Boston – T:119.1, 128.8, 121.75 (Helicopters); G:121.9; D:121.65; A:120.6, 118.25, 127.2; DEP:133.0; AT:135.0. Chicago (O'Hare) – T:126.9, 120.75; G:121.9, 121.75; D:119.25, 121.6, 129.05; A:119.0, 125.7; DEP:125.0, 127.4, 125.4; AT:135.4. Cincinnati – T:118.3, 118.975; G:121.7, 121.3; D:127.175; A:119.7, 123.875; DEP:125.65, 128.7; AT:135.3, 134.375. Dallas-Fort Worth – T:126.55, 124.15; G:121.8, 121.65, 134.05; A:119.05, 125.8; DEP:127.75, 124.25, 118.55;

Orlando Tower. (Leo Marriott)

AT:117.0, 134.9, 135.5. Dallas (Love Field) – T:118.7; G:121.9; D:123.7, 127.9; A:123.9; AT:114.3. Las Vegas – T:119.9; G:121.1, 121.9; D:118.0; A:127.15; DEP:133.95, 125.9; AT:132.4, 125.6. Los Angeles – T:120.95, 133.9; G:121.65, 121.75; D:121.4; A:124.9, 124.5, 128.5; DEP:125.2, 124.3; AT:133.8, 135.65. Memphis – T:118.3, 119.7; G:125.2; A:119.1, 125.8; DEP:124.65, 124.15; AT:127.75, 119.45. Miami – T:118.3, 123.9; G:121.8, 127.5; D:135.35, 120.35; A:124.85; DEP:119.45, 125.5; AT:117.1, 119.15. Newark – T:118.3; G:121.8, 126.15; D:118.85; A:127.6, 128.55, 132.7, 132.8, 128.55; DEP:119.2, 124.75; AT:115.7, 132.45, 134.825. New Orleans – T:119.5; G:121.9; D:127.2; A:120.6, 125.5, 123.85; AT:127.55. New York (Kennedy) – T:119.1, 123.9; G:121.9, 121.65, 130.775; D:135.05; A:127.4, 132.4; DEP:135.9, 123.7, 124.75; AT:117.7, 115.4, 128.725, 115.1. New York (La Guardia) – T:118.7, 126.5; G:121.7, 121.85; D:135.2; A:118.8, 134.9, 132.7, 127.05, 124.95; DEP:120.4, 128.8; AT:125.95, 127.05. Orlando – T:124.3, 118.45; G:121.8; D:134.7; A:135.3, 119.4, 121.1, 120.15, 124.8; AT:121.25. San Francisco – T:120.5, 125.6; G:128.65, 121.8, 124.25; D:118.2; A:134.5, 135.65; DEP:120.9, 135.1; AT:108.9, 113.7, 118.85, 135.45. Tampa – T:119.5; G:121.7, 121.35; D:133.6; A:118.8, 134.25, 118.15, 118.5; AT:126.45. Washington (Dulles) – T:120.1; G:121.9, 132.45, 129.55; D:127.35; A:120.45, 126.1, 124.65; DEP:125.05, 126.65; AT:134.85. Washington (National) – T:119.1, 120.75; G:121.7; D:128.25; A:124.2, 124.7; DEP:121.05, 118.9, 125.55, 125.65; AT:132.65.

Dallas-Fort Worth, which has a total of seven runways, including a STOL strip for commuter aircraft.

Many areas of the USA have the largest densities of air traffic in the world and thus it is not surprising that the nation's ATC system is so highly developed and automated. R/T phraseology ranges from the very verbose to the clipped, for example 'Ground point nine' for 'Contact Ground 121.9.' The only way ground movement controllers can move large numbers of aircraft along complex taxiway systems is to issue a continuous stream of instructions without expecting an acknowledgement, unless it be for a 'Stop immediately!' Certain procedures are unique to the USA, as are its airspace divisions which are as follows, with ICAO airspace classifications appended:

Continental Control Area (Class A): The airspace above the 48 contiguous states, the District of Columbia, and Alaska above 14,500 ft AMSL, but not including the airspace less than 1,500 ft above the earth's surface nor Prohibited and Restricted Areas.

Positive Control Area (Class A): The airspace within the CCA from 18,000 ft AMSL up to and including FL 600. All aircraft must operate on IFR Flight Plans and communicate with ATC.

Control Areas (Class A): From the ground to the base of the CCA (14,500 ft). They consist mainly of Federal airways and VOR airways.

Terminal Control Areas (Class B): Extend from the surface (or higher) to specified altitudes which vary from airport to airport. They are established around the busiest airports.

Airport Radar Service Areas (ARSA) and Terminal Radar Service Areas (TRSA) (Class C): Surround lower-density airports where ATC provides radar vectoring and sequencing on a full-time basis for all IFR and VFR traffic.

Control Zones (Class D): May include one or more airports and are normally a circular area with a radius of five statute miles and any extensions necessary to include instrument approaches and departure paths. Extend from the surface up to the CCA.

Transition Area (Class D): Designated to contain IFR operations in controlled airspace during descent into a TCA or CTZ and while transitting between the terminal and en route environment.

Airport Traffic Areas (Class D): Equivalent to ICAO Aerodrome Traffic Zone.

Airways Systems

VOR (Victor) Routes: From 1,200 ft above the surface (sometimes higher) up to but not including 18,000 ft. Alternate airways are identified by their location with respect to the associated main airway. For example, V9 West indicates an alternate airway to the west of V9.

Jet Route System: Established from 18,000 ft up to FL 450. An example is J9 (spoken as Jet or Juliet 9) from Los Angeles to Las Vegas.

Random Area Navigation (RNAV): Not charted except in Alaska. As a fuel

Grand Forks International, North Dakota, a typical US regional airport with much general aviation traffic.

saving measure the Federal Aviation Authority (FAA) encourages airline and business aircraft to file direct between two points for any flight in the Continental USA of at least 1,500 nm at or above 39,000 ft. Alaskan RNAV Routes are identified by an R suffix to the Jet Route number, e.g. J804R.
High Altitude Area System: The airspace structure above FL 450 is designed to permit free selection of routes.
Special User airspace protects sensitive areas and certain military activities. A typical Prohibited Area is the White House; Restricted Areas include gunnery and missile ranges.

A total of 20 Air Route Traffic Control Centres (ARTCC) are responsible for the airways system and are located at strategic points to cover the whole country via remote radio and radar antenna sites. An ongoing plan is to consolidate ATC services into Area Control Facilities (ACF), the Seattle ARTCC being the first to be reorganized in 1996. En route and airport approach control units will be served by specially designed large terminal control units, such as the new Metroplex Central Control facility in Southern California.

TRACON (Terminal Area Radar Control) is a system used in a number of areas where several major airports are in close proximity. ATC is centralized, allowing co-ordination of arrival and departure routes and thus avoiding conflictions. It also reduces controller workload and allows more traffic to be handled. An example is the New York TRACON which covers JF Kennedy, Newark, and La Guardia Airports, as well as several general aviation airfields.

Congested parts of US airspace are subject to Flow Management as in Europe. It is co-ordinated from the Washington ATC System Command Centre (formerly the Central Flow Control Facility) and uses very large computerized data displays capable of showing traffic across the entire USA. Each aircraft can be identified by data label, track, departure point, or level, if the system is programmed accordingly. Advanced warning is given of bottlenecks on similar displays at all the ARTCCs, enabling corrective action to be taken immediately.

The following is an outline of a typical airways flight adapted from an information booklet issued by the FAA.

A Boeing 737 packed with 120 Chicago-bound passengers is waiting in the customary queue on the holding pan at the end of Runway 18 at Washington National Airport. The 737 captain, who has already received a thorough briefing on weather conditions, preferential routeings, and other factors that will affect his flight to Chicago's O'Hare Airport, nods to his co-pilot who presses his mike button and says:

'Washington Tower, United 483 is ready for departure Runway 18.'

'United 483, taxi into position and hold' is the reply from the tower. The jet turns on to the runway and then receives another message from the tower: 'United 483 cleared for take-off.' As the aircraft climbs out over the Potomac, tower instructs the crew: 'United 483 contact Departure Control.' Following departure instructions, the pilot stays aligned with the runway until Departure issues a clearance six miles south of the airport: 'United 483 turn right direct Casanova, climb and maintain Flight Level 230.' Then he banks the aircraft right towards the Casanova VOR beacon.

Progress of the flight is monitored closely by the radar departure controller at National to ensure that the aircraft remains safely separated from all other traffic within the Terminal Control Area. As the flight approaches the boundary of the National Airport Control Area (approximately 30 miles) the departure controller prepares to handoff control of the flight to the Washington ARTCC. When ready, he or she makes a computer entry by means of a keyboard which causes the data tag to begin blinking on the controller's radarscope in the Washington Centre.

When the Centre controller is ready to accept the handoff, he or she likewise makes a computer entry and the data tag on the departure controller's scope begins to blink. The departure controller then tells the pilot: 'United 483 contact Washington Centre on 134.3.' Once the pilot has done that the transfer of control is complete.

The Washington Centre is located about 40 miles west of Washington near the town of Leesburg, Virginia. It is responsible for 140,000 square miles of airspace and 20,000 miles of airways over all or parts of six eastern states. On any given day it will handle more than 6,000 flights. During peak periods as many as 150 controllers will be on duty in the huge control room, staffing the Centre's 34 radar sectors. Each of these sectors represents a specific block of airspace over a particular geographical area. There are both high and low altitude sectors so any point on the ground may have two, three, or even four airspace sectors layered above it.

At least two and as many as four controllers work at each sector position. The voice the pilot hears belongs to the radar controller who monitors the scope to keep the traffic separated. Next to him sits the handoff controller who handles the transfer of flights between sectors or between facilities. When traffic is light only these two may be needed to staff a sector. When it is heavy a manual and assistant controller may be added to look after clerical and other duties.

The handoff of United 483 from Washington National Departure Control to the Washington ARTCC requires a minimum of voice communication since both facilities are equipped with computer-based systems for displaying aircraft identity and altitude. Still, the controller at Washington Centre will ask Flight 483 to 'ident' or identify itself by means of its transponder. This device sends out a coded signal which causes the radar target to enlarge and brighten, thus permitting the controller to make a positive identification. This is generally acknowledged with a cryptic 'Radar contact'. The automated equipment, now in operation in all US centres, also obviates the need for routine position reports and other non-essential conversation between pilots and other controllers. This leaves the radio channels free for more urgent communications.

Ten miles west of the Casanova VOR, the co-pilot of United 483 observes an ominous row of thunderheads in the distance. A brief discussion with the captain follows: Can we steer round them? Does the aircraft's weather radar show a comfortable detour? The consensus is no, so the co-pilot calls centre: 'Washington Centre, United 483.' 'United 483, go ahead.' 'We see some thunderheads up front. Request to detour south.' The controller scans the traffic situation south of 483 and responds: 'United 483 deviation approved. Report back on the airway.'

As Flight 483 turns south, its crew can rest assured that their aircraft is being watched on radar and controllers will issue appropriate instructions should a possible traffic confliction arise. The detour takes 15 minutes and generates another radio transmission when completed. 'United 483 turning back to Juliet 149,' says the co-pilot, using the verbal shorthand for Jet Route 149. 'Roger,' the centre responds, 'Washington Centre requests a PIREP.'

'Roger Washington,' says the co-pilot, responding to the call for a pilot's in-flight report on weather conditions. 'We got some light rime ice and moderate turbulence inside the clouds but we were in and out in 10 seconds. 483.' PIREPS are an important aid in gathering aviation weather information. In this case, the data obtained from Flight 483 is forwarded by teletype to FAA Flight Service Stations and other facilities coping with the line of thunderstorms for use in briefing other pilots operating in the area. Information on actual icing conditions is very valuable.

From Washington Centre, United 483, by now cleared to and level at FL 350, is handed off first to Indianapolis Centre, then to the Cleveland Centre, and finally to the Chicago Centre. In each case the procedure is virtually identical to that employed in the original transfer of the flight from Washington Departure to the centre. As the aircraft nears Chicago O'Hare, the captain tunes in the O'Hare Automatic Terminal Information Service. This facility provides the pilot with a continuous broadcast of recorded air-port weather and landing information.

On this occasion the following is received: 'O'Hare Airport Information Bravo. Measured ceiling 2,000 overcast, visibility three miles, blowing snow. Temperature three zero. Wind 340 degrees at 25. Altimeter two niner eight. ILS Runway 32 Left approach in use. Advise you have Bravo.' But, despite the blowing snow, the ceiling and visibility at O'Hare are well with-in limits for an instrument approach. Now the flight is handed off for the last time.

'United 483,' says the controller at the Chicago Centre, 'descend and maintain one zero thousand, report leaving one two thousand.' An acknowledgement follows and the 737 begins its descent, the altitude tick-ing off in 100-foot increments on the controller's console. A clearance for an ILS approach is received and in a matter of minutes the flight is slotted into the approach sequence and vectored on to the ILS. The final transfers of control involve the tower and the ground movements controller, the latter guiding the aircraft along the network of taxiways to the terminal gate.

A very large number of US airports and airstrips, including some which handle limited airline traffic, are totally uncontrolled or only have a Flight Service Station (FSS) operator or Unicom. Where there is no ground opera-tor, Multicom is used, a common channel on which arriving and departing aircraft broadcast their intentions, using the name of the airfield and the callsign *Traffic*. Unicom is a step up from Multicom; ground operators (they are *not* controllers) use it to pass 'field advisories', i.e. the windspeed and direction, altimeter setting, runway-in-use, and traffic information. As with Multicom, pilots are expected to announce their departure and direction of flight, for example: 'Mudville Traffic, Cessna 24 Zulu is departing Runway 27 northbound.' The airport's published common frequency is used and again *Traffic* indicates the absence of a tower. Several uncontrolled fields in the same area may share a single frequency and it is important to identify the airfield in each transmission.

Arriving aircraft will also make blind broadcasts of their intentions and position in the traffic pattern. The standard pattern entry is a 45° leg to join mid-downwind, but direct downwind and crosswind joins are also permitted. Straight-in approaches are a definite no-no! After take-off an aircraft should climb straight out and upon reaching pattern altitude make a 45° left turn and continue climb before setting course. The frequency is then monitored for about 10 miles for any conflicting traffic inbound to the field. 'See and avoid' is the paramount principle.

Some US airports are one-way in that, for one reason or another, take-offs and landings are made to and from the same direction, in other words, on opposite runways. Maybe the runway has a severe downhill slope (as at Prescott, Arizona). Another reason might be noise when there is a town or city close to the end of the runway (such as Bader Field, New Jersey). A third reason may be steeply rising terrain in one direction as at Aspen, Colorado, or Los Alamos, New Mexico.

Approximately 275 Flight Service Stations (FSS) are maintained by the FAA to provide assistance to General Aviation (GA) pilots. Included in the information on offer is pre-flight and in-flight weather, suggested routes, altitudes, indications of turbulence, icing, and any other factors affecting the safety of flight. FSSs are the direct descendants of the airways communications stations established in the 1920s to supply weather data and other assistance to the early mail pilots. Most FSSs are located at airports and the operators relay ATC instructions (using the phrase 'ATC clears ...'), assist pilots in emergency situations, provide airport advisory services, and participate in searches for missing or overdue aircraft.

Two or more parallel runways are a common feature of the larger US airports. For simultaneous independent IFR approaches to each, the parallel runways must be a minimum of 4,300 ft apart and 2,500 ft for non-simultaneous, i.e. 'staggered' IFR approaches. For the latter a diagonal separation of two miles and a minimum separation of three miles in trail is required during final approach. It is hoped that the introduction of precision runway monitoring using rapid-scan radar will reduce these criteria. The new Denver International Airport is capable of handling triple simultaneous approaches in IFR to three parallel runways and a planned fourth parallel runway will make quadruple approaches possible. The technology exists but it remains to be seen whether procedures and pilot confidence will allow it to become operational.

Obviously, any deviation from track on simultaneous approaches is dangerous so two extra radar controllers are provided, known as Final Approach Monitors. Each monitors the Radar Director handling a specific runway and the video map on his radar display has an additional marking made up of parallel broken lines either side of the final approach track. It is the Monitor's responsibility to override the R/T and issue go-around instructions immediately if an aircraft is seen to go out-side the parallel lines into the 'no transgression zone', which is at least 2,000 ft wide. The presence of the Monitor allows the Radar Director to carry out co-ordination and other ancillary tasks which might otherwise temporarily distract his attention.

Simultaneous instrument approaches are permitted to converging runways where a procedure has been approved. Another FAA practice is the 'Land and hold short' clearance, when two crossing runways are in simultaneous use. Although currently only authorized in visual conditions it may be extended to IFR operation as the FAA has success-fully tested a system of runway warning lights. It consists of a bar of high intensity pulsing white lights flush with the runway and marks the limit of roll-out after landing. If adopted, the use of the land and hold short procedure in IFR conditions would increase movement capacity considerably. Pilots,   however, are not entirely happy with the existing practice, let alone extending it to IFR. One European 747 captain on short final to an American airport, when told an aircraft landing on an intersecting runway would hold short, replied: 'How do you know?'

The USA has shelved its long term Microwave Landing System (MLS) programme, despite ICAO's decision (currently put 'on hold') for it to replace existing ILS equipment for precision landing. Instead, the FAA is confident that GPS will provide precision landing in low or zero visibility conditions – Category 2/3.

Glossary of expressions unique to US ATC

Abbreviated Flight Plan: Basic information such as type of aircraft, location, and route of flight or pilot's request, necessary for ATC to issue an IFR clearance on an ad hoc basis, usually to aircraft already airborne.

Airport Traffic Area: The airspace within five miles of the centre of an airport with an operating control tower, extending up to, but not including, 3,000 ft above ground level.

Abort: Terminate, for example, take-off run.

Advise intentions: What do you plan to do next?

Airep: Weather report from an aircraft in flight.

Altimeter: Equivalent of QNH.

Approach Gate: An imaginary point used by ATC as a basis for vectoring traffic to an airport final approach course. It is usually no more than five miles from the runway threshold.

Charted VFR Flyways: Flight paths recommended to VFR aircraft to by-pass areas heavily used by large transport aircraft.

Circling Approach: Visual re-alignment to an into-wind runway after an instrument approach.

Clearance void if not off by (time): An ATC advisory to IFR aircraft that if it is not airborne by a certain time the clearance is cancelled and must be re-requested.

Cleared for the option: ATC authorization for a pilot to make a touch-and-go, low approach, missed approach, stop and go, or full stop landing at his discretion.

Closed traffic: An aircraft remaining in the traffic pattern for practice take-offs and landings.

Contact Approach: May be requested by pilots operating under IFR, provided they are clear of clouds and have at least one mile flight visibility and can reasonably expect to continue to the destination airport in those conditions. Must be authorized by ATC.

Controlled Departure Time: A flow control procedure whereby aircraft are held on the ground, rather than in the air, when en route delays are expected.

Flight Watch: En route Flight Advisory Service.

Gate Hold Procedures: Used to hold aircraft on the ground or at their gates whenever departure delays exceed 15 minutes.

Handoff: Transfer of control from one radar controller to another.

Have numbers: Informal method of confirming that the pilot has the ATIS information, etc.

Hold for Release: Departure clearance is not valid until a release time has been given.

Intersection departure/take-off: Departure from a runway intersection along its length.

Low Altitude Alert: ATC phrase to alert a pilot to close proximity to terrain or obstructions.

Make short approach: ATC instruction to make a tight base leg on to short final.

Non-compulsory: US equivalent of an on-request reporting point.

Overhead approach or 360 overhead: Procedure for VFR arrival of military aircraft for pattern entry.

Pilot's discretion: When used after a climb or descent clearance, this advises the pilot that he may begin the manoeuvre when convenient.

Profile descent: An uninterrupted descent (except where level flight is required for speed adjustment, e.g. 250 kt at 10,000 ft) from cruising level to interception of a glideslope. It normally terminates at the approach gate (qv).

Radar contact: Phrase informing a pilot that he is positively identified on radar and may discontinue position reporting. Also a tacit understanding that the aircraft may enter the controller's airspace.

Ramp: US equivalent of apron.

Say altitude: Advise ATC of your current altitude.

Say your indicated: Advise your indicated airspeed.

Target: Primary radar return.

Taxi into position and hold: Tower instruction to an aircraft to line up on the runway and await take-off clearance.

Traffic advisory: Issued by ATC to alert a pilot to the presence of other aircraft in the area.

Unable: Cannot comply.

When able: Pilot must comply at the first opportunity.

Caribbean Islands

For space reasons I have not detailed the ATC systems – often rudimentary and sometimes non-existent – of these island groups. In some areas all operations have to be VFR. Most of the Lesser Antilles from St Kitts south to Trinidad are contained within the latter's Piarco FIR. The Netherlands Antilles fall inside Venezuela's Maiquetia FIR. HF networks known as CAR-A and CAR-B serve aircraft flying the West Atlantic Route System, using stations such as New York, San Juan, and Panama. The major airports can be very busy and rely almost wholly on procedural control. Aruba, for example, handles over 200 movements per day, many of them by widebodied aircraft. With no taxiways, extensive backtracking of the runway is necessary. Radar coverage is generally poor but Barbados is fortunate in having 200 nm range area equipment. Trinidad and Tobago's land area is quite small, but the islands' geographical position makes them an international crossroads between North America and the Caribbean and South America, and between the Caribbean and Africa and Europe. Piarco ACC looks after a vast area of oceanic airspace bordering with that controlled by Senegal, New York, and Santa Maria in the Azores.

Although farther north in the Atlantic, Bermuda has been included in this section. Because its commercial airport was shared with a naval air station until recently, the ATC system was managed by the US Navy and all controllers were military personnel, but it has now been civilianized. Puerto Rico is a self-governing federal state of the USA so ATC is run by the FAA. Main facility is the San Juan ARTCC which administers the San Juan Domestic and Oceanic CTAs. International air routes are supported by an unusual domestic system designated Route 1, 2, 3, etc. The very large island of Cuba, with a developing tourist industry, has several international airports, as well as a domestic airport in each province. The whole island is surrounded by an ADIZ. Within the Santiago TCA is the Guantanamo Naval Air Station and harbour, a US treaty facility which survived Castro's takeover.

Bahamas and Turks & Caicos
Freeport – T/A:118.5; G:121.7. Nassua – T:119.5, 122.5; G:121.7; D:118.3; A:121.0; AT:118.7.

Barbados
Barbados (Grantley Adams) – T:118.7; G:121.9; A:129.35.

Bermuda
Bermuda – T:118.1, 121.7; G:124.5; A:119.1, 128.5.

Cuba
Camaguey – T/A:118.5. Havana – T:118.1; A:120.3; AT:132.5.

Dominican Republic
Santo Domingo (Las Americas) – T:118.1; G:121.9; A:119.3.

French Antilles
Fort de France – T:118.5; A:121.0; AFIS:128.4; AT:127.85. Pointe à Pitre – T:118.4; A:121.3; AT:127.6.

Grenada
Point Salines – T:118.9; A:119.4.

Haiti
Port au Prince – T:118.3; A:119.8.

Jamaica and Cayman Islands
Grand Cayman – T/A:120.2; AT:115.6. Kingston – T/A:120.6; G:121.7; AFIS:121.6. Montego Bay (Sangster) – T/A:120.8; G:121.7; AT:127.9.

Leeward Islands
Antigua (VC Bird) – T/A:119.1; G:121.9. St Kitts – T:118.3; A:119.6.

Netherlands Antilles
Aruba – T/A:120.9, 118.0; G:121.9. Curacao – T:118.3; A:119.6. St Maarten (Juliana) – T:118.7; A:128.95.

Puerto Rico
San Juan – T:118.3, 126.4; G:121.9; D:126.4; A:120.9, 119.4; AT:125.8.

Trinidad and Tobago
Port of Spain (Piarco) – T:118.1; G:121.9; A:119.0; ACC:125.4, 123.7.

Virgin Islands
St Croix – T:118.6; G:121.7; A:128.65. St Thomas – A/G:127.3; G:121.9.

Windward Islands
St Lucia (Vigie) – T:118.0. St Lucia (Hewanorra) – T:118.3; A:119.8

Central America

Working from an ACC in the Honduran capital, Tegucigalpa, the Corporacion Centroamericano de Servicios de Navigacion Aerea (COCESNA) controls all airspace above 20,000 ft over the six states it represents – Belize, Costa Rica, El Salvador, Guatamala, Honduras, and Nicaragua. This and a significant amount of oceanic airspace over the Caribbean and Pacific is entirely contained within the Cenamer FIR. COCESNA dates from 1960 and is a direct equivalent of Eurocontrol. Political settlements are being reached in this troubled region and resulting economic growth will boost aircraft movements. Due to be completed in 1997, the Euromaya project will provide secondary radar coverage over much of the region and complete an ATC radar chain stretching from northern Alberta in Canada to Colombia and Venezuela, a distance of 4,000 miles. For maximum range the 250 mile radars are sited on high ground, one to the north of Guatamala City being on a 2,770 m mountain top. Despite such co-operation, the COCESNA states are very sensitive about their sovereignty and the charts are sprinkled with warnings about unauthorized overflights and the importance of prior radio contact when requiring to cross territorial boundaries. In the words of the Guatamala AIP: 'Aircraft not complying will be considered suspicious and suffer the consequences.' Belize is still under British protection and a Short Range Air Defence Engagement Zone is in force within eight miles of the international airport, up to 19,000 ft.

Belize
Belize Intl – T:118.0; G:121.9; A:121.0.

Costa Rica
Alajuela – T:118.6; A:119.6, 120.5. Liberia Intl – AFIS:118.8. Limon – AFIS:118.8.

El Salvador
San Salvador – T:118.0; G:121.7; A:119.9.

Guatamala
Guatamala City – A/G:5.568 (HF).

Honduras
Tegucigalpa – T:118.7; A:119.1; AFIS:126.9.

Nicaragua
Managua – T:118.1; A/G:126.9.

Mexico
Acapulco – T:118.5; A:125.2; AT:125.9. Cancun – T:118.6; A:120.4; AT:127.7.

Guadalajara – T:118.1; G:121.9; A:120.8; AT:127.9. Mexico City – T:118.1, 118.7; G:121.9, 121.0; A:121.2, 120.5, 119.7; AT:127.7. Monterrey – T:118.1; A:121.4, 119.6; AT:127.7.

ATC at Mexico City is housed in a modern ACC and tower. A new ACC at Mazatlan, on the Pacific coast, became operational in 1986. Two other ACCs at Monterrey and Merida complete ATC for the country. Mexico was one of the first countries to switch to SSR without long-range primary radar for en route control. The large revenue from tourist charter flights makes it possible to maintain a continuous upgrading and re-equipment programme. The airways system follows the US Victor and Jet Route pattern. (See USA entry.)

Panama
Balboa (Howard AFB) – T:126.2; A;119.2, 119.7. Panama City – T:118.1, 129.8, 122.8; G:121.9; A:119.7, 119.2.

The country is surrounded by an ADIZ. US influence can be seen in several Victor airways designators.

South America
South American ATC is often rudimentary, using either procedural methods or providing advisory service only. Radar coverage is relatively sparse and HF radio has to be used in many regions where VHF would be screened by the Andes. Traffic is still relatively light, however, so the large procedural separations are rarely a problem.

Argentina
Buenos Aires (Aeroparque) – T:118.3; A:119.5. Buenos Aires (Ezeiza) – T:119.1; G:121.7; A:119.9; AT:116.5. Mar Del Plata – A/T:120.5.

Second largest country in South America after Brazil, Argentina has a complex web of ATS routes connecting its widely scattered towns and cities. TCAs surround all the major airports, the most southerly being the Punta Arenas and Williams TCA complex in the vicinity of Cape Horn. From here extends one of the world's most southerly air routes, Whiskey 56, stretching into Antarctica. A procedure peculiar to Argentina is that all reporting points are compulsory for aircraft with a speed of less than 180 kts. Those with greater speeds need report only at compulsory reporting points.

Bolivia
La Paz – A:119.5. Santa Cruz – A:123.7.

The installation of area radars at Santa Cruz and Trinidad has enabled wide coverage of Bolivian airspace. TCAs surround both these airports as well as three others in the country.

Brazil
Rio De Janeiro (Galeao) – T:118.0, 118.2; G:121.9; A:119.0, 119.7, 120.0; D:121.0; AT:127.6. Salvador – T:118.35, 122.8; G:121.9; A:119.1, 119.3, 128.95. Sao Paulo – T:118.1, 118.4; G:121.7; A:119.4, 119.8, 129.75; D:121.0; AT:127.75.

ATC is an entirely military function in this vast country. Some of the air routes over the interior are uncontrolled and aircraft on upper airways, when converging on a crossing point with another airway, are expected to transmit blind, position, level and estimate for crossing point at 15, 10 and 5 minutes flight time from such a point. If a difference in crossing time is less that 15 minutes, the aircraft which has traffic on its right must alter its flight level by 500 ft (if FL 280 or below) or 1,000 ft (if at or above FL 290) when 33 nm from centre-line until 33 nm past centre-line. There are seven FIRs and their associated ACCs: Belem, Brasilia, Curtiba, Manaus, Porto Velho, and Recife. All make extensive use of HF to supplement limited VHF coverage. A 10 year expansion plan due for completion in 1998 will provide full radar coverage for both NE Brazil and the Amazon region.

Chile
Concepcion – T:118.1; G:121.9; A:119.9. Iquique – T:118.9; A:119.7. Santiago – T:118.1; G:121.7, 121.95; AT:132.1. Santiago (Los Cerillos) – T:118.5.

Although Chile has a relatively low volume of air traffic, it provides airspace services over an enormous area. The distance from its northern to southern extremities is 2,078 nm (3,849 km), added to which are the Chilean Antarctic Territories which extend to the South Pole. The country is divided into five FIRs: Antofagasta (northern area), Santiago (central area), Puerto Monnt (southern), Punta Arenas (extreme south), and Isla de Pascua (Easter Island-Pacific Ocean area extending to the Pole). Each has its own ACC but by 1995 a new unified centre at Santiago will tie together all the FIRs, solving problems of co-ordination and permitting a much more flexible handling of traffic, which is both variable and seasonable. Over much of Chile the Andes make long-range radar impracticable and the authorities are considering ADS as an alternative.

Colombia
Barranquilla – T:118.1; G:121.9; A:119.1. Bogota – T:118.1; G:121.9; A:119.5, 121.3; D:121.6; AT:114.7. Cali – T:118.1; G:121.9; A:119.1. Cartagena – T:118.3; A:120.3.

Entirely within the Bogota FIR, Colombia has a complex system of domestic and international air routes. An 'open skies' policy with neighbouring Venezuela has increased traffic considerably. An indication of the extent of the country's drug problem are the special procedures to deal with aircraft landing within certain restricted areas. Military aircraft detecting a civil aircraft on an unauthorized aerodrome will circle it, rocking the wings and trying to make radio contact on 122.1 or 118.1. Aircraft must not start engines as this will be interpreted as an attempt at evasion and the military aircraft will take 'corresponding measures'.

Ecuador
Guayaquil – T: 118.3; G:121.9; A:123.9, 119.3. Quito – A/G:126.9.

Bisected by the Andes, Ecuador is heavily reliant on air transport for its communications and has a remarkably complex air route system. The only radar service currently provided is by the approach control units at Quito and Guayaquil. However, radar coverage is planned over land and most of the airspace over its territorial waters, including the Galapagos Islands.

Falkland Islands
Mount Pleasant – T:133.35; G:130.3; A:118.5.

Although they are nominally within Argentina's Comodoro Rivadavia FIR, ATC in and around the Falklands is firmly in the hands of the Royal Air Force. The Mount Pleasant TCA surrounds the islands almost out to the Exclusion Zone and two airways, W50 and W54, connect them to the mainland. However, it is doubtful if either is in active use. An interesting anomaly is that the original civil airport at Port Stanley has the ICAO code SFAL while Mount Pleasant has the UK code EGYP as if to underline its Britishness!

Paraguay
Asuncion – T:118.1; G:121.9; A:119.7; ACC:124.1, 128.4.

Within the single FIR, Asuncion, there are six ATS routes and a TCA around the capital's airport. Much of the airspace is over Argentinian territory but is delegated to Asuncion Approach.

Peru
Cuzco – AFIS:126.7. Iquitos – AFIS:126.9. Lima – Not published. Trujillo – AFIS:126.9

Most of Peru's ATS routes are concentrated over the coastal areas with branches to Iquitos in the north-east and Cuzco, a tourist centre for the Inca site at Maccu Piccu. Over the Andes many of the minimum en route altitudes exceed FL 200. Peru has an ADIZ and no aircraft may leave or enter the country other than by specified corridors. The north-eastern borders with Colombia are often violated by drug trafficking aircraft and in an attempt to prevent incursion the Peruvian Air Force is responsible for the control of aerodromes in this area. Considerable use is made of HF for internal communication, VHF being of little use in such a mountainous country.

Uruguay
Montevideo (Carrasco) – T:118.1; A:119.2, 123.2.

The country's relatively simple ATS route structure lies entirely within the Montevideo FIR. Busiest sector is the Carrasco TCA which surrounds the capital's airport and several others. At present it has the only en route and terminal area radar system.

Venezuela
Caracas (Maiquetia) – T:118.1, 118.4, 126.18; G:121.9; A:120.1, 120.4; AT:114.8.

Venezuela is contained within the Maiquetia FIR, with TMAs around Caracas, Margarita, and Maracaibo. Very unusual is Caracas's use of three tower frequencies: one for arrivals, one for departures, and a third for military aircraft.

North Atlantic and Polar Routes
The highest density of oceanic air traffic in the world is to be found over the North Atlantic. At peak times more than 850 aircraft make the crossing over a 24 hour period and the 1994 total exceeded 250,000. The airspace is the responsibility of Shanwick Oceanic Area Control Centre (OACC), a hybrid of Shannon-Prestwick, which serves aircraft between roughly latitude 45°N and between longitude 10°W and 30°W; Iceland OACC at Reykjavik for traffic north of 61°N; and Gander, which looks after aircraft to the west of 30°W.

For sub-sonic aircraft over the Atlantic there is a procedure known as the Organized Track System (OTS). As a result of passenger demands, time zone differences, and airport noise restrictions, much of the North Atlantic air traffic is contained in two flows – westbound in the morning and eastbound in the evening. Because of the concentration of the flows and the limited vertical height band which is economical for jet operations, the airspace is comparatively congested. The track system is thus designed to accommodate as many aircraft as possible on the most suitable flight paths, taking advantage of any pressure systems to provide a tail wind where possible.

Prestwick OACC is responsible for the day track system and Gander for that at night. In each case, planners on both sides of the Atlantic consult with one another and co-ordinate as necessary with adjacent OACCs, as well as with domestic ATC agencies, to ensure that the system provides sufficient tracks and Flight Levels to satisfy anticipated traffic demands.

On completion of negotiations the OTS is sent out from the OACC concerned by signal to all interested parties in Europe and North America. The daytime system is usually published by Prestwick between midnight and

01:00 hours UTC. In addition, the track co-ordinates are broadcast on frequency 133.8 and this can be heard in many parts of the United Kingdom on a normal air band radio. The tracks are known as Alpha, Bravo, Charlie, and so on, the most northerly being Alpha. For night use the tracks are designated Zulu for the most southerly, Yankee for the adjacent one to the north etc. For aircraft not equipped with HF radio there are several routes, known as *Blue Spruce*, which follow short hops between Iceland, Greenland, and Canada within VHF coverage.

Military colour-coded routes are another special case. Intended for transatlantic tactical fighter deployments with mid-air refuelling, they include Blue Route which terminates at Macrihanish TACAN, Red Route terminating at Lands End VOR, Gold Hi East terminating at 56°N 10°W, and its reverse Gold Hi West starting at the same point. Brown and Yellow Routes are further south into Spanish airspace. Another series of colour routes was developed primarily for USAF transport aircraft to facilitate the activation of short-notice altitude reservations over the Atlantic. Black Route feeds into the UK military TACAN Route system (see *Air Band Radio Handbook*, page 84). Orange and Purple Routes enter France and Spain respectively.

Each oceanic flight plan received from the departure airport includes the track, Flight Level, and cruise Mach number requested (Mach number being a proportion of Mach 1, the speed of sound). When the pilot requests an oceanic clearance, the Planning Controller attempts to fit the flight into the planned slot according to the aircraft's requested level, Mach number, and boundary estimate.

Once the clearance is accepted by the pilot, the information is relayed to the relevant OACC and, where necessary, to adjacent OACCs. Then the clearance is fed into Prestwick's Flight Data Processing System (FDPS) which presents the information on the controller's Electronic Data Display and also passes the information to Gander's computer. This data, which resembles the old printed flight progress strips, gives all relevant flight details and computed times of arrival at specific reporting points along the track, normally at intervals of 10° of longitude. This display is used by the controller to monitor the progress of the flight through the Oceanic Control Area.

Most flights across the North Atlantic are handled in this way, but some aircraft may wish to operate outside the Organized Track System, for example on flights between Europe and the Caribbean, or between Europe and the West Coast of the USA. These so-called random tracks are also handled by Shanwick, as are transatlantic flights by Concorde. Over the Atlantic, position reports are passed in a similar fashion to those on VHF, i.e. the present position and a forward estimate for the next one. The positions are given in terms of latitude and longitude, 56 North 10 West being an example, or as a reporting point or beacon when nearing a land mass. Approximately one aircraft per hour is requested by the Oceanic Control Centre to 'Send Met' and will include weather information with each position report. This consists of outside air temperature, wind speed and direction derived from INS equipment, plus any other relevant observations. A typical position report is: 'Position Swissair 100 56 N 20 W 1235 Flight Level 330 estimate 56 N 30 W 1310, next 56 N 40 W.' Some phraseology is unique to HF R/T. For example, 'Charlie Charlie' is an obsolete way of saying 'received and understood'. Since the communicators are monitoring several frequencies, aircraft on first contact are expected to give the frequency they are using but if there is no possibility of confusion only the first two digits are required, e.g. 'Shanwick American 55 on 88'. Full frequency here is 8864 Khz.

The airspace between 27,500 ft and 40,000 ft over most of the North Atlantic is known as MNPS (Minimum Navigation Performance Specification) airspace. Aircraft flying within it are required to carry a certain scale of navigation equipment so that they can be flown accurately within the parameters of the ATC clearance. In this congested area, mostly unmonitored by radar, any deviation could be dangerous.

This is reflected in the fairly large lateral separation between flights, vertical separation being the same as that described on pages 47-48. Aircraft which do not meet the MNPS requirements are separated laterally by 120 nm, which is reduced to 90 nm in certain designated airspace. A spacing of 60 nm is allowed for aircraft which meet the MNPS.

The same applies to supersonic aircraft operating at or above FL 275. The rules for longitudinal spacing, i.e. one aircraft following another on the same track, are too complicated to list here but vary from 15 down to 10 minutes and sometimes less. It all depends upon speed, which is expressed as a Mach number. Satellite navigation, coupled with the replacement of HF by VHF satellite communications, is likely to reduce separations considerably over the next few years.

The Oceanic Controllers at Prestwick do not talk to the aircraft directly but teletype their instructions to specialized, usually ex-marine, radio operators at Ballygireen just north of Shannon Airport. The latter talk to the aircraft and teletype the responses back to Prestwick. This is not as inefficient as it sounds because HF communications can be so distorted that experienced radio operators, officially known as communicators, do better than the controllers themselves and the short delay in reply is insignificant with such long distances between aircraft. On the other side of the Atlantic,

ARINC communicators perform the same function for the US OACCs.

The North Atlantic HF network is divided into 'families' of frequencies to obtain a balanced loading of communications on the Oceanic Track System. They are designated NAT-A to F and a new NAT-G is rumoured. Each family uses a primary frequency with a secondary one nominated for use when reception is poor. The frequencies are shared by Shanwick, Reykjavik, and Gander.

Santa Maria in the Azores looks after traffic south of Shanwick's area, New York OACC controls flights over a large proportion of the south-west of the North Atlantic, and with favourable reception conditions those from the Caribbean and South America can be heard as well. San Juan in Puerto Rico is responsible for aircraft south of New York's area, using the same frequencies.

Twin-engined aircraft on trans-oceanic routes, such as the Boeing 757 and 767, are subject to ETOPS procedures – Extended Range Twin Engine Operations. They require the aircraft to be never more than three hours or 1,170 nm from an alternate airport in the unlikely event of engine failure. If a diversion becomes necessary, maximum thrust is set on the live engine in order to maintain the assigned Mach Number, and thus separation from other traffic, for as long as possible. A 90° turn is then made off the oceanic track towards the ETOPS alternate. When at least 30 nm from the original track, course is set for the alternate and long range cruise altitude and speed is attained.

Concordes operate along fixed tracks, normally between 50,000 ft and 60,000 ft. Because of the extremely small number of aircraft flying within this height band it is usually possible for the OACC to issue a clearance before take-off. This allows Concorde to operate on a supersonic 'cruise climb profile', which is the best in terms of fuel economy. Concorde has special, unvarying oceanic tracks, known as 'Sierra Mike' when westbound and 'Sierra November' when eastbound. 'Sierra Oscar' is a reserve track in both directions. Air France Concorde flights to North America depart from Paris Charles de Gaulle and enter the London UIR south-west of Lands End. They then route to the same oceanic entry point at 50°N 08°W. Supersonic Link Routes numbers SL1 to SL7 connect the oceanic tracks with domestic airspace.

North Polar Track Structure
Like most other North Atlantic traffic flows, traffic on the Europe–Alaska axis is predominantly unidirectional. In the Reykjavik CTA the westbound peak is between 1200 and 1800 UTC and the eastbound peak is between 0001 and 0600 UTC. To avoid the complications of random routes, a Polar

Track Structure consisting of 10 fixed tracks has been established for use during these periods. Use of the PTS is not mandatory but strongly recommended, especially between FL 310 and 390. Abbreviated clearances are issued, which include the track code number, cleared flight level, and cleared Mach Number. Position reports may also be abbreviated by replacing the normal latitude co-ordinate with the word 'Polar' and the track number. For example: 'Position Japanair 422 Polar 3 20 West 1537, estimating Polar 3 40 West 1620 next Polar 3 LT.' (LT is the Alert NDB in Canada's North West Territories.) West of 60°W, as they pass just south of the Pole, the tracks enter the Edmonton Arctic CTA. HF frequencies of the NAT-D family are used by such ground stations as Cambridge Bay and Churchill.

Ascension
Wideawake – T:126.2.

This island in the middle of the South Atlantic is an important staging point for traffic between the UK and the Falklands.

Azores
Lajes – T:122.1; G:121.9; A:135.0; AT:120.3. Santa Maria – T:118.1; A:119.1.

The strategic position of this Portuguese island has made it ideal to share the responsibility for oceanic control over the mid-Atlantic. The Santa Maria OCA stretches from 45°N to around 20°N and as far west as the New York OCA boundary at 40°W. However, its functions are soon to be transferred to Lisbon ACC following the installation of a new automated oceanic ATC system.

Faroes
Faroe Radar – 118.1, 122.2. Vagar – AFIS:124.85.

Lying to the south-east of Iceland, these Danish islands have their own Traffic Information Zone with the Reykjavik CTA (Faroe Sector) above it.

Greenland
Narssarssuaq – AFIS:119.1; A/G:121.3. Sondrestrom – T:126.2; A:118.3; FIS:121.3. Thule – T:126.2; A:119.9.

The world's largest island, mostly covered by an uninhabitable ice cap, Greenland is a Danish territory. Most of the settlements are on the west coast and, since there are no roads, the only connections are by air or sea.

Iceland
Keflavik – T:118.3; G:121.9; A:119.3, 118.7, 126.18, 134.1; AT:128.3, 112.0, 120.3; OPS:131.9. Reykjavik – T:118.0; G:121.7; A:119.0; AT:128.1; ACC:119.7, 125.7, 123.7, 132.2, 132.3.

Iceland's area of responsibility covers an enormous distance, from the 61st parallel to the North Pole and from the Greenwich Meridian to 75°W. Although this area is mostly oceanic, it also extends over Greenland above FL 195 through a special agreement with Denmark. To provide air navigation services for North Atlantic flights, a joint financing agreement was arranged by ICAO as long ago as 1949. At present 22 states with civil aircraft flying the North Atlantic are parties to the agreement. Approximately 35 per cent of the North Atlantic traffic flow enters the Reykjavik FIR/CTA, as well as polar traffic between Alaska and Europe. Radar cover is provided out to about 200 nm from the island and, via a remote site in the Faroes, south-east to Northern Scotland. There is still, however, a large area with no coverage but it is expected that the use of ADS will eventually solve the problem. Iceland Radio uses HF frequencies of the NAT-B, C, and D families, as well as VHF 127.85 and 126.55 remoted from mountain top sites.

Appendix 1

Principal Worldwide Air Routes

The following are those most commonly noted on HF, although other reporting points may be heard when an aircraft is re-routed by the controlling authority for operational reasons. The appropriate radio navigation charts are essential for plotting the beacons and five-letter waypoints listed! Note that European routes have not been included, as all are controlled on VHF frequencies.

Africa
Nairobi-Egyptian Coast
Lodwar (LV) – AMRAD – KUMRU – Kenana (KNA)/VHF/Merowe (MRW) – Abu Simbel (SML) – New Valley (NVA) – KATAB.
Djibouti-Egyptian Coast
RAGAS – TATGU – Asmara – TOKAR – Port Sudan (PSD) – ALEBA – UMINI – Luxor.
Nairobi-Egyptian Coast
Lodwar (LV) – NAGIR – Malakal (ML) – El Obeid (OBD) – ALVOR – ORNAT – KUFRA – Sarir (GS).
Harare-North
Lubumbashi (LUB) – Kamina Base (KB) – DETSU.
Kano-Khartoum
Maiduguri (MD) – N'Djamena (FL) – KIRBO – AMTIT – Geneina (GN).
Lagos-Kano
Oshogbo (GO) – Bida (BD) – Kaduna (KU).
Douala-Kano
OBUDU – AMKOR – Jos (JS).
Brazzaville FIR-Niamey FIR
N'Gaoundere (TJN) – Garoua (TJR) – EBIMU – Maiduguri (MU) – ENBUT – INISA.
Kano-Algiers
AMSIN – Agades (AS) – EREBO – RATIT – Tamanrasset (TMS) – El Golea (MNA).

AMSIN – Agades (AS) – EDAGO – KEMAL – ATAFA – Bordj Omar Driss (BOD).
Niamey-Algiers
APERO – AMTES – MISTO – In Salah (NSL) – KSOUR – El Golea (MNA).
GASON – INAMA – ANISU – Tamanrasset (TMS) – HOGAR – Bordj Omar Driss (BOD).
Bamako-Algiers
ONETA – LILAS – REGAN – RAHIL – El Golea (MNA).

Asia
Sharjah-Karachi
APNIS – Jiwani – LOTAT.
Shiraz-Delhi
PANUR – GASIR – RK – TIGER – LUNKA.
Karachi-Calcutta
TELEM – SONIR – SASRO – DAMAK – MMS.
Sharjah-Bombay
AVARA – BULVI – BILAT – BEMAN.
Colombo-Arabian Gulf
LASES – GUXOV – KATKI – GURVA – PAPON.
KAGLU – GIVIL – ELMIN – DOSGO – BITEP – ALTAS.
Delhi-Calcutta
Lucknow (LK) – KUSMI – Gaya (GC) – Dhanbad (DB).
Karachi-Calcutta
Mandasore (MMS) – Sihora (SA) – MANGO – RUPUR – Jameshedpur (JS).
Bombay-Calcutta
Nagpur (NP) – NIPAD – Rourkela (RCK) – Jameshedpur (JS).
Nagpur-Rangoon
Nagpur (NP) – PORUS – Bhubaneswar (BBS) – BILIL – BULRA.
Vishakhapatnam-Bangkok
VZ – ANSIT – TOLIS – URDIS.
Madras-Singapore
RUPOK – GIVAK – SUKRA – BULPO.

North/South America
South America-East Coast USA
MORRS – ROLEY – LOPPS/VHF/BOURS – LEARS – TALLO – MANNA – MERCI – CHAMP.
GRANT – GINNY – PRISS – DANER – FLANN.
GRANT – ENDER – CATCH – SWAPS – CHAMP.
KRAFT – ENDER – MANNA – BACUS.
ELMUC – TOOMS – TALLO – MANNA – MERCI – CHAMP.

Appendix 2

Selected HF Frequencies

Do not expect to hear the distant ones routinely. Major World Air Route Areas (ICAO), frequencies and main ground stations involved: AFI = African; CAR = Caribbean; CEP = Central East Pacific; CWP = Central West Pacific; EUR = European; MID = Middle East; NP = North Pacific; SAM = South America; SAT = South Atlantic; SEA = South East Asia; SP = South Pacific. Virtually all frequencies listed are USB.

NAT-A (southern tracks) 3.016 5.598 8.825 8.906 13.306 17.946 New York, Gander, Shanwick, Santa Maria

NAT-B (N/S Am-regd a/c) 2.899 5.616 8.864 13.291 17.946 Gander, Shanwick, New York

NAT-C (Eur/Asia-regd a/c) 2.872 5.649 8.879 11.336 13.306 17.946 Gander, Shanwick, New York

NAT-D (polar routes) 2.971 4.675 8.891 11.279 13.291 17.946 Gander, Shanwick, Iceland

NAT-E (south) 2.962 6.628 8.825 11.309 13.354 17.946

NAT-F (Mid-Atlantic) 3.476 6.622 8.831 13.291 New York, Santa Maria tracks

EUR-A 3.479 5.661 6.598 10.084 13.288 17.961 Berlin, Malta

CAR-A 2.287 5.550 6.577 8.846 8.918 11.396 13.297 17.907 New York, Paramaribo, San Juan, Panama

MID-1 2.992 5.667 8.918 13.312 Ankara, Baghdad, Beirut, Damascus, Kuwait, Bahrain, Cairo, Jeddah

MID-2 3.467 5.601 5.658 10.018 13.288 Bahrain, Karachi, Bombay, Lahore, Delhi, Calcutta

SEA-1 3.470 6.556 10.066 13.318 17.907 Calcutta, Dhaka, Madras, Colombo, Male, Cocos, Kuala Lumpur

SEA-2 3.485 5.655 8.942 11.396 13.309 Hong Kong, Manila, Kuala Lumpur

SEA-3 3.470 6.556 11.396 13.318 13.297 Manila, Singapore, Jakarta, Darwin, Sydney, Perth

AFI-1 3.452 6.535 6.673 8.861 13.357 17.955 Casablanca, Canaries, Dakar, Abidjan, Roberts

AFI-2 3.419 5.652 8.894 13.273 13.294 17.961 Algiers, Tripoli, Niamey, Kano

AFI-3 3.467 5.658 11.300 13.288 17.961 Lagos, Brazzaville, Luanda, Windhoek, Johannesburg, Lusaka

AFI-4 2.878 5.493 6.586 8.903 13.294 17.961 Lagos, Brazzaville, Luanda, Windhoek, Johannesburg, Lusaka
AFI-5/INO-1 3.476 5.634 8.879 13.806 17.961
CEP-5 2.869 3.413 5.547 5.574 8.843 11.282 13.261 13.354 17.904 Honolulu, San Francisco
CWP-1/2 2.998 4.666 6.532 6.562 8.903 11.384 13.300 17.904 21.985 Hong Kong, Manila, Guam, Tokyo, Honolulu, Port Moresby
NP-3/4 2.932 5.628 6.655 10.048 11.330 13.273 13.294 17.904 Tokyo, Cold Bay, Anchorage, Honolulu
SP-6/7 3.467 5.643 8.867 13.273 13.300 17.904 Sydney, Auckland, Nandi, Tahiti, Honolulu, Pascua
SAM-C/NE/SE 3.479 5.526 8.855 10.096 13.297 17.907 Belem, Bogota, Maiquetia, Rio de Janeiro
SAM-NW\SW 2.944 4.669 6.549 10.024 11.360 17.907 Barranquilla, La Paz, Ascuncion, Buenos Aires, Santiago
SAT-1 3.452 6.535 8.861 13.357 17.955 Brasilia, Canarias, Dakar, Paramaribo, Recife
SAT-2 2.854 5.565 11.291 13.315 17.955 Canarias, Dakar, Paramaribo, Recife, Rio

Base Stations: Portishead (UK) 4.807 5.610 6.634 8.170 8.960 10.291 11.306 12.133 14.890 15.964 16.273 17.335 18.210 19.510 20.065 23.142; Berne (Switzerland) 4.654 6.643 8.936 10.069 13.205 15.046 18.023 21.988 23.285 25.500; Stockholm 3.494 5.541 8.930 11.345 13.342 17.916 23.210; ARINC (San Francisco, New York, Houston, Honolulu) 3.013 3.494 5.529 6.640 10.075 11.342 13.330 13.348 13.354 17.925 21.964; Rainbow Radio (Canada) 3.378 5.604 8.819 10.264 13.285; Sydney SkyComms 3.007 4.666 8.903 9.040 11.342

Company frequencies (may be used by other carriers as well):
Aero Lloyd 13.327; Air France 6.637; Air India 8.930 10.072; American Trans-Air 13.333; Britannia 5.535 6.556 8.921 10.072 13.333; Cathay Pacific 13.333; Cyprus 11.363; El Al 13.04; Gulf Air 5.380; Hapag Lloyd 10.690; Iberia 5.529 13.327; KLM 13.336; Balkan-Bulgarian 11.382; LTU 10.030 13.324 13.327; MEA 13.330; PIA 8.930; Qantas 6.637 13.342; Royal Jordanian 13.255; Tarom 10.021; South African 8.933 13.330; Saudia 5.544 11.288; United 5.604; British Airways (*Speedbird London*) 5.535 8.921 10.072 13.333 17.922 21.946

Volmet: RAF 4.739 11.78; Shannon: 3.413 5.505 8.957 13.264; Gander/New York: 3.485 6.604 10.051 13.270; St John's: 4.703 6.706 6.754

Rescue: 5.680 (primary) 3.023 3.085 5.695 8.364 (International Distress)

Military frequencies: RAF Strike Command Integrated Comms System (*Architect*): 2.591 4.540 4.742 5.714 6.739 8.190 9.031 11.205 11.247 13.257 15.031 18.018 23.220; US Global High Frequency System (callsign *Croughton/Ascension/Incirlik/Lajes* etc): 11.175 4.724 6.712 8.968 8.992 13.200 15.016 17.976; Royal Canadian Air Force: Trenton, St John's Military etc: 6.683 5.718 9.006 11.233 13.257 15.031.

NB The decimal point is normally omitted when frequencies are referred to during communications.

Appendix 3

ICAO Location Indicators

All airfields and Area Control Centres on the Aeronautical Fixed Telecommunication Network (AFTN) are allocated a four-letter code known as a Location Indicator. Primarily designed as a teleprinter address, it is used also on flight progress strips, and frequently in HF radio messages to overcome poor reception where a spoken place name might be unintelligible. It is not to be confused with the International Air Transport Association (IATA) three-letter codes which are used by operators for domestic purposes such as ticket and baggage handling, examples being AMS (Amsterdam), FRA (Frankfurt) and AUH (Abu Dhabi). These codes are not normally heard in an ATC environment.

ICAO divides the world into non-overlapping Aeronautical Fixed Service Routeing Areas, each of which is assigned a separate identifying letter. Their boundaries do not necessarily coincide with those of any state or Flight Information Region and are decided solely to expedite message traffic routeing. The second letter of the code identifies the state, the third and fourth the individual location. Examples are LEMD (Madrid), EHAM (Amsterdam) and EPWA (Warsaw).

Most of the larger airports have codes which abbreviate the name, but the USA, a special case, is able to employ the last three letters and this makes a large proportion of the codes immediately identifiable, e.g. KJFK (John F. Kennedy), KSFS (San Francisco) and KDEN (Denver). The list below is merely a selection, but will help HF listeners and those able to intercept RTTY communications. The complete listing (over 10,000 entries) is to be found in ICAO Doc 7910 *Location Indicators*. The basic four letter group is not specific enough to address or originate messages on the AFTN; additional letters have to be added. For example, a message intended for the ATC tower at Hamburg would be addressed EDDHZTZ. Other pairs of letters are: ZAZ Approach Control, ZOZ Oceanic Control, ZRZ Area Control Service. To avoid lengthy groups of addressees on international flights, a single combination address is used. For example, a flight from London to Jeddah routeing over Egypt will cross 17 different FIRs, all of whose ACCs will need to know about it. The single code EGZYEJDA will alert them all, OEJD being the designator for Jeddah ACC; the only other addressees required are OEJNZGZ (ATC at Jeddah International) and EGTTZGZP (London ATCC traffic load prediction.)

AA	Australia	DB	Benin	EHRD	Rotterdam
AAYE	Ayers Rock	DBBB	Cotonou	EHSB	Soesterburg
AB	Australia	DF	Burkina Faso	EHVB	Valkenburg
ABBN	Brisbane	DFFD	Ouagadougou	EI	Ireland
ABCS	Cairns	DG	Ghana	EICK	Cork
ABTL	Townsville	DGAA	Accra	EIDW	Dublin
AF	French Antarctic	DI	Ivory Coast	EINN	Shannon
	Territory	DIAP	Abidjan	EK	Denmark
AFDU	Dumont d'Urville	DN	Nigeria	EKBI	Billund
AG	Solomon Islands	DNKN	Kano	EKCH	Copenhagen
AGGH	Honiara/	DNMM	Lagos	EKVL	Vaerlose
	Henderson	DR	Niger	EL	Luxembourg
AM	Australia	DRRN	Niamey	ELLX	Luxembourg
AMML	Melbourne Intl	DT	Tunisia	EN	Norway
AN	Nauru	DTMB	Monastir	ENBO	Bodo
ANAU	Nauru Island	DTTA	Tunis	ENBR	Bergen
AP	Australia	DTTX	Sfax	ENFB	Oslo/Fornebu
APAD	Adelaide	DX	Togo	ENZV	Stavanger
APDN	Darwin	DXXX	Lome	EP	Poland
APPH	Perth	EB	Belgium	EPKK	Krakow
AS	Australia	EBAW	Antwerp	EPWA	Warsaw
ASSY	Sydney	EBBR	Brussels	ES	Sweden
AY	Papua New Guinea	EBOS	Ostend	ESGG	Goteborg
AYPY	Port Moresby	ED	Germany	ESMS	Malmo
BG	Greenland	EDAF	Rhein-Main	ESSA	Stockholm/Arlanda
BGBW	Narssarssuaq	EDBT	Berlin/Tegel	ET	Germany (Military)
BGSF	Sondre Stromfjord	EDDB	Berlin (Schoenefeld)	ETAA	Frankfurt
BGTL	Thule	EDDF	Frankfurt Main	ETAS	Spangdahlem
BI	Iceland	EDDH	Hamburg	ETAR	Ramstein
BIKF	Keflavik	EDDI	Berlin (Tempelhof)	ETAS	Sembach
BIRK	Reykjavik	EDDK	Cologne/Bonn	FA	South Africa
CY	Canada	EDDL	Dusseldorf	FACT	Cape Town
CYEG	Edmonton	EDDM	Munich	FADN	Durban
CYHM	Hamilton	EDDN	Nuremburg	FAJS	Johannesburg
CYHZ	Halifax	EDDR	Saarbrucken	FR	Botswana
CYMX	Montreal/Mirabel	EDDS	Stuttgart	FBSK	Gaborone
CYOW	Ottawa	EDDT	Berlin (Tegel)	FC	Congo
CYQG	Windsor	EDDV	Hanover	FCBB	Brazzaville
CYQX	Gander	EF	Finland	FD	Swaziland
CYUL	Montreal/Dorval	EFHK	Helsinki	FDMS	Manzini
CYVR	Vancouver	EFTP	Tampere	FE	Central African
CYWG	Winnipeg	EG	United Kingdom		Republic
CYXE	Saskatoon	EGCC	Manchester	FEFF	Bangui
CYYC	Calgary	EGKK	London/Gatwick	FG	Equatorial Guinea
CYYR	Goose Bay	EGLL	London/Heathrow	FGBT	Bata
CYYT	St John's	EGPF	Glasgow	FH	Ascension
CYYZ	Toronto	EGPK	Prestwick	FHAW	Wideawake
DA	Algeria	EGSS	London/Stansted	FI	Mauritius
DAAG	Algiers	EH	Netherlands	FIMP	Mauritius
DABB	Annaba	EHAM	Amsterdam	FJ	British Indian
BABC	Constantine	EHEH	Eindhoven		Ocean Territory

FJDG	Diego Garcia	GQ	Mauritania	LATI	Tirana
FK	Cameroun	GQNN	Nouakchott	LB	Bulgaria
FKKD	Douala	GS	Sahara Occidental	LBBG	Burgas
FKKR	Garoua	GSVO	Villa Cisneros	LBSF	Sofia
FL	Zambia	GU	Guinea	LBWN	Varna
FLLS	Lusaka	GUCY	Conakry	LC	Cyprus
FM	Comores and La	GV	Cape Verde	LCLK	Larnaca
	Réunion	GVAC	Amilcar Cabral Intl	LCPH	Paphos
FMCH	Moroni	HA	Ethiopia	LCRA	Akrotiri
FMEE	Saint-Denis	HAAB	Addis Ababa	LD	Croatia
FM	Madagascar	HB	Burundi	LDDU	Dubrovnik
FMMI	Antananarivo	HBBA	Bujumbura	LDPL	Pula
FN	Angola	HC	Somalia	LDZA	Zagreb
FNLU	Luanda	HCMM	Mogadishu	LE	Spain
FO	Gabon	HE	Egypt	LEAL	Alicante
FOOL	Libreville	HEAX	Alexandria	LEBB	Bilbao
FP	Sào Tomé	HECA	Cairo Intl	LEBL	Barcelona
FPST	Sào Tomé	HELX	Luxor	LEIB	Ibiza
FQ	Mozambique	HF	Djibouti	LEMD	Madrid
FQBR	Beira	HFFF	Djibouti	LEMG	Malaga
FQMA	Maputo	HK	Kenya	LEMH	Minorca
FS	Seychelles	HKMO	Mombasa	LEPA	Palma
FSIA	Seychelles Intl	HKNA	Nairobi	LEST	Santiago
FT	Tchad	HL	Libya	LEVC	Valencia
FTTJ	N'Djamena	HLLT	Tripoli	LEZL	Seville
FV	Zimbabwe	HR	Rwanda	LF	France
FVHA	Harare	HRYR	Kigali	LFBD	Bordeaux
FW	Malawi	HS	Sudan	LFBO	Toulouse
FWCL	Blantyre	HSSS	Khartoum	LFLY	Lyon
FWKI	Lilongwe	HT	Tanzania	LFML	Marseille
FX	Lesotho	HTDA	Dar-es-Salaam	LFML	Nice
FXMM	Maseru	HTKJ	Kilimanjaro	LFPB	Le Bourget
	Moshoeshoe	HU	Uganda	LFPG	Charles de Gaulle
FY	Namibia	HUEN	Entebbe	LFPO	Orly
FYWH	Windhoek	K	USA	LFQQ	Lille
FZ	Zaire	KATL	Atlanta	LFRG	Deauville
FZAA	Kinshasa	KBOS	Boston	LG	Greece
GA	Mali	KBGR	Bangor	LGAT	Athens
GABS	Bamako	KBNA	Nashville	LGIR	Heraklion
GB	Gambia	KDEN	Denver/Stapleton	LGKR	Corfu
GBYD	Banjul	KDET	Detroit	LGKV	Kavala
GC	Canaries	KDFW	Dallas-Fort Worth	LGMK	Mikonos
GCLP	Las Palmas	KDOV	Dover AFB	LGRP	Rhodes
GCXO	Tenerife Norte	KEWR	Newark	LGSA	Souda
GF	Sierra Leone	KIAD	Washington/Dulles	LGSK	Skiathos
GFLL	Freetown	KJFK	New York/Kennedy	LGSR	Santorini
GG	Guinee-Bissau	KLAX	Los Angeles Intl	LGTS	Thessalonika
GGOV	Bissau	KMCO	Orlando	LH	Hungary
GL	Liberia	KMGE	Dobbins AFB	LHBP	Budapest
GLRB	Monrovia/Roberts	KMIA	Miami Intl	LI	Italy
GM	Morocco	KMSP	Minneapolis-St Paul	LICC	Catania
GMAA	Agadir	KORD	Chicago/O'Hare	LICZ	Sigonella
GMME	Rabat/Sale	KPHL	Philadelphia	LIMC	Milan/Malpensa
GMMN	Casablanca	KRDU	Raleigh/Durham	LIMF	Turin
GMMX	Marrakech	KSLC	Salt Lake City	LIMJ	Genoa
GMTT	Tangiers	KTEB	Teterboro	LIML	Milan/Linate
GO	Senegal	KTPA	Tampa	LIPA	Aviano
GOOY	Dakar	LA	Albania	LIPE	Bologna

LIPZ	Venice	MKJP	Kingston	OI	Iran
LIRA	Rome/Ciampino	MKJS	Montego Bay	OIII	Tehran
LIRN	Naples	MM	Mexico	OJ	Jordan
LIRP	Pisa	MMAA	Acapulco	OJAI	Amman
LIYW	Aviano (USAF)	MMGL	Guadalajara	OP	Pakistan
LJ	Slovenia	MMMX	Mexico City	OPKC	Karachi
LJLJ	Ljubljana	MMMY	Monterrey	OPLA	Lahore
LK	Czech Republic	MN	Nicaragua	OPPS	Peshawar
LKMT	Ostrava	MNMG	Managua	OPRN	Islamabad
LKPR	Prague	MP	Panama	OR	Iraq
LL	Israel	MPHO	Howard AFB	ORBS	Baghdad/Saddam
LLBG	Tel-Aviv	MPTO	Panama	OS	Syria
LM	Malta	MR	Costa Rica	OSAP	Aleppo
LMML	Luqa	MROC	Alajuela	OSDI	Damascus
LN	Monaco	MS	El Salvador	OT	Qatar
LNMC	Monaco Heliport	MSLP	San Salvador	OTBD	Doha
LO	Austria	MT	Haiti	OY	Yemen
LOWG	Graz	MTPP	Port-au-Prince	OYAA	Aden
LOWI	Innsbruck	MU	Cuba	OYHD	Hodeidah
LOWK	Klagenfurt	MUHA	Havana	OYSN	Sana'a
LOWL	Linz	MW	Cayman Is	OYTZ	Taiz
LOWS	Salzburg	MWCB	Cayman Brac	PA	Alaska
LOWW	Vienna	MWCR	Georgetown	PAEI	Eielson AFB
LP	Portugal	MY	Bahamas	PAFA	Fairbanks
LPAZ	Santa Maria	MYNN	Nassau	PANC	Anchorage
	(Azores)	MZ	Belize	PG	Mariana Is
LPFR	Faro	MZBZ	Belize	PGSN	Saipan
LPFU	Funchal (Madeira)	NC	Cook Is	PGUA	Guam
LPLA	Lajes (Azores)	NCRG	Rarotonga Intl	PH	Hawaii
LPPR	Oporto	NF	Fiji & Tonga	PHIK	Hickam AFB
LPPT	Lisbon	NFFN	Nandi	PHNA	Barbers Point
LR	Romania	NFNA	Nausori	PHNL	Honolulu
LROP	Bucharest/Otopeni	NFTF	Tongatapu	PJ	Johnston Is
LS	Switzerland	NG	Kiribati	PJON	Johnston
LSGG	Geneva	NGTA	Tarawa	PK	Marshall Is
LSZH	Zurich	NI	Niue	PKMJ	Majuro Atoll
LT	Turkey	NIUE	Niue Intl	PM	Midway Is
LTAC	Ankara/Esenboga	NS	American Samoa	PMDY	Midway/Henderson
LTAG	Incirlik	NSTU	Pago Pago	PT	Micronesia
LTBA	Istanbul	NT	French Polynesia	PTYA	Yap
LTBL	Izmir/Cigli	NTTO	Hao	PW	Wake Is
LX	Gibraltar	NV	Vanuatu	PWAK	Wake Is
LXGB	Gibraltar	NVVV	Port Vila	RC	China
LY	Yugoslavia	NW	New Caledonia	RCKH	Kaohsiung Intl
LYBE	Belgrade	NWWW	Noumea	RCTP	Taipei
LY	Bosnia-Herzegovina	NZ	New Zealand	RJ	Japan
LYSA	Sarajevo	NZAA	Auckland	RJAA	Tokyo
LZ	Slovakia	NZCH	Christchurch	RJFF	Fukuoka
LZIB	Bratislava	NZHN	Hamilton	RJNN	Nagoya
MB	Turks & Caicos	NZWN	Wellington	RJOO	Osaka
MBPV	Providenciales	OA	Afghanistan	RJTT	Tokyo/Haneda
MD	Dominican Republic	OAKB	Kabul	RK	South Korea
MDSD	Santo Domingo	OB	Bahrain	RKPC	Cheju
MG	Guatamala	OBBI	Bahrain	PKPK	Kimhae
MGGT	La Aurora	OE	Saudi Arabia	RKSS	Seoul/Kimpo
MH	Honduras	OEDR	Dhahran	RO	Japan
MHTG	Tegucigalpa	OEJN	Jeddah	RODN	Kadena AFB
MK	Jamaica	OERK	Riyadh	RP	Philippines

RPMK	Clark AFB	TKPK	Basseterre	VH	Hong-Kong
RPMM	Manila	TL	St Lucia	VHHH	Hong-Kong Intl
SA	Argentina	TLPC	Castries	VI	India
SAEZ	Buenos Aires/Ezeiza	TLPL	Hewanorra Intl	VIDP	Delhi
SB	Brazil	TN	Netherlands Antilles	VL	Laos
SBEG	Manaus	TNCC	Willemstad	VLVT	Ventiane
SBGL	Rio de Janeiro	TNCM	Philipsburg	VM	Macau
SBGR	Sao Paulo	TT	Trinidad & Tobago	VMMC	Macau
SBSP	Sao Paulo/	TTPP	Port of Spain	VN	Nepal
	Congonhas	TX	Bermuda	VNKT	Kathmandu
SBSV	Salvador	TXKF	Bermuda	VO	India
SC	Chile	UA	Kazakhstan	VOMM	Madras
SCEL	Santiago	UAAA	Alma Ata	VQ	Bhutan
SE	Ecuador	UB	Azerbaijan	VQPR	Paro
SEGU	Guyaquil	UBBB	Baku	VR	Maldives
SEQU	Quito	UE	Russian Fed	VRGN	Gan
SF	Falklands	UEEE	Yakutsk	VRMM	Male
SFAL	Stanley	UG	Armenia & Georgia	VT	Thailand
SG	Paraguay	UGEE	Yerevan	VTBD	Bangkok
SGAS	Asuncion	UGGG	Tbilisi	VTCC	Chiang Mai
SK	Colombia	UH	Russian Fed	VTSP	Phuket
SKBO	Bogota	UHWW	Vladivostok	VV	Vietnam
SKBQ	Barranquilla	UK	Ukraine	VVNB	Hanoi
SKCG	Cartagena	UKKK	Kiev	VVTS	Ho Chi Minh
SKCL	Cali	UKOO	Odessa	VY	Myanmar
SKMD	Medellin	UL	Russian Fed	VYYY	Yangon
SL	Bolivia	ULLI	St Petersburg	WA	Indonesia
SLLP	La Paz	UL	Estonia	WABB	Biak
SLVR	Santa Cruz	ULTT	Tallin	WB	Brunei
SM	Surinam	UM	Belarus	WBSB	Brunei Intl
SMJP	Zandery	UMMS	Minsk 2	WB	Malaysia
SO	French Guiana	UM	Latvia	WBGG	Kuching
SOCA	Cayenne	UMRR	Riga	WBKK	Kota Kinabalu
SP	Peru	UM	Lithuania	WI	Indonesia
SPIM	Lima Intl	UMWW	Vilnius	WIII	Jakarta
SU	Uruguay	UN	Russian Fed	WIMM	Medan
SUMU	Montevideo	UNOO	Omsk	WM	Malaysia
SV	Venezuela	UR	Russian Fed	WMKK	Kuala Lumpur
SVMI	Caracas	URRR	Rostov	WMKP	Penang
SY	Guiana	URWW	Volgograd	WP	East Timor
SYTM	Georgetown	US	Russian Fed	WPAT	Atauro
TA	Antigua	USKK	Kirov	WR	Indonesia
TAPA	St Johns	UT	Uzbekistan	WRRR	Bali
TB	Barbados	UTTT	Tashkent	WS	Singapore
TBPB	Bridgetown	UU	Russian Fed	WSSS	Singapore/Changi
TD	Dominica	UUWW	Moscow/Vnukovo	ZB	China
TDCF	Canefield	UW	Russian Fed	ZBAA	Beijing
TF	French Antilles	UWKD	Kazan	ZG	China
TFFF	Fort-de-France	VA	India	ZGGG	Guangzhou
TFFR	Pointe-a-Pitre	VABB	Bombay	ZK	North Korea
TG	Grenada	VC	Sri Lanka	ZKPY	Pyongyang
TGPY	Point Salines	VCBI	Colombo	ZM	Mongolia
TI	US Virgin Is	VD	Cambodia	ZMUB	Ulan Bator
TIST	St Thomas	VDPP	Phnom-Penh	ZS	China
TISX	St Croix	VE	India	ZSSS	Shanghai
TJ	Puerto Rico	VECC	Calcutta	ZU	China
TJSJ	San Juan	VG	Bangladesh	ZULS	Lhasa
TK	St Kitts & Nevis	VGZR	Dhaka		

Appendix 4

Aircraft Nationality Markings

Code	Country	Code	Country	Code	Country
AP	Pakistan	HC	Ecuador	P4	Aruba
A2	Botswana	HH	Haiti	RA	Russian Federation
A3	Tonga	HI	Dominican Republic	RDLP	Laos
A40	Oman	HK	Colombia	RP	Philippines
A5	Bhutan	HL	Republic of Korea	SE	Sweden
A6	United Arab Emirates	HP	Panama	SP	Poland
A7	Qatar	HR	Honduras	ST	Sudan
A9C	Bahrain	HS	Thailand	SU	Egypt
B	China	HZ	Saudi Arabia	SX	Greece
C, CF	Canada	H4	Solomon Islands	S2	Bangladesh
CC	Chile	I	Italy	S5	Slovenia
CN	Morocco	JA	Japan	S7	Seychelles
CP	Bolivia	JY	Jordan	S9	Sào Tomé and Principé
CR, CS	Portugal	J2	Djibouti		
CU	Cuba	J3	Grenada	TC	Turkey
CX	Uruguay	J5	Guinea Bissau	TF	Iceland
C2	Nauru	J6	Saint Lucia	TG	Guatemala
C5	Gambia	J7	Dominica	TI	Costa Rica
C6	Bahamas	J8	Saint Vincent and the Grenadines	TJ	Cameroon
C9	Mozambique			TL	Central African Republic
D	Germany	LN	Norway	TN	Congo
DQ	Fiji	LQ, LV	Argentina	TR	Gabon
D2	Angola	LX	Luxembourg	TS	Tunisia
D4	Cape Verde	LY	Lithuania	TT	Chad
EC	Spain	LZ	Bulgaria	TU	Côte d'Ivoire
EI, EJ	Ireland	N	United States	TY	Benin
EK	Armenia	OB	Peru	TZ	Mali
EL	Liberia	OL	Lebanon	T3	Kiribati
EP	Iran	OE	Austria	T7	San Marino
ER	Moldova	OH	Finland	T9	Bosnia and Herzegovina
ES	Estonia	OK	Czech Republic		
ET	Ethiopia	OK	Slovakia	UK	Uzbekistan
EW	Belarus	OO	Belgium	UR	Ukraine
EX	Kyrgyzstan	OY	Denmark	VH	Australia
EY	Tajikistan	P	North Korea	VP-F	Falkland Islands
EZ	Turkmenistan	PH	Netherlands	VQ-H	St Helena/Ascencion
F	France, Colonies and Protectorates	PJ	Netherlands Antilles	VP-L	Virgin Islands
G	United Kingdom	PK	Indonesia	VQ-T	Turks and Caicos
HA	Hungary	PP, PT	Brazil	VR-B	Bermuda
HB	Switzerland and Liechtenstein	PZ	Suriname	VR-C	Cayman Islands
		P2	Papua New Guinea	VR-G	Gibraltar

VR-H	Hong Kong	ZA	Albania	60	Somalia
VT	India	ZK, ZL,		6V, 6W	Senegal
V2	Antigua and	ZM	New Zealand	6Y	Jamaica
	Barbuda	ZP	Paraguay	70	Yemen
V3	Belize	ZS, ZT,		7P	Lesotho
V4	St Kitts and Nevis	ZU	South Africa	7QY	Malawi
V5	Namibia	3A	Monaco	7T	Algeria
V6	Micronesia	3B	Mauritius	8P	Barbados
V7	Marshall Islands	3C	Equatorial Guinea	8Q	Maldives
V8	Brunei	3D	Swaziland	8R	Guyana
XA, XB,		3X	Guinea	9A	Croatia
XC	Mexico	4K	Azerbaijan	9G	Ghana
XT	Burkina Faso	4L	Georgia	9H	Malta
XU	Cambodia	4R	Sri Lanka	9J	Zambia
XV	Vietnam	4X	Israel	9K	Kuwait
XY, XZ	Myanmar	5A	Libya	9L	Sierra Leone
YA	Afghanistan	5B	Cyprus	9M	Malaysia
YI	Iraq	5H	Tanzania	9N	Nepal
YJ	Vanuatu	5N	Nigeria	9Q	Zaire
YK	Syria	5R	Madagascar	9U	Burundi
YL	Latvia	5T	Mauritania	9V	Singapore
YN	Nicaragua	5U	Niger	9XR	Rwanda
YR	Romania	5V	Togo	9Y	Trinidad and
YS	Salvador	5W	Samoa		Tobago
YV	Venezuela	5X	Uganda		
Z	Zimbabwe	5Y	Kenya		

Appendix 5

Callsign Prefixes

These three-letter codes and word prefixes are allocated by ICAO on a worldwide basis, and are listed separately as many operators use them rather than the allocated company designator. An example is ESY instead of *Exco Air*, either being permissible. Designators are registered only for aircraft operating agencies running scheduled services and companies which, in the opinion of the state of jurisdiction, have a need for an exclusive designator. The three-letter code should reflect to the maximum extent practicable the name of the operator and version spoken on R/T – the telephony designator. It should also be easily pronounceable and suitable phonetically in at least one of the following languages: English, French, or Spanish. Ideally, it should reflect correlation between the three-letter code and the name of the operator, for example MNX = Manx = Manx Airlines, and ARO = Arrow = Arrow Aviation. Certain restrictions apply to the registration of designators to prevent confusion. For obvious reasons, PAN and SOS will not be allocated, nor will combinations which conflict with surviving groups in the largely obsolete Q-Code. To avoid clashing with the Telex Start-of-Message Signal, combinations utilizing 'ZC' or 'CZ' will not be used, nor will those with 'NN', the End-of-Message Signal. Codes with the letter 'I' as the third letter will not be used, to avoid confusion with the number one. In order to reduce the length of transmissions, the telephony designator should be brief, comprising, if possible, one word of two or three syllables, and should not exceed two words. The complete ICAO listing runs to many thousands, so the following are merely an international sample of those most commonly heard.

R/T callsign	Operator	R/T callsign	Operator
Adria	Adria Airways	Aeromonterrey	Aeromonterrey (Mexico)
Aerocancun	Aerocancun (Mexico)	African Airlines	African Airlines (Kenya)
Aerocaribbean	Aerocaribbean	Aigle Azur	Aigle Azur
Aeroflot	Aeroflot	Airafric	Air Afrique
Aero Lloyd	Aero Lloyd	Air Belgium	Air Belgium
Aeromexico	Aeromexico	Air Berlin	Air Berlin

Air Canada	Air Canada	Canada	Worldways Canada
Airevac	USAF Ambulance	Canadian	Canadian Airlines
Air Force One	US President	Canforce	Canadian Armed
Air Force Two	US Vice-President		Forces
Air France	Air France	Cannon	Cent Safair Freighters
Air Hong Kong	Air Hong Kong		(S Africa)
Air India	Air India	Cargolux	Cargolux Airlines
Air Lanka	Air Lanka	Cargosur	Cargosur (Spain)
Air Malta	Air Malta	Caribjet	Caribbean Airways
Air Martinique	Air Martinique		(Barbados)
Air Mauritius	Air Mauritius	Cathay	Cathay Pacific
Air Mil	Spanish Air Force	Cedarjet	Middle East Airlines
Air Mike	Continental Micronesia	China	CAAC
	(Guam)	China Eastern	China Eastern Airlines
Air Portugal	Air Portugal	Condor	Condor Flugdienst
Air Rwanda	Air Rwanda Air Service	Continental	Continental Airlines
Air Sweden	West Air Sweden		(USA)
Air Van	Air Vanuatu	Corsair	Corse Air (France)
Tahiti	Air Tahiti	Cotam	French AF Transport
Air Zaire	Air Zaire	Croatia	Croatian Airlines
Air Zimbabwe	Air Zimbabwe	Cross Air	Cross Air (Switzerland)
Alitalia	Alitalia	CSA Lines	Czech Airlines
All Nippon	All Nippon	Cubana	Cubana
Alyemda	Yemen Airlines	Cyprus	Cyprus Airways
Ambassador	Ambassador Airways	Dairair	Dairo Air Services
American	American Airlines		(Uganda)
Amtran	American Trans Air	Dantrans	Danish Air Transport
Ansett	Ansett Airlines	Delta	Delta Airlines
	(Australia)	Dominicana	Dominicana
Argentina	Aerolineas Argentinas	Dynasty	China Airlines
Arkia	Arkia (Israel)	Egyptair	Egyptair
Ascot	RAF No 1 Group	El Al	El Al
ATI	Aero Transport Italiani	Emirates	Emirates
Atrans	Aviatrans (Russian Fed)	Empress	CP-Air
Austrian	Austrian Airlines	Ethiopian	Ethiopian Airlines
Austrian Charter	Austrian Air Transport	Eurocypria	Eurocypria Airlines
Aviaco	Aviaco (Spain)	Excalibur	Excalibur Airways
Avianca	Avianca (Colombia)	Express	Federal Express
Balair	Balair (Switzerland)	Finnair	Finnair
Balkan	Balkan-Bulgarian	Foxtrot Mike	French Air Force
Bangladesh	Bangladesh Biman	Foyle	Air Foyle (TNT)
Beatours	British Airtours	Fred Olsen	Fred Olsen (Norway)
Belgair	Trans European Airways	French Lines	AOM French Airlines
Belgian Carriers	Belgian International	Futura	Futura (Spain)
Belstar	Eurobelgian Airlines	Gabon Cargo	Air Gabon Cargo
Big A	Arrow Air (USA)	Garuda	Garuda Indonesian
Biscayne	Miami Air International	Ghana	Ghana Airways
Braathens	Braathens (Norway)	Gibair	GB Airways
Britannia	Britannia Airways	Greenlandair	Greenlandair Grid
Brunei	Royal Brunei Airlines	Gulf Air	Gulf Air
Buffalo Air	Buffalo Airways (USA)	Hapag Lloyd	Hapag-Lloyd
Bul Air Cargo	Bulgarian Air Cargo	Heavylift	Heavylift Cargo
Busy Bee	Busy Bee of Norway	Hotel Yankee	Liberia World Airlines
Cactus	America West Airlines	Iberia	Iberia
Calypso	Regal Bahamas	Iceair	Icelandair
	International	Indair	Indian Airlines
Cam-Air	Cameroon Airlines	Indonesian	Garuda Indonesian
Cameo	Cam Air	Iranair	Iran Air

Japanair	Japan Airlines	Saudi	Saudi-Arabian Airlines
JAT	Jugoslovenski-Aerotransport	Scandi	Scandinavian Airlines System
Jordanian	Royal Jordanian	Scanvip	Air Express (Norway)
Kenya	Kenya Airways	Scanwing	Malmo Aviation
Kiwi	Royal New Zealand Air Force	Schreiner	Schreiner Airways
		Selair	Sierra Leone Airways
KLM	KLM	Seychelles	Air Seychelles
Koreanair	Korean Airlines	Shamrock	Aer Lingus
Kuwaiti	Kuwait Airways	Singapore	Singapore Airlines
Lair	Lionair (Luxembourg)	Southern Air	Southern Air Transport (USA)
LAN	LAN Chile		
Lauda	Lauda Air	Speedbird	British Airways
LCN	Lineas Aereas Canarias	Springbok	South African Airways
Leisure	Air UK (Leisure)	Sterling	Sterling European Airways
Libair	Libyan Arab Lifeline		
Lithuania	Air Lithuanian Airlines	Sudanair	Sudan Airways
LTU Sud LTU	Lufttransport	Sunturk	Pegasus (Turkey)
Lufthansa	Lufthansa	Sunwing	Spanair
Luxair	Luxair	Surinam	Surinam Airways
Maerskair	Maerskair (Denmark)	Swazi Cargo	Air Swazi
Malawi	Air Malawi	Swedair	Swedair
Malaysian	Malaysian Airlines	Swedline	Linjeflyg
Malev	Malev (Hungary)	Swissair	Swissair
Marocair	Royal Air Maroc	Syrianair	Syrian Arab Airlines
Merair	Meridiana (Italy)	Tango Lima	Trans Mediterranean
Midland	British Midland	Tarom	Tarom (Romania)
Mike Romeo	Air Mauritanie	Tee Air	Tower Air
Monarch	Monarch Airlines	Territorial	NWT Air (Canada)
Namibia	Namib Air	Thai Inter	Thai International
Nationair	Nation Air (Canada)	Tiger	Flying Tiger
Navy	Royal or US Navy	Time Air	Time Air (Canada)
New Zealand	Air New Zealand	Tomcat	Cologne Commercial Flight
Nippon Cargo	Nippon Cargo Airlines		
Nitro	TNT International	Tourjet	Airtours
NOAA	National Oceanographic and Atmospheric Administration	Transamerica	Transamerica Airlines
		Trans Arabian	Trans Arabian (Sudan)
		Transat	Air Transat
Northwest	Northwest Orient	Transatlantic	Transatlantic (Gambia)
Okada Air	Okada Airlines (Nigeria)	Transavia	Transavia (Holland)
Olympic	Olympic Airways	Transcon	Trans Continental
Orange	Air Holland Orion	Transcorp	Transcorp Airways
Pacific	Air Pacific (Fiji)	Triangle	Atlantic Island Air (Iceland)
Pakistan	Pakistan International		
Paraguaya	Lineas Aereas Paraguayas	Tunair	Tunis Air
		Turkair	Turkish Airlines
Philippine	Philippine Airlines	Tyrolean	Tyrolean Airways
Pollot	LOT (Poland)	Uganda	Uganda Airlines
Portugalia	Portugalia	Ukay	Air UK
Qantas	Qantas	Ukraine Cargo	Air Ukraine Cargo
Reach	USAF Air Mobility Command	Ukraine	International Air Ukraine International
Rubens	VLM (Belgium)	Uni Air	Uni Air (France)
Rushair	AVIAL (Russian Fed)	United	United Airlines
Ryanair	Ryanair	Universair	Universair (Spain)
Sabena	Sabena	UPS	United Parcel Service (USA)
Sam	Special Air Mission (USAF)		
		US Air	US Air

UTA	UTA (France)	ANA	All Nippon Airways
Uzbek	Uzbekistan Airways	ANZ	Air New Zealand
Varig	Varig Brazil	AOM	AOM French Airlines
Viasa	VIASA (Venezuela)	APW	Arrow Air
Victor Victor	US Navy	ARG	Aerolineas Argentinas
Virgin	Virgin Atlantic	ATI	Aero Transport Italiani
Viva	Viva Air (Spain)	ATQ	Air Transport Schiphol
Volare	Volare (Russian Fed)	AUA	Austrian Airlines
Volga-Dnepr	Volga-Dnepr Airline (Russian Fed)	AUI	Air Ukraine
		AVA	Avianca
WDL	WDL Flugdienst	AYC	Aviaco
Witchcraft	Flugdienst Fehlhaber	AZR	Air Zaire
World	World Airways	AZW	Air Zimbabwe
Yemeni	Yemen Airways	BAT	Bohemian Air Transport
Yugair	Air Yugoslavia	BBB	Balair
Zambia	Zambia Airways	BBC	Bangladesh Biman
ZAS Airlines	ZAS Airlines Egypt	BCS	European Air Transport
Zebra	African Safari	BEX	Benin Air Express
		BIC	Belgian International Air Carriers

Suffixes to the flight number have various meanings:

A – Extra flight on the same route. If more than one, then B, C, etc may be used. (Britannia Airways use A for outbound flights from UK, and B for the return sector.)

F – Freight

P – Positioning flight

T – Training flight

Heavy – Reminds ATC that aircraft is wide-bodied with a strong vortex wake.

ICAO 3-letter codes

AAF	Aigle Azur	BSK	Miami Air International
AAL	American Airlines	BVA	Buffalo Airways
ABB	Air Belgium	BWA	BWIA International
ADB	Antonov Design Bureau (Ukraine)	CCA	Air China
		CDN	Canadian Airlines International
ADR	Adria Airways		
AEK	African Express Airways	CFG	Condor Flugdienst
AFC	African West	CKS	Connie Kalitta Services (USA)
AFM	Affretair		
AFN	African International	CKT	Caledonian Airways
AFP	Portuguese Air Force	CLC	Classic Air (Switzerland)
AGS	Air Gambia	CLG	Challenge Air (France)
AGX	Aviogenex	CLX	Cargolux Airlines
AHD	Air Holland	CMI	Continental Micronesia
AHK	Air Hong Kong	CMM	Air 3000 (Canada)
AIA	Air Atlantis	CNA	Centennial (Spain)
AIK	African Airlines (Kenya)	COA	Continental Airlines
AJM	Air Jamaica	CPA	Cathay Pacific
ALK	Air Lanka	CRL	Corse Air International
AMC	Air Malta	CRN	Aero Caribbean
AME	Spanish Air Force	CRX	Cross Air
AML	Air Malawi	CSA	Czech Airlines
AMM	Air 2000	CTA	Compagnie De Transport Aerien
AMR	Air America		
AMT	American Trans Air	CTN	Croatia Airlines
AMX	Aeronaves De Mexico	CUB	Cubana
		CWS	Air Swazi Cargo
		CYP	Cyprus Airways
		DAH	Air Algerie
		DAL	Delta Airlines
		DAT	Delta Air Transport
		DCN	German Federal Armed Forces
		DQI	Cimber Air
		DSR	Dairo Air Services (Uganda)
		DYA	Alyemda Democratic Yemen Airlines